DEATH AND MASTERY

NEW DIRECTIONS IN CRITICAL THEORY

New Directions in Critical Theory
Amy Allen, General Editor

New Directions in Critical Theory presents outstanding classic and contemporary texts in the tradition of critical social theory, broadly construed. The series aims to renew and advance the program of critical social theory, with a particular focus on theorizing contemporary struggles around gender, race, sexuality, class, and globalization and their complex interconnections.

DEATH AND MASTERY

Psychoanalytic Drive Theory and the Subject of Late Capitalism

Benjamin Y. Fong

Columbia University Press   New York

Columbia University Press

Publishers Since 1893

New York   Chichester, West Sussex

cup.columbia.edu

Copyright © 2016 Columbia University Press

Paperback edition, 2018

All rights reserved

Library of Congress Cataloging-in-Publication Data

Names: Fong, Benjamin Y., author.

Title: Death and mastery: psychoanalytic drive theory and the subject
   of late capitalism / Benjamin Y. Fong.

Description: New York: Columbia University Press, [2016] |
   Series: New directions in critical theory | Includes bibliographical
   references and index.

Identifiers: LCCN 2016014150| ISBN 9780231176682 (cloth) |
   ISBN 9780231176699 (pbk.) | ISBN 9780231542616 (e-book)

Subjects: LCSH: Death instinct. | Death—Psychological aspects. |
   Capitalism—Psychological aspects.

Classification: LCC BF175.5.D4 F66 2016 | DDC 150. 19/5—dc23

LC record available at https://lccn.loc.gov/2016014150

Cover design: Rebecca Lown

You are using one part of your force to fight the other part.

—Sigmund Freud

Contents

Acknowledgments

This book grew out of dialogue with a diverse set of intellectually stimulating and nourishing colleagues, mentors, friends, and family members for which I am tremendously grateful. I would like specifically to thank Mark C. Taylor and Wayne Proudfoot, for the extraordinary guidance and feedback; Kevin Kelly, whose perspicuous exposition of Freudian metapsychology helped lay the foundation for this project; Fred Neuhouser, for his valuable comments on a longer paper that eventually became chapters 1 and 2, but also for directing me to the Columbia University Center for Psychoanalytic Training and Research, where I was an Affiliate Scholar for two years; Lisa Cerami, who helped me work through some of the more impenetrable passages in Adorno; Joshua Dubler, a sounding board of unusual warmth and clarity; Yonatan Brafman and Liane Carlson, for the continuing education; Andrea Sun-Mee Jones, who is in many ways responsible for the existence of this project; that remarkable organization that is the Society for Psychoanalytic Inquiry, and in particular Jeremy Cohan, Chris Crawford, Greg Gabrellas, Scott Jenkins, Ben Koditschek, Christie Offenbacher, and Allan Scholom for their leadership; Gil Anidjar, Fabian Arzuaga (and the Social Theory Workshop at the University of Chicago), Courtney Bender, Alison Brown, Ashleigh Campi, Shanna Carlson, Bernard Faure, Daragh Grant, Jack Hawley, Phillip Henry, Andy Junker, Jonathan Lear, Mark Loeffler,

Birte Löschenkohl, Moishe Postone, Jonathan Schorsch, and Simon Taylor for discussing various chapters with me; and Isaac Balbus, Jared Holley, Gabriel Levine, and Eric Santner, all of whom read the entire manuscript at critical moments in its development and whose lucid feedback gave me the confidence to move forward.

I presented a portion of this book's introduction at the American Psychoanalytic Association's Annual Meeting in January 2015 as an APsaA Fellow, and I would like to thank Charles Amrhein, Rosemary Johnson, and Lynne Zeavin for coordinating the fellowship and Bruce Reis and Paul Schwaber for responding to my presentation. Parts of chapters 1 and 2 were presented at the Hans W. Loewald Conference in February 2014 at the New School; thanks go to Ryan Gustafson and Hunter Robinson for organizing the conference, Brian Kloppenberg and Aleksandra Wagner for responding to my paper, and Elliot Jurist for organizing the special issue of *Psychoanalytic Psychology* in which the proceedings were published.

More generally, thanks to the Jacob K. Javits Foundation, Julia Clark-Spohn, Meryl Marcus, Deborah Neibel, and the Society of Fellows at the University of Chicago for their support, and to all fellow Fellows for their friendship and collegiality. Thanks also to Amy Allen, Wendy Lochner, Christine Dunbar, the two anonymous readers, and the team at Columbia University Press for the excellent feedback, encouragement, and patient attention to my many questions and requests.

To my parents, Hon and Jo Fong, my sister, Christina Fong, and my mother-in-law, Rosemary Easter, who are all unjustifiably supportive of my work, I owe a debt that far transcends the bounds of this project. Finally, not a day goes by where I do not feel an overwhelming appreciation for the love and support of my wife, Alison Easter, who is kind enough to welcome unsolicited ramblings about the conditions under which it possible to say "I," and my kids, Jaya and Ziggy, baffled as they justifiably are that their second-favorite grown-up disappears for large swaths of time in order to drink coffee and stare blankly at a laptop.

* * *

A very early version of chapter 5 appeared as "Death Drive Sublimation: A Psychoanalytic Perspective on Technological Development" in *Psychoanalysis, Culture, and Society* 18, no. 4 (December 2013): 352–67. Bits of chapters 1 and 2 appeared as "Hans Loewald and the Death Drive" in *Psychoanalytic Psychology* 31, no. 4 (October 2014): 525–36. I am grateful to these journals for their permission to reprint materials here.

DEATH AND MASTERY

The theory of the instincts [Triebe] is so to say our mythology. Instincts are myth-ical entities, magnificent in their indefiniteness. In our work we cannot for a mo-ment disregard them, and yet we are never sure that we are seeing them clearly.
—Sigmund Freud, *New Introductory Lectures on Psycho-Analysis*

Introduction

In Defense of Drive Theory

One could say that this book is an attempt to illuminate the var-ied psychic and social impediments to the achievement of mastery. When we hear the word *mastery*, it is natural to turn to Hegel or to think of some kind of domination or subjugation, but we very often use the word in a more everyday sense to designate the acquisition of a skill, a certain deftness of practice, or even the possession of a basic grip on a difficult situation. It is the obstacles to mastery in the latter sense of the term, and thus the question of why human beings are particularly bad at just get-ting along, that primarily concerns me here. One might argue that it is a mistake cleanly to separate these two: the critical theorists, after all, con-vincingly argued that the Enlightenment quest for mastery in the second sense has dissolved into a crisis of mastery in the first.[1]

Part of what I try to do in this book is to offer an explanation of this dissolution and thus to propose a theory of the relationship between these two senses of mastery. To admit, however, that they are related, even *neces-sarily*, is not to say that we should collapse the distinction: indeed, I take the question of how we work toward a stability and equanimity that allows us to get through the day (mastery$_2$) without going on, whether through frustration, overeagerness, or fear, then to seek the kind of excessive and controlling stability that is bought at the expense of others (mastery$_1$) to be a fundamental one for both psychology and social theory. To give up on this distinction—to hold, in other words, that domination is bound inextricably to the task of getting the hang of life—is to fall prey to an irremediable cynicism about the possibility of psychic and social transformation.

My interest in this problematic stems from Karl Marx, who conceives of alienation as an inversion of the human being's natural relationship of mastery over the environment. For Marx, human beings as a species are defined by their capacity consciously to "*produce* their means of subsistence";[2] in capitalism this capacity is turned against the being in whom it is manifest. Thus, we do not hone and perfect our capacities *through* work but are rather dulled and fragmented *by* work; we do not deploy our intellects toward the solution of our problems but submit to a scientific organization that demands conformity; we do not gain the satisfaction that follows from successfully furthering our abilities but rather stew in a general anxiety about losing our places in processes over which we have no control; we do not work in order to live better, in order to make a difficult but pliable world warm and inviting, but live merely in order to work and according to the demands of a world made icy and hostile. These are the basics of what, in *Capital*, is commonly called the "immiseration thesis."[3]

In brief, when Marx claims that the human being is "alienated" under capitalism, he means that an animal whose essence it is to master its environment is itself *mastered by its environment*.[4] What I find lacking in Marx, and also in the general tradition that carries his name, is any recognition of a part of our nature that actually works *against* our own mastery and thus willingly accepts this "inversion." If, to simplify Marx's point in *The German Ideology* tremendously, we are what we do, then surely some place must be made in our conception of ourselves for all the destructive behavior that serves to *erode* our mastery, that welcomes the destabilization wrought by capitalism, and that actively embraces, rather than passively imbibes, cultural "opiates." On this last point the ideal, as I see it, would be to view the beliefs, activities, and organizations too casually labeled distractions not as ancillary to the capitalist mode of production, nor as bearing their own autonomous logic, but rather as speaking to something else about the human being left untheorized by Marx. This would be to recognize all those things we take to provide some relief from alienation to be not so different from less socially accepted ways of attaining that relief, detrimental to the mastery of our own lives, but nonetheless actually providing real satisfaction to some part of ourselves.

Despite knowing precious little about the "communist system" upon which he would so casually cast judgment, Sigmund Freud proposed the basics of an incisive critique of Marx's understanding of alienation as inverted mastery: if "human nature" is not exhausted by the drive to mastery, and if, more radically, there exists an even more primordial counterforce to this drive, a drive to undo our own mastery and return to heteronomy, then Marx's theory and its attendant vision of liberation must, at the very least, be rethought.[5] Indeed, if something like what Freud called the "death drive" exists, capitalism could actually be said to provide a form of perverse psychic gratification in undermining the individual's mastery. That satisfaction might be ultimately damaging to our general fulfillment, but its very existence nonetheless implies that the theory of alienation could benefit from a new proposal as to what constitutes our "nature," one that takes into account a psychic force that works against our own mastery. The current project first took root when I realized that it was in the same text (*Beyond the Pleasure Principle*) in which Freud proposed the existence of this drive that two conceptions of mastery, roughly corresponding to what I have dubbed mastery$_1$ (in Freud, *Bemächtigung*) and mastery$_2$ (*Bewältigung*), became conceptually fused in his metapsychology. My intuition and hope, more or less stubbornly enacted in the pages that follow, was that a more robust understanding of how precisely we are alienated today could be formulated by working out the relations between the death drive and these two forms of mastery.[6]

As Marx was the soil and Freud the seed, I naturally accepted a great deal of help in cultivating my little plot from the so-called Frankfurt School. Largely under the influence of early friend and later foe Erich Fromm, the Frankfurt School famously turned to psychoanalysis to supplement Marxism with a psychological analysis of the motivations behind ideological subjectification.[7] While generally faithful to Freud in his early years, Fromm rejected outright his later metapsychology, and specifically his theory of the death drive.[8] The "integration of psychoanalysis" that took place under his watch thus self-consciously neglected the drive theory that Freud defended from the 1920s to his death. Though Fromm's influence on the inner circle of the Frankfurt School was to be short-lived, his understanding of the late metapsychology as essentially pessimistic and thus unserviceable in its original form remained at the core of critical theory. Thus, even Herbert Marcuse, Fromm's greatest detractor, could only theorize that which "seems to defy any hypothesis of a non-repressive civilization" as a by-product of frustration.[9] Like most marriages, the critical theorists' "marriage of Marx and Freud" involved a bit of both repression and suppression.[10]

The stage is now more or less set: a problem of mastery in Marx, a possible solution in Freud, and a very interesting conversation by proxy unfortunately structured around the neglect of that solution. What I have just described is a simplification, of course, and what follows will, without a doubt, spill over the sides of this narrative. I nonetheless hope it is enough to entice the reader into following me through the perils of execution. I would further hope, however, that the grand "what if" question at the heart of this project finds answers, or at least echoes thereof, in the present. Of course, a great deal of time separates us from Marx and Freud, and even the Fordist-Keynesian paradigm in which the Frankfurt School operated seems somewhat distant from the present; but no energy need be spent demonstrating the continued relevance of the contradictions inherent in capitalism as described by Marx, the contradictions inherent in the psyche as described by Freud, and the strange intermingling of those contradictions as described by the critical theorists. To those who would decline engagement with my argument ahead of time, and even to those who think I was born fifty-some years too late, I am afraid any such effort would be a plunge into the void.[11]

I will, however, attempt to do more focused justificatory work in the remainder of this introduction, specifically pertaining to the nature of psychoanalytic drive theory. It was not so long ago that discussion of these psychic forces proudly bore the label *scientific*. Today, however, they have been relegated to the mythological, the realm that Freud, in any case, thought was their natural home. Rather than lamenting this reversion, I take it as a positive opportunity to reassert the nature and value of drive theory free of the scientism that plagued the American psychoanalytic scene for so many years. In a sense, now that the wave of anti-Freudianism has subsided,[12] and along with it the fury at Freud's misguided biologism, it has been given a clean slate, like so many theories that are chewed up and spit out by history. Having been placed right in that wonderful no-man's-land between irrelevance and outmodedness, I find it an opportune time to revisit Freud's grand mythology.

Drive, Psyche, and Interpretation Before 1920 . . .

It is customary to divide Freud's corpus into three main periods: 1. his prepsychoanalytic writings of the late 1800s; 2. his "early" psychoanalytic work beginning with *The Interpretation of Dreams* (1900), in which he develops the "topographical" model of unconscious, preconscious, and conscious; and 3. his "late" work beginning with *Beyond the Pleasure Principle* (1920), in which he develops the "structural" model of id, ego, and superego. The drive theory that will be examined and expanded upon in the chapters that follow was first developed in the last of these three periods, during which time Freud came to a radically new understanding not only of the drives but also of the nature of the psyche and of psychoanalytic therapy. It is my aim in the next few sections of this introduction to explain how Freud's understandings of drive, psyche, and interpretation changed between his early and late periods as well as how these three fundamental concepts became more intimately related after 1920.

For the early Freud, drive (*Trieb*) is primarily somatic in origin (though it is unclear whether or not drives themselves are strictly somatic forces) and is thus not primarily a force *of* the psyche but rather one applied *to* the psyche. When impinged upon by the drives, it is the psyche's task then to "process the incoming stimuli [and] to discharge them again in some modified form."[13] Since the psyche is understood here to be a kind of stimulus-processing mechanical instrument, we might call this the "mechanism model" of the psyche.[14] For my present purposes, all that I wish to emphasize here is that drive, in this early model, is essentially an *external* and *disturbing* force, a source of chaos upsetting to a psychic apparatus seeking stability, order, and repose. For the most part, a healthy tension is maintained, but at those life-defining moments when Dionysus runs roughshod over Apollo, the latter draws upon its own proprietary tactic for coping with its failure: repression. By banishing the memory of its having been overcome to the unconscious, the psyche is able to return quickly to the status quo but without learning from the experience and thus to the detriment of its own health. The task of interpretation is then to name particular instances during which the psyche was unable to manage the demands placed upon it, with the aim not of quelling, or otherwise altering, the drives, but rather of bringing said failure to consciousness and thereby replacing "hysterical misery" with "common unhappiness."[15]

As an example: a wealthy young Russian named Sergei Pankejeff comes to see Freud in 1910 with a variety of maladies all circulating around a state of deep depression.[16] In the course of reviewing his personal history, Freud discovers conflict in virtually all of Pankejeff's early relationships. Shortly after his birth, his mother begins to suffer from abdominal disorders and as a result has relatively little to do with his rearing (despite hanging about as a cold, distant presence). Throughout his childhood, his precocious older sister regularly seduces him into a variety of sexual practices while planting wild ideas in his head. He recalls, on one occasion, her playing with his penis while telling him by way of explanation that his Nanya (the peasant nurse who was caring for him in his mother's absence) regularly did the same with their gardener's genitals. As a result of these experiences, the boy takes on a passive attitude toward sexual activity—it is something *done to* him—and begins to distrust the sole source of maternal warmth in his life. His Nanya does her part to confirm that distrust: catching him playing with his penis in front of her, she threatens that he will get a "wound" there. Finally, and perhaps on account of all of these factors, the child develops a great attachment to his father, who is frequently away in sanatoriums and who overtly prefers his more boyish elder sister.[7]

These are the basics of the case study that Freud would publish in 1918 under the title "From the History of an Infantile Neurosis,"[18] known more affectionately (or cruelly) as the case of the "Wolfman," so called on account of an anxiety dream that Pankejeff has just before his fourth birthday wherein he opens a window to find wolves sitting silently and motionlessly in a tree. There is a great deal more to this case, perhaps Freud's most elaborate and important,[19] but we can already see the basic ingredients for depression here. However, rather than chalk up his adult neurosis to this set of infantile factors (undoubtedly the most sensible route to take), Freud instead posits the existence of a repressed "primal scene" that relates to all of these factors but is, according to Freud, the *real* cause of Pankejeff's illness. The infamous scene runs essentially as follows: at the ripe young age of eighteen months, Pankejeff wakes up from an afternoon nap to find his parents engaged in coitus *a tergo* (from behind). On Freud's explanation, while the young boy does not know precisely what to make of this scene at first, it slowly comes to bear an overwhelming significance: as his mother grows increasingly ill, he cannot help but feel that the violent motions he had witnessed that afternoon had somehow caused her infirmity. Even more important: both as a result of being the passive object of his sister's sexual researches and of his intense affection for his father, he comes to identify himself in his mother's position, simultaneously wishing to occupy her role as love object while fearing the violence that this position entails, vividly demonstrated to him in the primal scene.

In "discovering" and articulating the repressed primal scene to the Wolfman, Freud understood himself to have "liberated" his patient in one particular way: having been debased by his sister and threatened by his Nanya, the boy had overcompensated for these early wrongs with an aggressive masculinity, expressed first in an early phase of cruelty (Pankejeff was, by his own admission, a sadistic child) and then later in his adolescence in an exaggerated enthusiasm for military affairs. This "masculine protest" was cover for a wish that had been engendered by the very passivity to which he was protesting: in short, to be penetrated by his father as his mother had been in the primal scene. The repression of this homosexual object cathexis was in large part responsible for the disconnect between the Wolfman's affective life and his intelligence: his critical faculties had been impaired by his positive wish *not* to confront his desires, leading to a state of general depletion and indifference accented by bizarre rituals and erratic behavior within which the repressed current forced its way to the surface. In bringing the primal scene to consciousness, the Wolfman recognized that toward which his drives were propelling him and in so doing relieved himself not of the drives themselves but of the neurotic misery they were causing.

Everything I have said thus far of this case has been explained according to Freud's *early* understandings of drive, psyche, and interpretation. In conjunction with later experiences that "activated" its implications,[20] the "primal scene" had forcefully awakened Pankejeff's sexual and aggressive drives, and he had dealt with the overwhelming and conflicting feelings that followed by repressing it. The drives, however, remained active, leading him to a variety of activities in which could be found an unstable mixture of desire and aggression. Freud's interpretation then named the *actual moment* of having been overwhelmed and, in so doing, was able to rob the primal scene of its unconscious power.

. . . and After 1920

Like many readers of this case, I have always taken Freud's interpretation to be so patently absurd that mere rejection somehow misses the mark. I thus feel comfortable in claiming that if we understand this case as the "early" Freud did, there is little reason to read it as anything more than a document of the wild ramblings that a self-appointed seer once offered to a fragile young man in need of real help. Fortunately, around the time that the Wolfman's (first) analysis with Freud was terminating (and perhaps on account of what transpired in this wild case),[21] the "early" understandings of the drives, the psyche, and the task of interpretation that I have just outlined all began to fall apart.[22] As if in an effort to reorient himself, Freud set out, at the end of 1914, to systematize his metapsychology—his stock of theories concerning the general nature and structure of psychic life—in a twelve-chapter treatise that he hoped would be a landmark of psychology. The project never materialized, and, in the five papers that did eventually see the light of day,[23] it is easy to see why: what begin as earnest attempts to illuminate a particular pillar of psychoanalytic theory quickly introduce contradictions and tangents that find no resolution within their pages.

None of the so-called metapsychology papers demonstrates this tendency to unravel better than "Instincts and Their Vicissitudes" (1915), a veritable mess that foreshadows, in marking off the limits of one line of thought, the Freudian turn to come. The paper aims to outline the basics of the aforementioned "mechanism model" of the psyche, which, as Hans Loewald aptly observes,[24] assumes two rigid distinctions: first, that between psyche and soma (drives impinge on the psyche from without, i.e., from the body) and, second, that between psyche-soma and world (drives arise not from the environment but only from the body). Though Freud means to uphold these two distinctions at the outset of the paper, both very quickly deteriorate. Shortly after defining drive as a "stimulus applied to the mind," he claims that a drive "appears to us as a concept on the frontier between the mental and the somatic, as the psychical representative of the stimuli originating from within the organism."[25] One must immediately wonder: is drive the stimulus or is it the psychic representative of the stimulus (or does it only "appear to us" as a psychic representative)? And how would we know the difference? As James Strachey hints already in his introduction to the piece, the definition of drive here seems to undo the psyche-soma relation it is meant to explain.[26] Similarly, as important as the distinction between stimuli arising from internal and external worlds is at the beginning of the paper, the external world is soon claimed to be thoroughly imbued with internal conflicts: "At the very beginning," Freud speculates, "it seems the external world, objects, and *what is hated* are identical."[27] How exactly are we to differentiate external and internal stimuli in this situation?

Not six months after completing "Instincts and Their Vicissitudes," Freud would complain to Karl Abraham that it and its eleven companion pieces were little more than "war-time atrocities."[28] No one could have thought more differently of these papers than Freud's enthusiastic

Hungarian colleague and perhaps his most active wartime correspondent, Sándor Ferenczi,[29] who would tell "the Professor" of his metapsychology papers in general that "only now does one comprehend the structure of the psychic apparatus."[30] Of the many lessons Ferenczi would learn in reading through the drafts of the metapsychology papers, he expressed particular appreciation for one in a letter from February 1915: in brief, "that the terms pro- and introjection should be taken cum grano salis."[31] Three years later, in February 1918, he would reiterate that the developments of the metapsychology papers have made it "necessary to revise *the concept of introjection* on the basis of the new findings."[32] What Ferenczi claims to have "learned" from Freud in both instances—though it is unclear who was teaching whom—was that the psyche is not so much a receiver and manager of external stimuli as it is the product of a "constant, oscillating process" of projection and introjection.[33]

Five years after the completion of "Instincts and Their Vicissitudes," Freud would emerge from the morass of the Great War with *Beyond the Pleasure Principle* (1920), announcing in its very title a revolution of no small scale: whereas human beings had previously been understood as oriented fundamentally toward the pursuit of pleasure, Freud asserts in this text that that pursuit is conditioned by a more primary drive of all organic matter toward self-destruction. It is easy to see in this proposal of a "death drive" a product of its times: the problem of death had, after all, become *the* central preoccupation of all European thinkers, and Freud's beloved daughter Sophie had died shortly before the text's publication.[34] Much more interesting, to my mind, than the external factors involved in the genesis of the theory are the *internal* ones: metapsychology clearly ran aground with the collapse of the distinctions between psyche, soma, and world (uncomfortably on display in "Instincts and Their Vicissitudes"), and the floundering, unsystematic nature of everything Freud published during the war attests to a full-fledged *theoretical* crisis to complement the personal and social crises he was undergoing.

The overcoming of this theoretical crisis in *Beyond* involved a decisive abandonment of the smoking wreck produced by "Instincts and Their Vicissitudes" and the formulation of a radically new psychic architecture that Loewald calls the "organism" model of the psyche. In this new model the human being is understood as "embedded in its environment in such a way that it is in living contact and interchange with it; it modulates and influences the environment by its own activity, and its activity is modulated and influenced by the environment."[35] Whereas the world had no sway over the drives in the early model, it is thus afforded no such strict externality after 1920. Similarly, whereas the drives were before understood to be external forces disruptive to an apparatus seeking repose, in this new model the drives themselves seek the quietude that was previously the aim of the psyche (Freud now claims that the aim of all drive is to reestablish a previous state). As Loewald summarizes, "the gain, from the present point of view, was that instincts and the psyche were no longer at loggerheads with each other, as they had been when . . . seen as disturbing an apparatus that wanted to be unstimulated."[36] In short, the drives become "forces *within* the psychic organization and not stimuli which operate on the system from without."[37] Under the influence of the organism analogy, Freud is thus compelled to arrive at a different conclusion than the one he sought in 1915: namely, that drives are *psychic* forces shaped *in relation to the environment*.[38]

With this new understanding of drive in mind, it only makes sense that Freud would become a fervent supporter of Jean-Baptiste Lamarck, hopeful that psychoanalysis might eventually explain his theory of biological adaptation. In a letter to Abraham, he expressed his desire "to put Lamarck entirely on our ground and to show that the 'necessity' that according to him creates and transforms organs is nothing but the power of unconscious ideas over one's own body."[39] His ambition to ground psychoanalysis in the biology of his day might be a retrospective embarrassment, given the discrediting of Lamarck's "soft inheritance" theory, but the introduction of the organism model to drive theory is a case of new wine bursting old wineskins. For if drives are *acquired* in the early stages of life in relation to the environment, how can they be solely our "inheritance from the animal world"?[40] The environment in which the human organism comes to maturity is, after all, a distinctively human one, shaped by forces that have as much to do with culture and society as they do biology. The basic insight that drives are formed in relation to the environment need not be implicated in Freud's misguided biologism, and one might even say that his turn to an explicitly biological metaphor paradoxically and definitively differentiates drive theory from biology.[41]

Although Freud would spend the rest of his life grappling with the implications of this new "organism" model of the psyche, he unfortunately did little in the way of indicating how it required a new conception not simply of what the drives are but rather of what *drive itself is*. Once again, we may follow Loewald's lead in articulating the consequences of

Freud's "late" views. According to Loewald, drive, in the late model, is indeterminate at first and comes only to acquire aim and force in the complex interchanges of early life, i.e., in relation to the environment. We are held, caressed, cooed at, coddled, fed at the breast, or in close bodily contact and we can also be neglected and cared for in an impersonal way. Later we are encouraged, corralled, admonished, disciplined, screamed at, etc. It is in these experiences that drives are not elicited but *formed*—we *learn* what it is to love, to master, to aggress[42]—and their formation coincides with the development of psychic life itself.[43]

This new conception of drive thus goes hand in hand with a new conception of the psyche: instead of being *opposed* to the disturbing force of the drives, the psyche is now understood to be more primarily *composed* of the drives and the structures to which they give rise *in their conflict*.[44] We want to love that which we also want to aggress, to master that which we also want to reject, to be hurt by that which we want to hurt, and all of these conflicts *engender* the basic structures that are responsible for the existence of that special domain that Freud calls "psychical reality."[45] In a late paper, "The Dissolution of the Oedipus Complex" (1924), Freud offers the following formulation of oedipal conflict: "If the satisfaction of love in the field of the Oedipus Complex is to cost the child his penis, a conflict is bound to arise between his narcissistic interest in that part of his body and the libidinal cathexis of his parental objects. In this conflict, the first of these forces normally triumphs: the child's ego turns away from the Oedipus complex."[46] Behind the specific gendering of the conflict, one can see clearly here that the Oedipus complex, at bottom, is one of conflict between generally self-interested forces—narcissistic or ego drives—and sexual ones. The Oedipus complex is thus such a major developmental hurdle because in it the satisfaction of one of our primary drives imperils the satisfaction of another, and the same is true for every single one of the complexes, fantasies, and scenes of which "psychical reality" is composed.[47]

What, then, of interpretation? In the early conception, interpretation a) names an *actual occurrence* in the patient's history b) with the aim not of affecting the drives but simply of bringing the unconscious to consciousness. In the late paper "Constructions in Analysis" (1937), Freud would upset both components of this view of interpretation. First, he admits that an interpretation is only "real" in the context of an analytic relationship: in other words, that the reality of what is uncovered in analysis is determined by its impact on the therapeutic process.[48] He might have also said that since psychic reality is a product of conflict between the drives it need not have any *actual* reality in order to affect the course of our lives. Second, he talks about the constructions of interpretation "stirring to activity" the "'upward drive' of the repressed" (*der "Auftrieb" des Verdrängten*).[49] I take this to mean that interpretation does not simply uncover repressed material, leaving the drives unaltered, but rather that the drives are constantly reaching "upward" and latching on to constructions in order to find gratification in new forms of expression. When they find this new expression, the drives do not lessen or disappear in their force, but they do take on a new form, one that opens them, in Loewald's words, "to the dynamics of personal motivation."[50] This is to say that interpretations can facilitate not only *realization* (from hysterical misery to common unhappiness) but also *transformation* (from impersonal drive to personal motivation).[51] In this new view, the task of the psychoanalyst is not, like the scientist's, to discover an already existing unconscious occurrence but rather, more like the artist's, to take an unfinished kind of mental life that is incessantly reaching upward, clamoring for expression, and to give it *form* (or at least, a *better* form).[52] Psychoanalysis, in this view, is about not finding but *creating* reality.[53]

The Wolfman Revisited

It is possible now to redescribe the case of the Wolfman with these new conceptions of drive, psyche, and interpretation in tow. It is not, as before, that Pankejeff's early experiences *awakened* his already existent sexual and aggressive drives but rather that he *learned*—in the seduction by his sister, in the distance of his mother, in the threats of his Nanya, in the lack of his father's affection—*how* to love and aggress in these interactions. It is the drives that were *formed* during these early years that were then responsible for his childhood "naughtiness" and later neurosis. Perhaps even more important: when Freud articulates the fantastic "primal scene" to Pankejeff, its efficaciousness lies in the fact not that it actually happened but rather that it makes sense of the conflict between two desires: on the one hand, to be a strong male, an aim threatened by many of his early experiences and yet also encouraged by social pressure, and, on the other, to be the object of his father's love and attention, even (and, seemingly, especially) if this meant being penetrated and hurt by him.

Freud devotes the entirety of section 5 of "From the History of an Infantile Neurosis" to wondering himself about the nature of the primal scene, admitting that the particular construction under examination there—witnessing coitus a tergo at eighteen months—seems rather farfetched. He ultimately comes down in favor, provisionally, of the *actual occurrence* of the scene, but he also asserts that, even if it were a fantasy, "the carrying-out of analysis would not in the first instance be altered in any respect."[54] Much has been written about Freud's abandonment, in 1897, of the so-called seduction thesis—the view that all neurotic conflict can be traced back to *actual instances* of sexual abuse—for a theory that put fantasy center stage, and one might wonder if he does not return, in 1918, to his early view in asserting the actual occurrence of the coitus a tergo scene.[55] What the discussion of the reality of the primal scene in the Wolfman case makes clear, however, is that this problem—whether or not the constructions proffered in analysis actually occurred or not—*no longer mattered* for Freud: quite contentedly, he ends "the discussion of the reality of the primal scene with a *non liquet*."[56] It is not clear, and it *does not need to be clear*, as the legitimacy of the constructions of analysis does not stem from their historical actuality.

What interpretation did for Pankejeff was thus not to name the actual moment of being overwhelmed but rather to articulate a scene that would give expression to his drives in their conflict. Freud admittedly thought that he had "cured" Pankejeff in 1914,[57] but makes a much more modest claim in the case history itself: quite simply, to have liberated "his shackled homosexuality" and thereby to have freed his "intellectual activity" from impairment.[58] It is thus not that Pankejeff came to realize the truth of the repressed scene but rather that a portion of his drives found expression in Freud's articulation and in so doing enlivened his secondary process. Put more subjectively, instead of greeting Freud's construct with the realization "Oh, *that* happened," we can think of Pankejeff as instead hearing Freud articulate this wild speculation, and *even while finding it to be utter speculation*, feeling something like, "Here is something that hits upon the nature of my drives." What Freud gave Pankejeff, in short, was not the truth but *a fantasy within which drive met thought*.

In 1973, almost sixty years after the Wolfman had finished his first treatment with Freud, the journalist Karin Obholzer found and interviewed Pankejeff, who told her, among other things, that the primal scene as Freud described it was quite "improbable because in Russia [his birthplace], children sleep in the nanny's bedroom, not in their parents."[59]

Pankejeff offers many other recollections that impugn Freud or other analysts in some respect and conceives of himself as quite critical of psychoanalysis,[60] but his condemnation is by no means consistent: though he claims at one point to be "in the same state as when [he] first came to Freud," at others he expresses a belief in the idea "that improvement can be made by transference" and a real appreciation for his initial analysis.[61] One gets the impression throughout of a still compulsive, depressed, guilt-ridden, and frustrating person—he finds it quite normal to pay women for sex, he is obsessed with the behavior of "sluts," he cannot see how his taking of mistresses during his marriage had anything to do with his wife's suicide[62]—but also one who had managed to eke out a tolerable existence in spite of his childhood difficulties—the seduction by his sister, his distance from his mother, and the disappointment of his father are all confirmed in these interviews—and adulthood tragedies.[63] He is able to discuss homosexuality (in an admittedly defensive and distancing manner), takes an active interest in painting and literature, and cannot help but speak about his life in psychoanalytic terms, even while taking objection to many of them.

It would be quite impossible to argue, based upon these interviews, or even his own memoirs, that the Wolfman's analysis had been anything resembling a success, though I am not certain that either point definitively to its failure.[64] My discussion of Freud's changing views of drive, psyche, and interpretation in the previous two sections cannot help decide the matter either way, but it *can* help us establish what we would need to affirm if we *were* to consider his analysis meaningful: namely, not that the primal scene articulated by Freud was any "more than a construct," but rather that a previously unreflective person burdened by his own lack of satisfaction became a slightly more reflective and slightly less unsatisfied one in finding something in Freud's discourse onto which his drives found occasion to latch.

Society and Psyche

When it comes to explaining why human beings do what they do, two options are readily available to us: a *subjective* explanation (as found in statements like "she chose to do that," "you must take responsibility for your action," etc.) and an *objective* one ("he has a chemical imbalance," "it's all determined by genes," etc.). What I will reluctantly

call "social constructionism" has problematized both these kinds of explanation.[65] In this view, the best way to explain an individual's choice to
do X is to look neither to agency nor to brain chemistry but rather to the
individual's social, cultural, political, and economic milieu. The subjective explanation, for the social constructionist, typically does not account
for the preconditions of the subject's supposed "state of freedom": as
Durkheim said, the subject is a social product and not an ontological
substratum. The objective explanation, by contrast, lends itself to a rigid
fatalism in mistaking social constructions for objective facts.[66] When we
see that "undesirable" human behavior is not hard-wired, we can go about
changing the social conditions in which that behavior emerges.

Drive theory, in fact, shares a great deal with this mode of explanation, spurning both rigidified subjectivism and objectivism. Unlike the
"subjective" explanation, drive theory does not assume total, conscious,
volitional activity. And unlike the "objective" explanation, drive theory
does not assume nonconscious passivity: our actions are more than the
precipitates of our genetic makeup. Although it is never possible to be in
complete control or understanding of either drives or social conditions,
it *is* possible to *better* control and understand them. Drive theory is also
similar to social constructionism in being primarily *narrative*: since drives
are *acquired* during the early stages of life, there is a story to how they are
formed, and that story is just as essential to drive theory as the drives are
in themselves. Freedom *is*. Determinism *is*. But social formations and
psychic drives *come to be*, and they can also *be differently*. One could say
that both theories are kinds of *theodicy*, both in the etymological sense of
an attempt to do justice (*dike*) to the mystery (*theos*) of human being,[67]
but also in the more common sense of a narration that makes sense of
various evils in the world without demolishing its affirmability and our
capacity to enact change within it.[68]

Unfortunately, and perhaps since Michel Foucault's rise to patristic
status in the humanities, drive theory has been edged out of contempo-
raneity by social constructionism. Psychological theories, in this view, are
but reflections of larger discursive shifts in power relations, themselves to
be explained through historicization and contextualization. The critique
is both historical and substantive: on the one hand, the claim is that only
at a particular historical moment—for Nikolas Rose, "one that emerges
only in the nineteenth century"—and "in a limited and localized geographical space" is human being understood "in terms of individuals who
are selves, each equipped with an inner domain, a 'psychology,' which is

structured by the interaction between a particular biographical experience and certain general laws or processes of the human animal."[69] If drive theory has any purchase, in this view, it can only be one with limited temporal and geographical scope. On the other hand, the critique is that the object of psychology itself *does not exist*: there is no "unified psychological domain," only "culturally diverse linguistic practices, beliefs, and conventions."[70] Quite simply, there is no "unified self" because human beings are "heterogeneous and situationally produced."[71]

I have done some work to address this latter claim in the previous sections—for the late Freud, at least, drives ought to be understood as formed in relation to the environment and in conflict in such a way as to preclude the possibility of a "unified self"—and I will also deal with the historical specificity of the psyche beginning in chapter 4. No doubt, however, the critique goes deeper: in this view, it is wrong to speak of "drives" for the same reason it is wrong to speak of "selves" or "subjects," as if there are anything like universals when it comes to the myriad ways in which human beings conceive of their interiority (if, indeed, they do such a thing at all).[72] In different cultures and at different times, across lines of gender, race, socioeconomic status, etc., people are formed in a multitude of ways. Furthermore, where universals *are* invoked, one typically finds them in "continually repeated, motivated, and gendered act[s] of symbolic violence."[73]

While I agree with the critique that a particular discourse dominant in the modern West that pretends to universality has been oppressive, imposing, and simply inaccurate, I worry in two particular ways—one historically specific, the other more global and transhistorical—that the baby is being thrown out with the bathwater here (somewhat literally in this case).[74] First, while advanced capitalist society might be able to accommodate a wide range of subjectivities, it nonetheless must re-ensure that "living labour remains integral to the process of production of society as a whole" and thus produce subjects that abide by its "abstract form of social domination."[75] Insofar as this is true, it is premature to abandon talk of "subjects" with certain constant features, especially when it is in the interest of capitalism that its subjects see diversity and newness instead of a relentless reproduction of the same. In any event, when I turn to the language of "subject" in chapters 4 and 5 I mean it in this particular sense.

Second, I am in basic agreement with Peter Gay that "all humans share some inescapable universal preconditions"—in particular, bodies of certain kinds and a complete dependence on caretakers in early life—that dictate that they cannot be formed in just any way.[76] What mouths and their various acts *are* to human beings differs in various places and times, but *that we have mouths*, mouths that can do a limited number of things and that *must* ingest food, *does not*, and this fact provides a constraint on the range of meanings mouths can have for human beings. Even more important: what care *is* can be radically different in different societies,[77] but *that* human beings enter life completely dependent on the responses of other human beings (and for a fairly lengthy amount of time in comparison to other animals) is invariable.[78]

To be clear, I am not saying that there is some timeless bedrock of human *nature* that culture merely surrounds, but simply that there are a few important things about how we come to exist that pose particular problems for us and constrain the range of our possibilities.[79] Even though drives are formed in relation to the environment, from the existence of the "universal preconditions" of which Gay speaks it follows that there will be certain drives that all human beings share; but *how* these particular drives are formed—and, in turn, how they impact our lives and thus what they *mean* to us—as well as the *vicissitudes* available for their expression vary markedly in different societies and at different times.[80] I would thus agree with the claim that the "basic presuppositions of human life . . . imply very little when it comes to evaluating how humans, in relation to issues beyond mere survival, *lead their lives*," but would stress that we should nonetheless be extremely attentive to and unapologetic about what little they *do* imply.[81] If, thus, I dare to interpret the "death drive" in a transhistorical and universalist way, it is because I believe that *all* infants seek to maintain what I will call, in the first chapter, the "tension-within" position; but neither *how* this position is maintained, and thus what the death drive *is* for any particular individual, nor the modes of its expression are constant in the same way (the kind of death drive gratification I describe in chapter 4, for instance, is unique to the era of the culture industry).[82] The same basic argument goes for the drive to mastery and aggressivity.

In sum then, drives are formed in relation to the environment, but they are not just formed *in* any old thing: they appear in mammals with mouths, anuses, and genitals (not to mention opposable thumbs and large brains) that would, without fail, *die* upon birth were it not for an extended period of infancy in which they are *absolutely dependent* on their caretakers. What a strange and complex situation! No wonder, then, that "we are never sure that we are seeing [drives] clearly": it is impossible to know with exact precision how the infinite number of bodily, familial, and social factors combine in early life to form our unconscious motivational forces, but "we cannot for a moment disregard" these "mythical entities, magnificent in their indefiniteness," without abandoning depth psychology.[83] In one of those curious assertions that sowed the seeds of its own destruction (like so many of his defenses in his later years),[84] Freud offered a very precise articulation of the stakes and difficulties of this endeavor.

In Brief

I hope that the preceding defense of drive theory in general serves as a line of entry for a reconsideration of Freud's own drive theory, and in particular his strange proposal that all living things are driven to return to the inanimate ooze from which they sprang; in short, that "the aim of all life is death." In chapter 1 I turn directly to sections 4 and 5 of *Beyond the Pleasure Principle*, the wild "speculative" sections in which Freud constructs a grand narrative about the origins of life on earth as a curious and, most commentators would add, confused way of making sense of the novel clinical problems he had introduced in the first three sections, problems generally relating to what he calls the repetition compulsion. Through a close reading of these two sections, I recount Freud's understanding of how the first fledgling eruptions of life, interested only in reimmersing themselves in the primordial soup, refashion themselves into living organisms fighting against a "hostile environment" for their continued existence; that is, how the *death drive* becomes its own counterdrive, a *drive to mastery*.

This unfortunately undertheorized drive to mastery (*Bemächtigungstrieb*) is at the heart of my reinterpretation of Freudian drive theory and the key, in my view, to understanding the better-known instinctual antagonism of the late metapsychology: before the great struggle between Eros and Thanatos, there was a much more complicated self-subversion of the death drive resulting in the drive to mastery. At least as Freud describes it in *Beyond the Pleasure Principle*, the death drive is a drive to eliminate any self/other distinction, to cast off difference and be reimmersed in the environment. The drive to mastery, by contrast, is a drive to build and reinforce the living organism's protective structures. Whereas one aims to destroy the organism, the other aims to protect it; one seeks to stop the process of individuation, one to promote it. This is the basic form of ambivalence and the crux of this underexplored drive theory.

As biology, of course, Freud's mythological venture hardly holds water; as a theory of *psychic development*, however, it is perhaps more serviceable. In a creative interpretation of Haeckel's law, Loewald faithfully translates Freudian phylogeny into developmental ontogeny: thus, instead of a living organism, Loewald imagines an infant turning an urge to return to the care structure characteristic of the pre- and neonatal state into one for increased autonomy and mastery, into a drive to cope with the stark fact of separation that all human beings must endure. In chapter 2 I introduce Loewald's psychoanalytic vision through the lens of Freudian metapsychology with the hope of asserting the continued worth of this drive theory when rescued from biological anachronism.

No one has done more to keep the death drive in conceptual circulation than Jacques Lacan, who invokes Freud's theory at many different times in his oeuvre to a variety of effects. In chapter 3 I choose to focus on his treatment of the death drive through the notion of "specular aggressivity." By reading gestalt theory into *The Project for a Scientific Psychology* in *Seminar II*, Lacan comes to argue that the infant's aggressive struggle with a specular other is the primary motor of psychic development and that this seems to make sense of "the enigmatic signification" Freud expressed in the term *death drive*. What gets elided in this reading, I argue, is Freud's concern in these texts with psychic *mastery*, which is hastily translated into *aggressivity*. A critique of Lacan on this particular point proves to be a ripe occasion to formulate a new theory of aggressivity and thereby to clarify the distinctions between the concepts of death drive, drive to mastery, and aggressivity, which are often conflated in psychoanalytic theory.

In the last two chapters I employ the drive theory developed in the first three to sort out the critical theorists' appropriation of psychoanalysis. Chapter 4 examines Theodor Adorno and Max Horkheimer's claim that late capitalism engenders a "new anthropological type" resulting from a dissolution of the psychic tension that held together the bourgeois subject theorized by Freud. In order to analyze this new type, they employ the structural model of id, ego, and superego while thoroughly neglecting the drive theory that undergirded it. By reworking their articulation of this psychic transformation with a stronger metapsychological foundation, it is possible more clearly to specify the nature of the drive gratification provided by the culture industry and how that gratification works on the psyche.

In chapter 5 I look at this same process of psychic change from a slightly different angle. Throughout his work Marcuse flirted with the idea that technological progress provides an avenue for the sublimation of our aggressive and destructive tendencies toward social ends. Through a symptomatic reading of Marcuse's repeated rejections of this hypothesis, I attempt to salvage the idea of "aggressive sublimation" and to spell out its implications for thinking about psychic life under late capitalism. As the commodification of culture and aggressive instrumentalism settle into a comfortable obviousness, it is necessary to renew our efforts to understand the nature of the desire and satisfaction promised by cultural consumption and technological innovation. These last two chapters are written with this aim in mind: to break the spell of the array of programs and gadgets that are constantly being paraded in front of us by coming to a greater understanding of the drive fulfillment provided therein.

PART I

Dream

The "death drive" . . . is a concept which can only be correctly situated at a specific moment in the drama of the Freudian discovery. Outside of that context, it becomes an empty formula.
                    —Jean Laplanche, "The So-Called 'Death Drive'"

1   Death, Mastery, and the Origins of Life

Sigmund Freud's Strange Proposal

In this first chapter, I will be teasing out the basics of a metapsychological narrative first outlined by Sigmund Freud in *Beyond the Pleasure Principle*. I have already discussed, in the introduction, the deep theoretical crisis out of which this text emerged. For my present purposes, I want simply to emphasize that the metapsychology produced there, in the background of every theoretical innovation that Freud would make for the rest of his life, is indeed a narrative. Whereas the earlier metapsychological venture of the 1910s sought to lay out a set of categories that analysts could apply schematically, in Kantian fashion, to the empirical content of their analytic encounters, the later "metanarrative" provides more of a Hegelian schema-in-motion, a set of ideas that can only be properly grasped in the story in which they unfold. The various concepts that emerge from this development (id, ego, and superego) are not simple additions to the pre-1920 analytic toolbelt but rather characters in a fundamentally new story, the central personage of which is undoubtedly the death drive.[1]

Before turning to the narrative itself, however, I will offer a brief conceptual history of the death drive and its unfortunately undertheorized vicissitude, *the drive to mastery*.[2] Despite its recurrence throughout Freud's work, this latter concept has failed to receive due treatment; where it has been addressed, it is more often than not assimilated to more familiar concepts like aggression. It is my aim here to demonstrate that the drive to mastery is not a footnote in the history of psychoanalytic theory but a key to understanding Freud's later dual drive theory and, by extension, the structural model of id, ego, and superego. The death drive, on the other hand, though widely rejected by the professional analytic community, has been fruitfully developed in a number of directions. Unfortunately, this development has typically taken place *outside* the narrative of which it is the critical part.

In the effort thus to re-embed the death drive in its natural habitat and unveil the importance of the drive to mastery for psychoanalytic theory,[3] I will attempt a cohesive presentation of sections 4 and 5 of *Beyond the Pleasure Principle,* which contain what many would argue are the most ludicrous hypotheses to be found in Freud's grand corpus. Given the fragmented and wild nature of his endeavor there, this task will require some intensive textual work. To take another early cue from Jean Laplanche, the aim of this reading will be not so much to criticize Freud, nor simply to recapitulate his views, but rather to think *alongside* of him, to retrace his steps, and, if necessary, to veer slightly from his own path to inspect the conceptual surroundings.[4] My hope, by the end of this chapter, is to have elucidated the basic tension between the death drive and the drive to mastery, which, like eerily similar personalities whose opposition comprises a plot's intrigue, form the antithetical counterpoles of the drive theory that will occupy the attention of the remaining chapters of this book.

A Brief History of Mastery and Death

In 1920 Freud shocked the bourgeoning analytic community with the introduction of the death drive (*Todestrieb*),[5] the unsettling hypothesis that all living things are unconsciously driven to their own demise. This new drive theory was meant to provide a comprehensive solution to a set of conundrums that had hitherto eluded psychoanalytic explanation, most notably the "compulsion to repeat" traumatic situations and thereby retroactively attempt to gain some degree of *mastery* over them.[6] New as the speculations of *Beyond the Pleasure Principle* were, this concern with psychic mastery had been a mainstay of Freud's thought throughout his career.[7] Very early on, in a paper from 1894, he suggests the importance of "mastering somatic excitation" (*Bewältigung der somatischen Sexualerregung*),[8] a phrase that would repeat in a number of his most well-known essays: in "On Narcissism," where he calls "our mental apparatus . . . a device for mastering excitations [*Bewältigung von Erregungen*] which would otherwise be felt as distressing or would have pathogenic effects";[9] in the case of the Wolfman, where he discourses on the failure "to master the real problems of life" (*Bewältigung der realen Probleme des Lebens*);[10] and in "Instincts and Their Vicissitudes," where he emphasizes the importance of "mastering stimuli" (*Reizbewältigung*).[11]

A somewhat different concern with mastery is found in *Three Essays on the Theory of Sexuality* (1905), where Freud posits a "drive to mastery" (*Bemächtigungstrieb*) associated with "masculine sexual activity" and aggressive, anal behavior.[12] It is also, curiously enough, linked to "the instinct for knowledge," which is deemed "a sublimated manner of obtaining mastery."[13] Between the *Three Essays* and *Beyond the Pleasure Principle*, the phrase would appear sporadically and always in the limited sense accorded it in the *Three Essays*.[14] As Kristin White explains, Freud most likely had Alfred Adler's concept of *Machtstreben* (striving for power) in mind every time he used *Bemächtigungstrieb*.[15] Adler was an important but threatening interlocutor of Freud's throughout the 1900s, but rather angrily broke with the Vienna Psychoanalytic Society in 1911. It would thus make sense that Freud employed the term sparingly and to restricted effect.

Nothing in the pre-1920 appearances of the term *Bemächtigungstrieb* thus prepares us for the significance it acquires in *Beyond the Pleasure Principle*, where Freud explains the efforts of his grandson's *Fort/Da* game[16] in terms of an "instinct for mastery [*Bemächtigungstrieb*] that was acting independently of whether the memory was in itself pleasurable or not."[17] No longer a simple "component instinct" as it was in the *Three Essays*, *Bemächtigungstrieb* is now put forth as counterevidence to Freud's belief, held for some thirty years, that all life is governed by the pleasure principle. In addition, it is made responsible for the compulsion to repeat in that it is what causes us to return to traumatic scenes and retroactively "master or bind its excitations" (*die Erregung zu bewältigen oder zu binden*).[18] Jean Laplanche and Jean-Bertrand Pontalis help us make sense of this surprising conceptual transformation: during the war years, they argue, Freud came to realize that the "mastery of the object" characteristic of aggressive behavior "goes hand in hand with the binding together" of distressing stimuli.[19] In other words, the problematics of *Bewältigung* and *Bemächtigung* slowly began to fuse in Freud's mind, and by *Beyond the Pleasure Principle* "no strict distinction is drawn between the two terms."[20] We can thus only make sense of Freud's explanation of the *Fort/Da* game if we understand *Bemächtigungstrieb* to mean, for the first time, *Bewältigungstrieb*.[21] For all of their supposed translation sins, it seems then that the Stracheys were quite justified in rendering both *Bemächtigung* and *Bewältigung* as "mastery."[22]

Aside from *Beyond the Pleasure Principle*, the most striking usage of the drive to mastery comes in "The Economic Problem of Masochism" (1924), where the term is further equated with "the destructive instinct" (*Destruktionstrieb*) and, strikingly, "the will to power" (*Wille zur Macht*).[23] Freud is clearly struggling with the terminology here, as he even goes so far as to equate the destructive and the death drives (*Todes- oder Destruktionstrieb*).[24] Should we then, by the transitive property, take *Bemächtigungstrieb* to mean *Todestrieb*? As I intend to show in what follows, reconstructing Freud's metapsychological narrative in *Beyond the Pleasure Principle* reveals more terminological distinction between these concepts than he offers in "The Economic Problem of Masochism." Intimately connected as the two drives in fact are, the relationship is much more complicated than one of identity.

* * *

After Freud, not much is made of *Bemächtigungstrieb*;[25] but while his thoughts on psychic mastery withered from neglect, the theory of the death drive ironically caused a great disturbance within the psychoanalytic community and was the subject of much, albeit predominantly negative, discussion.[26] At first, Freud himself only ambivalently proposed the idea, but it eventually "acquired such a power" over him that he could "no longer think in any other way."[27] Freud's followers, despite their general obsequiousness, were not so charmed: indeed, as Freud's enthusiasm waxed, theirs waned. With the exception of Sándor Ferenczi, whose elaborate extensions of psychoanalytic metapsychology worried even Freud himself,[28] none in Freud's inner circle came to accept the death drive.[29] Despite epistolary pleas for their relevance to psychoanalytic theory, Ernest Jones and Oskar Pfister both sadly reported to Freud in 1930 that they simply could not endorse his views on the matter.[30] Many of the continental emigrants felt similarly and did not pass up the opportunity to say so. Fritz Wittels suggested that the wild speculations in *Beyond the Pleasure Principle* followed upon the death of Freud's daughter, Sophie Halberstadt, an accusation that Freud was quick to deny.[31] Otto Fenichel contended in typically reasoned fashion that the clinical facts "do not necessitate the assumption of a genuine self-destructive instinct."[32] As de facto leader of the school of ego psychology, Heinz Hartmann sought to develop the structural theory while "omitting Freud's other, mainly biologically oriented set of hypotheses of the 'life' and 'death' instincts."[33] Wilhelm Reich, one of the earliest opponents of the death drive, claimed simply that "'Death' was right. 'Instinct' was wrong."[34] One could go on like this for quite some time: the number of theorists who have entertained the death drive only to curtly dismiss it is rather astounding.[35]

The only psychoanalytic theorists who have affirmed the death drive, at least in some part, have generally belonged to one of two psychoanalytic "schools": Kleinian or Lacanian.[36] Hoping to draw more attention to the aggressive impulses she had discovered in her work with children, Melanie Klein was an early endorser of the concept of the death drive.[37] As many commentators have noted, however, Klein herself never really dealt with the death drive as it was described by Freud: her interest from the beginning was in aggression and destruction, concepts that she equated with *Todestrieb*.[38] Although Freud most certainly gave his adherents ample reason to relate the concepts of death drive, drive to mastery, and aggression beginning around 1923, the exact relation between these terms was never made clear. As Jean Laplanche argues, "Freud understands his death drive *retrospectively* as an aggressive drive;"[39] that is, in its initial formulation in *Beyond the Pleasure Principle* the death drive was most certainly not conceived as aggression.[40] Only later did Freud come to associate these terms. Although Klein did a great deal to advance and complicate Freudian theory, in taking this association, in rather uncomplicated fashion, to be equation, I do not believe she did any service to the concept of the death drive.

Indeed, one might argue that her work actually *prevented* any real discussion of the death drive in the English literature. In the early 1940s Klein and her followers were locked in an acrimonious debate with Anna Freud and other "orthodox" members of the British Psychoanalytic Society.[41] When the animosity passed and Kleinians began more freely to mingle in the so-called psychoanalytic mainstream, British and American analysts were also confronting the need to make sense of the metapsychology that undergirded the structural model of id, ego, and superego. In the simplest terms, their solution went something like this: "Freud had *actually* been struggling with the stark fact of aggression for some time, but in order to make himself seem different from Adler, he formulated the problem in *Beyond the Pleasure Principle* in alien terms. Recognizing as we do the distorting nature of Freud's ambition, we can dispose of his theoretical idiosyncrasies and focus on what we analysts all recognize to be of clinical importance: aggression." The fact that it was the controversial figure of Melanie Klein who most powerfully made the equation "death drive = aggression" led the psychoanalytic community to feel that it had made great progress in mending an internal conflict when it finally accepted aggressive drives alongside libidinal ones. The self-congratulation that followed virtually buried the concepts of the death drive and the drive to mastery under the weight of good will amidst the English-speaking psychoanalytic world.

Not everyone, however, fell victim to this conceptual "evolution": in France, free from the adaptive ideals in emigrant lands and under the spell of Jacques Lacan, the death drive was explored in all its enigmatic impenetrability. While there is a strain of the Lacanian appropriation that links the themes of death and aggression through the lens of the Hegelian "struggle unto death,"[42] Lacan employed the death drive in many different contexts toward many different ends, recognizing, at every turn, the real difficulty of understanding Freud's hypothesis.[43] This experimental approach of his theoretical encounters solidified into a generally centrifugal tendency in the works of his heirs, loyal or otherwise: the death drive became "unbound" (*deliée*) libido (Laplanche),[44] a "counter-evolutionary movement of disorganization" (Marty),[45] a "desire of non-desire" (Aulagnier),[46] semiotic *chora* (Kristeva),[47] an ever failing attack on primary narcissism (Leclaire),[48] negative narcissism (Green),[49] or else, even more radically, *différance vis à vis* the pleasure principle (Derrida),[50] an archiviolithic force (Derrida again),[51] body without organs (Deleuze),[52] "'undead' eternal life itself" (Žižek).[53] Without taking away from the inevitability of differential play, one wonders, given the theoretical implications of the present topic, about this desire to send the death drive out in ever new directions without first interrogating its source.[54]

The absent center around which these various forms of reception relate is a serious confrontation with the death drive that does not reduce it to aggression and remains *within* Freud's conceptual space in an attempt to see what this notion undoes and redoes. This project is no different from the one Freud himself undertook after 1920.

Life After Death: Freud's Account of the Origins of Life in Sections 4 and 5 of *Beyond the Pleasure Principle*

In this section I intend to follow the death drive in the metapsychological narrative of which it is the primary character and without which its significance cannot be fully appreciated. The death drive was a comprehensive solution to a fundamental problem for Freud, a thread that tied together seemingly disparate phenomena into a cohesive theoretical whole. What were those phenomena? How did it function as a solution?

Sections 1–3 of *Beyond the Pleasure Principle* introduce difficulties that challenge the dominance of the pleasure principle, including war neurosis and the repetitive nature of children's play (the *Fort/Da* game). The first appearance of the term *death instinct* comes at the beginning of section 6. Sections 4 and 5, which link the straightforward clinical observations of 1–3 to the introduction of the death drive in 6, are, for lack of better description, quite strange. They are an admittedly speculative attempt to account for the relation between the compulsion to repeat and the pleasure principle in a mythological narration of the genesis of life or, in Freud's terms, the emergence of the organic from the inorganic.[55] I will begin this reading in section 5 and work my way back to section 4, as section 5 contains the most explicit description of the genesis of life.

Freud has no doubt that "'inanimate things existed before living ones,'" and so the biogonic problem, for him, is one of the emergence of organic matter from the inorganic.[56] Yet the specifics of its genesis form something like the "navel" of this particular dream: "the attributes of life were at some time evoked in inanimate matter by the action of a force of whose nature we can form no conception" (38). Although the genesis of life itself is unfathomable, one can speculate that its first attempts were brief, given that the tension which "arose in what had hitherto been an inanimate substance endeavored to cancel itself out. In this way the first instinct came into being: the instinct to return to the inanimate state. It was still an easy matter at that time for a living substance to die; the course of its life was probably only a brief one, whose direction was determined by the chemical structure of the young life" (38).

Though Freud does not call it by its name, this passage is the first introduction of the death drive, which is described here as resulting from the organism's endeavor to cancel out what it sees as a tension that disturbs an inanimate repose. A question immediately arises: given that all factors determining the course of this hapless first organism point to its absorption back into the inorganic, how is it that death could be anything *other* than an "easy matter?" That is, how do we get development? Freud admits that "for a long time, perhaps, living substance was thus being constantly created afresh and easily dying, till *decisive external influences* altered in such a way as to oblige the still surviving substance to diverge ever more widely from its original course of life and to make ever more complicated *détours* before reaching its aim of death. These circuitous paths to death, faithfully kept to by the conservative instincts, would thus present us to-day with the picture of the phenomena of life" (38–39, my emphasis).

How is one to understand these "decisive external influences?" Are they equally unfathomable as the forces that brought about the organic in the first place? This statement is all the more puzzling given what follows: two possible explanations of the development of life from this primitive state based upon *internal* influences. First, Freud follows an "extreme" line of thought and imagines the self-preservative instincts to be "component instincts whose function is to assure that the organism shall follow its own path to death" (39). In other words, the death drive is already a kind of self-preservative drive insofar as it assures that the organism wards "off any possible ways of returning to inorganic existence other than those which are immanent in the organism itself" (39). Freud summarizes this first hypothesis with the conclusion that the "guardians of life" were originally "the myrmidons of death" (39). Although this possibility is immediately rejected, an element of truth is buried in this first "extreme view," which I will return to shortly.

The second hypothesis, which is promptly affirmed, is that certain "germ-cells" of primitive organisms "retain the original structure of living matter and, after a certain time, with their full complement of inherited and freshly acquired instinctual dispositions, separate themselves from the organism as a whole" (40). "The instincts which watch over the destinies of these elementary organisms that survive the whole individual" are deemed "the true life instincts" (40). This second hypothesis has the benefit of positing *real countervailing forces* to the death drive, as opposed to the first, which simply blurs the line between them. But the *existence* of these "germ-cells" still cannot be accounted for: in the first stirrings of life, Freud has only posited a drive to return to the inorganic. How is it that there was time for "germ-cells" to develop in such a hostile atmosphere? Even were this second hypothesis acceptable, Freud would still lack an explanation as to how the organism survives long enough for it to have any investment in procreation. Thus, if his genetic story is going to make sense beyond its humble beginnings, he must have recourse to something besides the "germ-cell" to explain the generation of instinctual conflict.[57]

And in fact, near the beginning of section 4, he has already explained how *death itself can lead to life*: Freud here worries that a "living organism in its most simplified possible form" "would be killed by the stimulation emanating from" . . . "an external world charged with the most power-ful energies" . . . "if it were not provided with a protective shield against stimuli."[58] Note the inverted problematic: whereas in section 5 he was concerned with how an organism could survive in the face of the death drive, here he is positing a hostile external world against which the organ-ism defends itself. Why does this organism devote its energy to develop-ing a protective shield, given that its only impulse is to die? In other words, how does Freud get from brief eruptions of life with little interest in remaining alive to a situation where life is actually defending itself from the external world? He explains as follows:

[The organism] acquires the shield in this way: its outermost surface *ceases to have the structure proper to living matter, becomes to some de-gree inorganic* and thenceforward functions as a special envelope or membrane resistant to stimuli. In consequence, the energies of the external world are able to pass into the next underlying layers, which have remained living, with only a fragment of their original inten-sity; and these layers can devote themselves, behind the protective shield, to the reception of the amounts of stimulus which have been allowed through it. *By its death [Absterben], the outer layer has saved all the deeper ones from a similar fate*—unless, that is to say, stimuli reach it which are so strong that they break through the protective shield [*Reizschutz*].[59]

A solution as elegant as it is strange: in *partly* attaining the aim of the death drive, the organism inadvertently *protects* itself through the construction of a "dead" psychic *Reizschutz*.[60] In the words of Benno

Rosenberg, we are confronted here with the "surprising possibility of diverting a part of the death drive and using it to defend against the death drive."[61] Without recourse to any other principle, then, Freud has found a reason why life might be preserved in an organism that has no intention to live. His statement that the guardians of life were originally the myrmidons of death is thus not unfounded: by fortuitous cosmic accident, the sole drive manifested in the first organism happened also to be, when only partially gratified in a very particular way, its own opposition.[62]

But something is not right about this picture: if the organism seeks a return to the inorganic, what exactly is so threatening about the external world that it needs to build a protective shield? Why would it not welcome death? Freud has described the *mechanism* for the construction of the protective shield but not the *reason* for it. Another question: if the organism's environment is inorganic matter, as Freud says it is, how does it distinguish the inorganic shield from the inorganic external world? In other words, what is the difference between dying and dying to protect oneself? If the organism is to have reason to construct a protective shield, the external world somehow must become charged with energies in a way that both transforms a longed-for origin into a hostile threat and that differentiates it from the organism's protective outer layer.

Once again, Freud addresses this precise problem when he turns his attention to a particular way in which the fledgling organism deals with an overabundance of stimuli: "There is a tendency to treat them as though they were acting, not from the inside, but from the outside, so that it may be possible to bring the shield against stimuli into operation as a means of defense against them. This is the origin of *projection*."[63] Is "projection," like the "germ-cell," yet another incomprehensible addition to Freud's story? Where does projection come from in an organism made up only of death drive?

I am tempted here to tackle this problem in a Kleinian fashion by seeing projection as implied in a *position*, as a concomitant of a certain orientation to the world, rather than as a psychic mechanism. Freud's account can be reasonably reconstructed in light of this understanding of projection as follows: in the beginning stages of its differentiation from the inorganic, the organism is not yet truly an "inside" distinct from an inorganic "outside." The tension constitutive of the death drive is thus both a tension *within* and a tension *between*: from one angle, the organic is a tension *within* a larger inorganic system. From another, there is a tension *between* organic and inorganic. These two views are both technically accurate, though they result in two very different relationships: in the first the inorganic is the tensionless home of the organic. In the second the inorganic is a hostile threat. This situation, where the very same force can be seen as both one of homecoming and one of destruction, is character- ized by a *primal ambivalence*.

Projection, in this view, is the assumption of what I will call the "ten- sion-between" position,[64] which would be of no particular importance in comparison to the "tension-within" position were it not for its effect of making the world something against which to develop a protective shield; that is, of making the world into an *external* world. The tension-between position thus has *performative* effects: when the questionably exterior is treated as definitively exterior, further differentiation via the development of the protective shield results. In other words, an inorganic/organic "inside" is recognized as an inorganic "outside" in contrast to an organic "inside," and this act itself leads to the increasing individuation of the organism. Projection, at this stage, is not the transposition of inside into outside but the simultaneous invention of both inside and outside.

Whether projection is a concomitant of a position or a psychic mecha- nism, as Freud most probably thought of it, its introduction at this point in the story casts doubt on the nature of the "decisive external influences" that were credited with the death drive's detours: *how is it possible now to maintain the externality of the external?*[65] In the paragraph that immedi- ately follows the one in which he describes the origin of projection, Freud defines "as 'traumatic' any excitations from outside which are powerful enough to break through the protective shield."[66] If this reading has so far been accurate, when the organism turns its energy to the problem of mastering this great amount of stimulus that breaks in as a result of trauma, it turns the death drive as reinforcer of the protective shield against the death drive "projected" as exterior threat. The death drive in its former capacity as protective shield builder is what "binds" the free- flowing energy that rushes through the traumatic breach by means of "anticathexis" into a dead, cortical layer; in other words, in this role, it operates as the *drive to mastery*.[67] In turning against itself in this way, the death drive (what might be called a drive to "self"-mastery, i.e., mastery of the tension of organic matter) is redirected outward into a drive to "other"- mastery (mastery of the tension caused by "external" impingement).[68]

One can glimpse here the importance of distinguishing between aggression and the drive to mastery: for Freud, the death drive is not sent outward into the world when it is deflected. Its destructiveness is still pointed at the self when it is exteriorized. In other words, "I want to annihilate myself" does not become "I want to annihilate others," but rather "Others are trying to annihilate me" and "I want to protect myself against others" (and this dual movement is itself the invention of both "I" and "other" in this formulation).[69] Admittedly, Freud himself does later speak of the externalization of the death drive into a sadistic drive: "Is it not plausible to suppose that this sadism is in fact a death instinct which, under the influence of the narcissistic libido, has been forced away from the ego and has consequently only emerged in relation to the object?"[70] This is commonly taken to mean that the death drive is an inward-pointing sadism, thus paving the way for the general equation of death drive and aggression.

What, however, is the "narcissistic libido" in this sentence?[71] Just before this passage, Freud writes: "the ego is the true and original reservoir of libido . . . ; it is only from that reservoir that libido is extended on to objects." Libido that returns to cathect the ego itself is "described as 'narcissistic.'"[72] Since the psychic structure of the ego must have some degree of existence if it is to be both a reservoir for and object of this energy, the very existence of narcissistic libido assumes a certain development of the psychic *Reizschutz* and thus that the drive to mastery has already been at work before the narcissistic libido manages to convert the death drive into sadism. This difference between aggression and the drive to mastery will be more fully explored in chapter 3.

In addition to differentiating mastery and aggression, Freud also makes it clear that mastery is more than mere defensiveness: before the development of the psychic stimulus-barrier, the organism is overwhelmed by the environment and thus does not *relate* to it as an external entity. It is only with the development of protective structure that a "favourable" condition is created "for the reception of stimuli."[73] In other words, although the drive to mastery emerges initially as a protective drive in relation to a hostile environment, it is also the condition of the possibility of receptivity to the outer world (and, in theory, it continues to be so after the "paranoid" relation to the world is overcome). As will become clearer in the next chapter, I believe that Freud's *Reizschutz* is best understood not only as a protective "carapace or armor" but *also* as a "matrix or medium" that allows "for a greater mobility and circulation of psychic energies."[74]

Freud's picture of the beginning of life can now be completed: the protective shield, the external threats, and the drive to mastery that deals with those threats can all in some way be related back to the death drive, the

concept that allows him to unite the diverse set of phenomena he introduced in sections 1–3 of *Beyond the Pleasure Principle*, just as the theory of
the primal horde allowed him to explain a diverse set of anthropological
data in *Totem and Taboo*. To recap the story:

1. "By the action of a force of whose nature we can form no conception," the organic emerges from the inorganic.

2. The first instinct, the death drive, arises from the tension inherent in organic matter and the desired return to the "zero-level" of the
inanimate.

3. By a certain partial and focused gratification of the death drive, the
primitive organism is able to form a protective and receptive outer layer
(*Reizschutz*).

4. The organism exists in a state of *primal ambivalence* in relation to
the inorganic: on the one hand, it is a tension within a larger inorganic
whole. On the other, there is a tension between it and the inorganic. The
assumption of the latter position is called *projection*.

5. Only with projection is the mechanism for the formation of a protective shield engaged against decisive "external" influences; this causes the
organism to devote a great amount of energy to the task of "mastering
stimuli" and to further developing its structure of "bound energy," which
serves to protect the organism with increasing strength.

"*Mastery of and through death*": this, in short, is the way one gets to a
Nietzschean will for ever greater forms of life from a simple living vesicle
that has no other wish than that it die.[75]

Primal Repression, or Tying off a Loose End in "The Economic Problem of Masochism"

At one point in Freud's description of his living vesicle, he writes
that excitations "give rise to feelings in the pleasure-unpleasure series":
these feelings are said to index "what is happening in the interior" of the
organism, which has hitherto been described solely in terms of death
drive.[76] In an important follow-up paper to *Beyond the Pleasure Principle*,
Freud directly confronts this "economic problem" introduced by his new
dual drive theory: if the death drive aims toward a reduction of tensions to
a zero level, how is it that it differs from the pleasure principle, which had

been previously defined in precisely the same terms? As Laplanche notes, the "principle of neuronic inertia" that Freud had posited in the *Project for a Scientific Psychology*, which asserted the tendency of neurones "to a *complete* discharge, to *inertia*, to a *zero level*," went through three stages: "first, at this initial stage, under the name of the principle of neuronic inertia; soon thereafter under the term of 'pleasure principle'; finally as the Nirvana principle or the principle of the death instinct."[77]

Given this conceptual confusion, Freud admits that his first impulse was to conflate the two:

> We have unhesitatingly identified the pleasure-unpleasure principle with this Nirvana principle. . . . The Nirvana principle (and the pleasure principle which is supposedly identical with it) would be entirely in the service of the death instincts, whose aim is to conduct the restlessness of life into the stability of the inorganic state, and it would have the function of giving warnings against the demands of the life instincts—the libido—which try to disturb the intended course of life. But such a view cannot be correct.[78]

Such a view cannot be correct because it would mean that the principle Freud had previously posited as governing all life would now be in the service of death; in this case the pleasure principle would not truly have a "beyond." He thus revises his conception of the pleasure principle, arguing that it deals not in "quantitative" reduction like the death drive but with some "qualitative characteristic" the nature and genesis of which he admits no knowledge.[79] But "however this may be, we must perceive that the Nirvana principle, belonging as it does to the death instinct, has undergone a modification in living organisms through which it has become the pleasure principle."[80]

It is interesting to note that both the pleasure principle and the drive to mastery, the two basic requirements of life, one demanding satisfaction and nourishment, the other building the young organism's strength so as to put it in a better position to provide satisfaction and nourishment for itself, are in this view redirections and modifications of the death drive. It is tempting to view this process of redirection in terms of *repression*, which Freud had understood, from his earliest writings on the subject, as involving a split between an idea and its corresponding affect, the redirection of that affective force, and a distortion of the original idea. Freud was constantly searching for new ways to name this split (neurone/charge, idea/affect, word/thing), this difference between some kind of structure and its associated force. Since in the beginning stages of life the zero principle of the death drive is transformed into the pleasure principle and its associated entropic force is split up into a hostile exterior force and the drive to mastery, I propose to dub the event that gives rise to the drive to mastery and the pleasure principle *primal repression*. Freud introduces this term in his metapsychological paper "Repression," though he provides it with very little content other than to say that it is the primal event upon which all subsequent repression is modeled.[81] Given its foundational role in the development of life, this event is most certainly the first instance of the distortion of an instinctual representative and the redirection of its force. This picture is consistent with Freud's argument that all development takes place as a result of instinctual repression.[82]

Curiously enough, it is *Eros* that is said to accomplish this task of redirection. What modifies the Nirvana principle of the death drive into the pleasure principle? "It can only be the life instinct, the libido, which has thus, alongside of the death instinct, seized upon a share in the regulation of the processes of life."[83] Later in the same paper, Freud tells us that Eros has another task: that of "diverting [the death drive] to a great extent outwards . . . towards objects in the external world."[84] Although in both cases Freud attributes a positive agency to Eros, it is not clear that he is justified in doing so: the drive to mastery, at least, being a self-subversion of the death drive, is generated without any outside help, and it is reasonable to assume that the pleasure principle comes into existence in the same movement. If this is true, then Eros is not the *motor* of primal repression but rather its *after-effect*,[85] a force that *will have been* only when a life-conducive organization (mastery + pleasure) gains enough stability to create a new kind of conflict with the death drive.[86] I will take up this idea in more detail in the next chapter.

* * *

Returning once again to the text of *Beyond the Pleasure Principle*,[87] my reading of Freud's "metanarrative" there elucidated an instinctual opposition between a drive toward self/other confusion (the death drive) and one toward self/other differentiation (the drive to mastery). The former, at least in its original state, is exhausted by the simple aim of casting off differentiation and returning to the repose of the "inorganic" environment, in which the organism wishes to be like "water in water," to use

Georges Bataille's words.[88] The drive to mastery, on the other hand, is a more complicated character. For the moment, I will sum up its basic characteristics in five points.

1. The drive to mastery provides protection for the organism by reinforcing its stimulus barrier (*Reizschutz*) when it is threatened, by harnessing "free" energy into a "bound" shield, and this protective structure creates a "favourable" condition "for the reception of stimuli."[89]

2. It is directed against "exterior threats" that, at a more fundamental level, are neither truly exterior nor threats; which is to say a) that the drive to mastery is itself the cause of differentiation, the separation of inside and outside, and b) that these threats are repressed objects of longing. Developmentally, this would mean that living beings must turn their reality into a threat for the purpose of individuation while at the same time maintaining a libidinal attachment.

3. Although the transition from the tension-within to the tension-between position involves something of a misrecognition, it is a necessary one: without turning its reality into a "hostile exterior," the organism has no counterforce against which to mobilize its own forces of development.

4. The protective shield formed by the drive to mastery is a "dead" cortical layer covering over an "organic" kernel, but, again, a kind of death that is necessary for the propagation of life. Long after Freudian drive theory would be rejected as bad biologism, Roberto Esposito would express this same idea while introducing his concept of "immunitary process": "unable to directly achieve its objective, it is forced to pursue it from the inside out. In so doing, it retains its objective in the horizon of meaning of its opposite: it can prolong life, but only by continuously giving it a taste of death."[90]

5. Due to the primal ambivalence of the organism, the *Reizschutz* can be neither too "thin" nor too "thick": on the one hand, the organism cannot survive without some form of protection. On the other, it cannot become too insulated from the external world.[91] The cultivation of death in life thus easily lapses into death itself. The organism thus must both have constant contact with its environment (else it slide definitively into the tension-between position) and at the same time be able to ward off engulfment (else it remain too comfortable in the tension-within position).

PART II

Interpretation

An invincible force impelled me to get rid of my existence, in one way or another. It cannot be said exactly that I wished to kill myself, for the force which drew me away from life was fuller, more powerful, more general than any mere desire. It was a force like my old aspiration to live, only it impelled me in the opposite direction.   —Leo Tolstoy, *Confession*

2   Between Need and Dread

Hans Loewald and the Primordial Density

In this chapter I will be arguing that the developmental theory of the psychoanalyst-philosopher Hans Loewald is the most intensive elaboration of the speculations that led to the introduction of the death drive and that it is possible, through Loewald's work, to formulate a demythologized version of the dialectic of death and mastery examined in the previous chapter, i.e., a more reasonable ontogenic version of Freud's phylogenic fantasy.[1] The connection is far from obvious. Though generally unafraid of tackling Freudian metapsychology to illuminate psychic development, nowhere does Loewald systematically work out his thoughts on the death drive—a fact that could be related to his aversion to the topics of hatred, aggression, etc. In fact, he goes so far as to deny that the death drive is anything particularly novel in Freud's work,[2] despite hinting in certain places that it touches on key concepts in his own. In a circuitous remark from a short book review, for instance, he writes: "If you say I am talking here not so much of a death instinct in Freud's sense, but more of an urge toward the bliss and pain of consuming oneself in the intensity of being lived by the id, you may be right."[3]

As the relation between Loewald's work and the theory of the death drive has largely gone unexplored, my aim here, in brief, is to provide a selective introduction to his developmental theory using the lens of the metapsychology examined in the previous chapter.[4] My hope is to bind Freud to Loewald with the aim of lifting the former's speculations from the pit of biological anachronism, but it is also further to bind Loewald to Freud and thus to stave off the notion that there could ever be a "Loewaldian" school of psychoanalysis. Loewald's work is not a development of Freud's but, for better or worse, a *nachträglich* re-presentation of the original. As I present it here, it is itself a work of *Eros*.[5]

The Primordial Density

In the "traditional" psychoanalytic understanding of mental development, the infant's psyche, under the duress of an unforgiving reality at odds with its wishes and fantasies, develops a stable protective structure called the ego that mediates between outer and inner worlds. The ego, in this view, "is the outer, cortical layer of the id and has as such become different from the inner stratum. The influence of external reality, which has brought forth the ego, is seen as essentially threatening and hostile. Correspondingly, the predominant function of the ego is a defensive one, not only against reality but also against the inner world of the id, which disregards reality."[6]

Buried underneath this official narrative, hidden away in the most questionable sections of Freud's most speculative work,[7] Loewald finds a different story, one in which the ego does not develop as protection against an already existent, objective reality but rather *coemerges with reality*: "in other words, the psychological constitution of ego and outer world go hand in hand."[8] If, however, reality is not the external menace Freud makes it out to be—that is, if the conflict between ego and reality is not baseline—what prompts psychic development? In Loewald's view, it is the "infant's repeated experience that something, in his original feeling a part of him, is not always available, this repeated experience of separateness" that first fractures the "primordial density" from which id, ego, and external world eventually blossom.[9]

There is, biologically and psychologically, an increasing emancipation from the mother that leads to an ever-growing tension. The less mother and child are one, the more they become separate entities, the more will there be a dynamic interplay of forces between these two "systems." As the mother becomes outside, and hand in hand with this, the child an inside, there arises a tension system between the two. Expressed in different terms, libidinal forces arise between infant and mother. As infant (mouth) and mother (breast) are not identical, or better, not one whole, any longer, a libidinal flow between infant and mother originates, in an urge towards re-establishing the original unity.[10]

Just as in Freud's account of the genesis of life, a tension arises that leads to an urge back to a tensionless state. Loewald describes this urge (what Freud would call the death drive)[11] as a desire to rid oneself of separateness and to return to a state where boundaries are lacking "and therefore there is no distinction between [id, ego, and environment]."[12] Since the child's first "reality" is a "global situation" that has resulted from a fracture of the primordial density, Freud was wrong to have portrayed reality as fundamentally threatening: in Loewald's words, "reality, understood genetically, is not primarily outside and hostile, alien to the ego, but intimately connected with and originally not even distinguished from it."[13] Far from wishing to fend off the threats of reality, the infant wants nothing more, at this developmental stage, than to be rid of the burden of separateness and to "return to an enclosure that effectively forecloses the anxious possibility of a hostile external world."[14]

How do we get from this first stage, in which "inner" and "outer" are separate but still components of a larger whole that the child wishes to reintegrate (I will call this the tension-within position), to the next, where id, ego, and reality are clearly distinct entities (the tension-between position)? Here Loewald invokes the idea of a "dread of women," first articulated by Karen Horney but more convincingly explained by Dorothy Dinnerstein,[15] to move his story along: at the same time that infants wish to maintain the wholeness of the tension-within position, they are also, he quizzically asserts, terrified of that same possibility. More concisely, "the positive libidinal relation to the mother is understood as consisting of the two components: need for union with her and dread of this union."[16]

Although this move perfectly parallels Freud's (one and the same "environment" signifies both a longed-for origin and a dreaded threat), it is not immediately clear what Loewald is proposing here. One might guess that he is offering something like Melanie Klein's theory of the "paranoid-schizoid" position, where one and the same object is split into "good" and "bad" parts. However, unlike Klein, who posits an inherent tendency within the psyche toward splitting, Loewald thinks that infants have a very good, if unfortunate, reason for their dual mindset, one rooted in their dual condition: on the one hand, far, far away from anything resembling independence and theoretically indistinguishable from their environments and, on the other, all too aware of the stark fact of separateness, inescapable in moments of parental absence.

Turning away from the reality of this impossible situation, the fragmentation of the child's tension-within world is managed psychically in fantasy: I am not my caretaker in reality, but I can nonetheless fantasize *being* this powerful and terribly needed person,[17] I can recreate a "confusion of subject and object" by *identifying* with the "other," thereby satisfying the urge to union in fantasy.[18] Immature as an imitative "erasure of difference" may be, Loewald believes that it is the first step toward real differentiation: by "imitating in order to be" their caretakers so that they do not need to be there themselves, by establishing their presence in their inner being, infants are able to build and further reinforce the psychic structures of their own "internal world."[19] "Identification," in other words, "is a way-station to internalization, but in internalization, if carried to completion, a redifferentiation has taken place by which both subject and object have been reconstituted, each on a new level of organization."[20] When this redifferentiation occurs, the loss of the primordial density has been successfully "mourned,"[21] and the child comes to experience the separation "not as deprivation or loss but as liberation and a sign of mastery."[22] In short, "the road leads from depression through mourning to elation."[23] It is this process, and not conflict with an objectively hostile reality, that leads to the genesis of the ego.

"Dread of union" follows, in Loewald's view, from successful coping with separation: elated at their newly acquired mastery and eager to maintain and further the ego boundaries they have so doggedly worked to construct,[24] children begin to perceive their caretakers as impinging, here and there, on their emergent autonomy. Caretakers in the tension-within position become sources of threatening domination in the tension-between position. If, as Adam Phillips writes, "the first world we find outside is, in part, a repository for the terror inside us," it must be added that that terror *coemerges* with the externality of the world.[25] From the vantage point of this new world, the possibility of returning to the tension-within position appears as a threat "to engulf the emerging ego into the original unity" and thereby reverse the painstaking accomplishments of internalization.[26] While it is undeniable that Loewald gravitates toward the positive aspects of the primordial density,[27] he avoids the trap of what Jonathan Lear has called a "secularized version of the fall" in emphasizing that it is also the primary source of dread.[28]

I should here make an important terminological clarification: Loewald often fails to distinguish reality in its primordial form from the person of the caretaker, and, as a result, "hostile reality," in Freud's sense, from the "dreaded other" in his own (perhaps, out of a fidelity to the metapsy-chological narrative outlined in the previous chapter). It is clear, however, that a distinction is necessary for Loewald's story to work.[29] I thus pro-pose the following: the caretaker (I will use the marking "other," other in quotation marks) is the condition of and most important part of the infant's primary tension-within reality, in which a fluid, continuous rela-tion between ego and world prevails. As this primary reality is sundered, a less continuous, more bounded relation between ego and reality comes into being through internalization. From the perspective of this new "tension-between" reality, the "other" toward whom the child bears a now partially repressed urge to union is transformed into the dreaded *other* that threatens engulfment of the ego and thus to destroy tension-between reality (I will use the marking *other*, other in italics, to designate this aspect of the caretaker's reality).[30]

For perfectly understandable reasons, then, having to do with the trials of dependence rather than any primordial "split" in the psyche, children acquire a schizoid relation to their caretakers and to reality. How are help-less parents to navigate this impossible situation? Should they quickly ferry their children out of the tension-within position, thus helping them along toward autonomy and avoiding, to the greatest degree possible, their fate as dreaded *other*? Although it is true that the infant gains a certain independence through this painful separation process, Loewald is not the kind of moralist who encourages training to the harsh realities of disappointment and loss: the "other's" absence, the inability properly to respond to the child's needs, and all the rest of the ingredients that go into the mourning process are inevitabilities, givens of our finite and flawed existences. The parental task is less to facilitate structure building than to prevent what might be called an "overbuilding" of structure in the face of lack, an overreaction resulting in what Loewald calls "ego rigidity."[31] The kind of intervention that minimizes the "discrepancy between the indi-vidual [child's] needs and the support of the environment" preserves the "wholeness" in the world reminiscent of the lost intimacy from which the ego is slowly severed.[32] Without this support, which responds and adapts to the emergence of autonomy, the child loses the fluid relationship with reality characteristic of the tension-within position and comes to see it as exclusively external and hostile.[33]

This outcome of failed mutuality is more than just one form of neurosis. Indeed, for Loewald, it is definitive of modernity:

> Freud as well as many others before and after him have been profoundly influenced in their way of experiencing life, and therefore in their thinking, by the overwhelming and increasing impact of social, political, economical, and cultural changes on the individual. The high degree of differentiation and complexity of our civilization, which seems to have run away from its human sources and foundations and to have taken a course all its own, seldom mastered and understood, has led to the view that culture and reality as a whole is basically and by definition inimical to the individual. The estrangement of man from his culture (from moral and religious norms that nevertheless continue to determine his conduct and thus are experienced as hostile impositions) and the fear and suppression of controlled but nondefensive regression is the emotional and intellectual climate in which Freud conceived his ideas of the psychological structure of the individual and the individual's relationship to reality. It is also the climate in which neurosis grows—and here we hark back to our exposition of the neurotogenic conflict situation. The hostile, submissive-rebellious manipulation of the environment and the repressive-reactive manipulation of inner needs, so characteristic and necessary for man who cannot keep pace with the complexity of his culture and for a culture that loses contact with its human origins, is the domain of neurotic development. It is the above-described discrepancy situation repeated and re-enacted on a different level.[34]

Out of sync with civilization, individuals are forced into defensive maneuvers and come to substitute a cold, oppositional reality for a more primary, dynamic one.[35] Alan Bass calls this rigidification *fetishism*—lacking the care structures supportive of a nondefensive psychic organization, the fetishist substitutes a "static, finished thing" for a "difference that overwhelms him or her," thus providing "the illusion of control of what is inside and what is outside, at the cost of a hostile relation between the two"—though one could just as well use *alienation*: in Rahel Jaeggi's formulation, alienation is an "impoverishment of the relation to self and world" effected in the act of relating to self and world, a mastery lost *in the very pursuit of mastery.*[36]

Born of alienation, then, "psychoanalytic theory has unwittingly taken over much of the obsessive neurotic's experience and conception of reality and has taken it for granted as 'the objective reality.'"[37] In other words, in positing a fundamentally hostile and disappointing reality, Freud universalized an "overbuilt" defensive psychic structure, one that suffers from a discrepancy between individual need and environmental support.[38] Loewald's criticism is all the more devastating in saddling psychoanalytic theory with the same diagnosis that Freud had made of the religious believer.

Superego and Eros

To sum up: wanting nothing more than to be cared for immediately, without delay and without distance, infants are inevitably thrust into situations where that care is absent. In the terrifying and devastating pain accompanying this loss, they explode, unable to stand this gratuitous threat to their being. Eventually a strategy is unwittingly devised: "The 'other' might not be here, but *I* can be this person, and thereby not really be without care" (and it must be kept in mind that this fantasy performatively creates the "I" it posits). When the "other" leaves again, the loss is not as severe. There may be moments of weakness, in which the newly solidified identification is not yet able to bear the necessary weight, but on the whole, as identification quietly morphs into internalization, separation slowly becomes an easier ordeal.

Yet the partial satisfaction of the urge to union—that is, its satisfaction in the fantasy constitutive of the ego—is at odds with the urge to union itself (in slightly different terms: *identification is a gratification in fantasy of the death drive that is at odds with actual death drive gratification*): "I am, after all, not the 'other,'" and cruel reminders of this fact abound. The child is thus forced into a schizoid existence, rent between the need to be cared for and the equally strong and opposing need to be able to bear parental absence, to be independent. Urge to union, need for independence: the primary conflict of childhood according to Loewald, and an opposition structurally analogous to the Freudian antagonism between the death drive and the drive to mastery.

Thankfully, this is not the end of the road. The internalization process, wherein infants "take in" pieces of their absent "others," inevitably reaches a critical point. Separate and proudly so, able to do a great deal themselves thanks to the imitative practice of "being the 'other,'"[39] children still cannot shake that first urge, and every once in a while their confident autonomy melts away in tears and frustration. The lure of the primordial density is too much; the schizoid push and pull between need and dread too difficult to bear any longer. They wish they could do away with everything standing between themselves and the primordial density so that they could enter it and *be* it once again, but they also understand that the actualization of this wish would amount to utter catastrophe for their own existences. Freud called it the Oedipus complex.[40]

In the standard telling of this story, the child's drives are conquered, beaten back and held under the tight lid of repression. If, however, repression involves a split between thought and affect, an expulsion of the thought from consciousness and the redirection of its associated force elsewhere, where does the force of the urge to union go with the waning of the Oedipus complex? How is the child able to stand finally giving up on that first drive? As Loewald very concisely explains, the primary urge to union is transformed at the height of oedipal struggle into a secondary "synthetic" drive that aims to restore, "on more and more complex levels of differentiation and objectivation of reality, the original unity."[41] Though both increasingly removed from the tension-within position and also cognizant of its "perfectly hellish" aspect, children do not give up on attaining its "wholeness": *within* the world of the tension-between position, they now seek to synthesize a totality resembling the primordial density from which they have departed, only in such a way that its pursuit does not eliminate self/other distinction.[42] In this way, the overwhelming desire for and fear of reimmersion in the primordial density is abandoned for the goal of reassembling its "wholeness" on a higher level (the *arche* become *telos*).[43]

It is this sublimation of a past fantasy into an ideal achievement,[44] Loewald contends, that animates a new psychic agency, whose task is to oversee the ego's progression toward this goal. This new agency, which "functions from the viewpoint of a future ego, from the standpoint of the ego's future which is to be reached, is being reached, is being failed or abandoned by the ego," is, of course, the superego, the ego's guide on its path to secondary unity.[45] In transferring the contractive energy of the primordial density toward the synthetic activity of Eros, the superego, in effect, hijacks the urge to union toward aims that are not its own. Like the

Greeks for Kierkegaard, children approach "wholeness" as "the past that can only be entered backwards";[46] but with the birth of the superego, they come to experience this same wholeness as something to be achieved in the future, thereby acquiring the "fullness of time."[47]

If I am correct in identifying Loewald's urge to union with Freud's death drive, then we have here a novel (but already foreshadowed) take on Freud's instinctual "dualism:" Eros and the death drive are not, on this account, opposing drives, but two admittedly contradictory manifestations of one and the same force.[48] Both threaten to undermine the ego's stability, but whereas the death drive/urge to union is at odds with growing autonomy, constantly threatening to tear down ego boundaries and reimmerse the psyche in utter dependence, Eros is only in healthy tension with the ego, forcing it to push beyond itself toward a "vital ego-ideal" without threatening extinction.[49] The accomplishment of Eros is thus *the transformation of a drive to ego-destruction into one of ego-transcendence.* One might say, then, that, with the waning of the Oedipus complex, the conflict between id and ego, which wreaks havoc on our early lives, is internalized in the more manageable tension between superego and ego, which is also to say that the ego comes to stability by appropriating for itself the very method of its own construction.[50]

The birth of the superego is thus, in Loewald's view, an overcoming of primal ambivalence, a repression of the urge to union (a primal repression, as I called it in chapter 1), but also a new avenue for the expression of this drive in the secondary process. One is tempted to call it a *sublation,* and the implicit Hegelianism here has already been noted by Joel Whitebook.[51] Like Hegel's *Geist,* Loewald's Eros brings contradictory tendencies into harmony, channeling a regressive force toward a progressive aim.[52] The psyche thereby reaches something of a dialectical resolution to the opposition of the tension-within and tension-between positions: guided by the superego, it is possible to accept the destabilizing effects of striving for wholeness without at every turn fearing the erasure of the accomplishments of individuation.

The Language of Eros

Loewald does a great deal to highlight the novelty of Eros in Freud's work as well as to expand and clarify its meaning, but one might still legitimately wonder what it is to bind into ever greater unities,[53] as

Freud says, or to seek secondary unity, as Loewald himself does. Abstract metapsychological concepts in general often suffer from a lack of a sense of how they are to be applied concretely, and it is Loewald's great strength to have articulated, very precisely, how his developmental model is also a theory of language acquisition and thus how we should understand the relation between drive theory and the psychoanalytic process.

One of the primary characteristics of the tension-within position, for Loewald, is a fluid relationship between "word" and "thing" (*Sache*), taken to mean not merely a thing but a "state of affairs, event, circumscribed action, etc.":

> Thing, in this wide sense, and words, in the early stages of mentation, in primary process—insofar as words come into play—are not separate. Words here are, on the contrary, indistinguishable ingredients of global states of affairs. The mother's flow of words does not convey meaning to or symbolize "things" for the infant—"meaning" as something differentiated from "fact"—but the sounds, tone of voice, and rhythm of speech are fused within the apprehended global event. One might say that, while the mother utters words, the infant does not perceive words but is bathed in sound, rhythm, etc., as accentuating ingredients of a uniform experience.[54]

Like Walter Benjamin, Loewald thus posits a primordial "language as such" in which there is "an absolute relation between name and thing."[55] How do we proceed from this "global state of affairs," where word and thing seamlessly flow together, to one where words are clearly separate from and designate "things" in the child's external reality?

The key event, predictably, is separation,[56] but more specifically the role that vocalization plays in managing that separation. In his view, the

> parental voice and speech take on a special significance for the child insofar as they come to convey the parents' closeness at a distance, their presence in absence. When the child is alone, cannot see or touch and smell the parents, hearing their voice tends to render them present in a somewhat remote and less global fashion. The parental voice, responding to the child's crying or other vocal utterance, for example in the dark, gives him a sense of their presence. Thus the child's utterances may conjure up parental presence, even if the parent does not visibly or tangibly appear.[57]

The child's own articulations simultaneously play two roles: on the one hand, they are employed by the urge to union *actually* to summon parental presence; on the other, they bear a unique capacity to conjure a "presence in absence," to maintain a parental presence in a "remote and less global fashion." I take this to mean that vocalization is a medium of internalization: by "taking in" the parental voice, infants (from *in-fans*, or "without language") are able to better manage separation, even if their utterances do not immediately bring their parents near. Vocalization thus plays an important role in the "mourning process" whereby the ego comes into being.[58] Perhaps this is another way of interpreting Freud's claim that the death drive is "mute": only when the primordial density is broken do drives begin to find a voice.[59]

In chapter 1 I highlighted Freud's recourse to the strange idea that the living vesicle "deadens" part of its outer layer in order to provide protection for itself from a hostile "external" reality. Loewald has already put his finger on the truth perhaps unintentionally expressed in this idea of partial death *qua* protection—that life in its primordial form is way too much, that its "bliss and pain" would lead to its own end were it not tempered by the deadening weight of the ego[60]—but this proposal finds even more concrete expression in his assertion that words distanced from "unconscious thing-presentations," words that acquire a "degree of autonomy" through internalization, become "lifeless."[61] When isolated from the global experience of the parent-child "field" (what he calls our "poetic-unconscious origin"), words become "deficient in experiential meaning"; in excessive isolation, insulated in "ego rigidity," they deteriorate "to more or less hollow echoes."[62]

Inasmuch as this linguistic "deadening" aids the individuation process, it serves a protective function and thus constitutes an act of mastery; but in addition to providing insulation from the lows of fragmentation, it also shuts out the highs of the tension-within position. For this reason, Loewald's internalized cluster of "deficient word-presentations," like Freud's stimulus barrier, must allow the infant to strike a "viable compromise between too intimate and intense closeness to the unconscious, with its threatening creative-destructive potentialities, and deadening insulation from the unconscious where human life and language are no longer vibrant and warmed by its fire."[63] The linguistic *Reizschutz* must thus be neither so weak and unformed as to be overtaken by the unconscious nor so rigid and fortified as to deaden psychic life completely.

As long as words remain a means of conjuring up a lost unity, however, there is an inherent limit to language acquisition: unwilling to stray too far from the unconscious fire, language can only remain in stunted form. The emergence of the superego represents a decisive step forward in terms of linguistic capacity: instead of seeking the primordial density directly, instead of attempting to recreate unity *with* language, the child comes to seek unity *within* language, *to cathect language itself with the urge to union.*[64] As the Greek *symbolon* indicates both a sundering and the promise of a new union, Lacan's notion of an "entrance into the symbolic" seems apposite here.[65] To enter the symbolic is to raise up and cancel the contradiction between recreating unity and managing separation that is endemic to early language acquisition into a new tension between ego and superego, between language in its capacity a) to provide a stabilizing mastery and b) to point beyond the ego's present configuration.

Neurosis, in this view, is a function of the ego's resistance to superego pressure. Haphazardly constructed and responding to crises of the moment without a grander architectural vision, the ego is an entity interested in immediate stability. When challenges arise, it is more likely to find stopgap solutions than to entertain more involved renovations. Thus, when a thing arises that poses a threat to its coherence (say, the deferred realization of infantile sexuality), the ego chooses to invest a great amount of energy into preventing the thing from being named, from finding a "word" for it; in Samuel Weber's formulation, "repression denies the translation of one kind of identity (object-cathexes) into another (word-cathexes)."[66] Similarly, when words lack a reference in the world (happiness, freedom, etc., what Lacan calls "master signifiers"), the ego prevents investigation into why these words lack things and how it might be possible to bring "things" into existence.

The task of analysis, to put it in disarmingly simple terms, is to find words for things and things for words; in other words, to bring about a greater linguistic unity, to follow Eros. This goal is accomplished, in Loewald's view, in two steps: in the first, through free association and regression, the analysand's words are "reabsorbed into that old memorial formation where thing and words are not yet distinguished as different."[67] In the second, interpretive phase, the analyst aims to reestablish differentiation "in such a way that renewed linking can be achieved;"[68] that is, in such a way that words are found for the previously-unprocessed "things" in the analysand's world and things are found for "deficient word-presentations" so that they become more than "mere sounds without meaning."⁶⁹ We should understand the term *find* here in the same sense as we understand the term *discover* in the sentence "Freud discovered the primal scene," that is, as involving not an encounter with an already existing reality but rather a process of creative reformulation wherein words and things are placed in a "new configuration."⁷⁰

Loewald thus sees no necessity in the analytic journey: the process of finding words for things and things for words is an interminable one, which can most certainly overcome particularly stubborn obstacles and reach certain plateaus, but can never find eternal rest until the body does. Indeed, taking into account the modern predicament of estrangement he invokes to explain Freud's universalization of obsessional neurosis, it is an inevitability today that all analyses will end in at least partial failure: in Loewald's view, an individual analysis can only proceed to the point of realizing that there will inevitably be "deficient word-presentations" in the modern world.

Urge to Union? Primary Undifferentiation?

My work thus far has been primarily expository, an attempt to show rather than to defend. Before concluding, however, I would like to address two objections to Loewald's developmental theory, one pertaining to the idea of an "urge to union," the other to the postulate of a "primary undifferentiation." In so doing, I will engage two psychologists, John Bowlby and Daniel Stern (representing, respectively, the contemporary fields of attachment theory and interpersonal theory), in an attempt both to defend and to highlight the distinctiveness of Loewald's theory.

In a seminal paper that would foreshadow his grand trilogy, *Attachment and Loss*, Bowlby claims that "the theory of Primary Return-to-Womb Craving," that "infants resent their extrusion from the womb and seek to return there" (a category within which one might include Loewald's "urge to union"), is "both redundant and biologically improbable": the former because his own theory of attachment better makes sense of the caretaker-infant bond than does the "return-to-womb" theory (represented, in his mind, primarily by the Kleinians) and the latter because "it is difficult to imagine what survival value such a desire might have."⁷¹ For Bowlby, infants are not libidinally tied to their caretakers by their nostalgic desire to return to the prenatal state but by the need "to ensure that [they obtain] parental care sufficient for [their] survival."⁷² The ways in which they accomplish this task ("sucking, clinging, following, crying, and smiling")[73] need not "invoke hypothetical instincts of sex and self-preservation as causal agents";[74] they are present, rather, because of the "survival value" of the "child's tie to his mother."[75]

Given its ubiquity today, everywhere from Dr. Sears's "attachment parenting" to Judith Butler's "passionate attachments," the language of attachment may seem like a better way to describe preoedipal relations than that of drives. Why, then, retain drive theory instead of opting for the postulation of "component instincts" that regulate "attachment systems?" My answer has simply to do with the partitioning of domains: the *psychologically* relevant fact about human infancy is not that the infant must form attachments for survival but that one is removed from the tension-within position and forced to endure failed attempts to recreate it at the same time that one must struggle, slowly and painfully, for one's own (partial) independence. Bowlby unsurprisingly spurns talk of "dependence" in order to differentiate attachment and drive satisfaction,[76] but that dependence, and its attendant horrors and comforts, again seems the *psychologically* relevant fact about the neonatal state.

No doubt the various activities of "attachment" have "survival value,"[77] but "survival" cannot serve the same centrally organizing function in psychology as it can in biology.[78] Indeed, the challenge of psychology is to explain why human beings do much more than survive and why they even do things that imperil their survival. In Adrian Johnston's words, drives, as opposed to instincts, are "beyond biological rationality."[79] The psychological relevance of the attachment behaviors that ensure the infant's survival is thus that they are *also* expressions of drive formations that lead to more than evolutionary benefits.[80] Bowlby had good reason to reject the "return-to-womb" hypothesis, taken literally, but not, on those same biological grounds, to dismiss the idea that there is something very attractive about the early care state that children seek to recreate and struggle to give up.[81]

Although Bowlby rejects the "return-to-womb" theory, he seems to allow the legitimacy of the idea of "mother-child undifferentiation."[82] For many today, the work of Daniel Stern has definitively laid this hypothesis to rest: according to Stern, "infants begin to experience a sense of an emergent self from birth. They are predesigned to be aware of self-organizing processes. They never experience a period of total self/other undifferentiation."[83] He argues further that "undifferentiation" is in fact an adult projection on the child's universe: "Only an observer who has enough perspective to know the future course of things can even imagine an undifferentiated state. . . . The traditional notions of clinical theorists have taken the observer's knowledge of infants—that is, the relative undifferentiation compared to the differentiated view of older children—reified it, and given it back, or attributed it, to infants as their own dominant subjective sense of things."[84]

Admittedly, Loewald does assert, without much nuance, an initial undifferentiation of mother and infant, one that I cannot affirm, being in agreement with Jessica Benjamin that the distinction between undifferentiation and separation is a form of splitting that reinforces gender domination in leaving only "the alternatives of [feminine] irrational oneness and [masculine] rational autonomy."[85] The heart of Loewald's work, however, lies less with the distinction between undifferentiation and differentiation than with the two psychic states that I have called the tension-within and the tension-between positions, the conflict between which captures what Benjamin calls the "real ambivalence of the maternal relation."[86] In one, "inner" and "outer" are components of a larger situation still experienced by the child to be relatively whole (note that one could concede to Stern that the neonate bears a limited sense of differentiation in this state).[87] In the other, that situation has been fractured by an overwhelming experience of separateness, and in this fragile state the child works to develop a protective psychic structure that clearly delimits id, ego, and reality. It is the conflict between these two positions, and not in psychic undifferentiation, that is at the center of Loewald's theory. Thus, though Loewald himself posited an "undifferentiated phase out of which id and ego develop," Alan Bass is right to assert that he would have done better with an "originally differentiated stage, in which differentiation itself is not understood in internal-external, subject-object, memory-perception terms"—something akin to what Bracha Ettinger calls "*jointness-in-differentiating*" or what Michael Eigen calls "dual union" or even what Stern himself calls "core relatedness."[88]

With all of this in mind, I would like to be clear about how I am conceiving of the urge to union/death drive and thus how I will be employing these two terms (taken to be synonymous) in what follows: while it would be possible to affirm the existence of a drive toward a state of undifferentiation without doing the same for that undifferentiation itself, I find it less problematic to say that the urge to union is a drive to reverse the differentiating process of separation and individuation. This reversal constitutes a drive toward "death" inasmuch as its pursuit constitutes an all-out assault on that entity that we call "I." What I want to emphasize in this conception of the urge to union/death drive is that it implies a certain *world* that the drive aims to maintain, a world where we are not off on our own, where we *belong* as one component of a larger "system," one "characterized by soft boundaries between self and other," a world that is experienced from what I have dubbed the tension-within position.[89]

As a final note, while I hope to have assuaged this concern pertaining to undifferentiation, I am not thereby acceding to the truth of the inter-personal/intersubjective framework in which it is couched, which I find to be an overreaction to the theory of primary narcissism, to the idea that infants are primarily self-centered, autistic creatures that must be forc-ibly brought into the social world.[90] This classical psychoanalytic idea is surely mistaken,[91] but no less so than that infants are "naturally social" from the beginning, that they are subjects from the very first moment.[92] Infants may interact with their environment much more than the first generation of psychoanalysts thought, but this does not mean that they do not have to go through a difficult ordeal on their way to becoming subjects. Eliding the yawning gap between the neonate and the linguistic subject transforms a qualitative difference into a quantitative one. More important, however, it turns the clock back on one of Freud's basic dis-coveries: that the subject is a *nachträglich* phenomenon, a linguistic "over-writing" of nonlinguistic forces. For Freud, the subject is not born, and it does not progress along a linear path to maturity. It rather *comes to be* where it was not and in such a way as to erase its own past. It is in this disjunctive repression that psychoanalysis gains its unique purchase.

What Is Mastery?

By connecting late Freudian drive theory to the developmental struggles of infancy and the acquisition of language, Hans Loewald pro-duced a lucid understanding of the psychoanalytic process based in the work of Eros. At the center of this vision is an ego both necessary and dangerous: as is clear from the transposition of Freud's metapsychologi-cal narrative into developmental terms, the ego is akin to the "dead" outer layer of Freud's living vesicle. It is but an "inorganic" shell protecting an "organic" inner core. While certainly a crucial developmental accom-plishment, in that the process of its erection goes hand in hand with the child's *mastery* over its environment, this "crust of indifference" can be as much of a poison as it is a gift, as too much structure building leads to the entombment of life.[93] Loewald's understanding of psychoanalytic health is thus "between two deaths," to purposefully misapply a phrase from Lacan: on the one side, there is death by ego fragility, where one's "boundedness" is swept away, a state that is both desired and feared; on the other, death by ego rigidity, where boundedness itself becomes a form of suffocation, where one loses contact with the environment from which springs vitality; and in between somewhere, in that delicate and liminal space as elusive as it is fleeting, mastery.[94]

For Loewald, the emergence of the superego represents a decisive victory in the pursuit of this end: unity is no longer sought *in itself*, and thus the urge to union—the instinctual foundation of human relatedness—need not threaten the child's individuation. The primary conflict of infancy does not, however, thereby disappear. It is rather *internalized* in the tension between ego and superego: instead of playing out the conflict between the urge to union and dread of that union in the world, instead of alternating in a bipolar fashion between the tension-within and the tension-between positions, the child slowly begins to take in the antagonism between self-reinforcing and self-negating tendencies, to make an "external" tension an inner tension, *to make a play of forces "outside" the self the primary dynamic of the self.* And this is achieved, Loewald asserts, when language itself becomes the stage of instinctual struggle.

With this in mind, we might distinguish preoedipal mastery, which pushes the tension between need and dread of union to a breaking point as it grows, from postoedipal mastery, the pursuit of which is allowed by the cathexis of language with the urge to union. The emergence of the superego is itself an act of mastery inasmuch as it is the condition of the possibility of achieving mastery without generating both nostalgic longing and environmental dread. Preoedipal mastery, generated against a "hostile" and "external" world, is attained *in spite of* an ambivalence that threatens to tear it down, postoedipal mastery by *harnessing* this ambivalence in the tension between ego and superego, a tension that allows us to see the world as neither wildly insufficient nor all-threatening. If the deadened ego is the precondition for relating to the world in a nonprojective manner and to others as separate centers of intentionality,[95] it is the reanimating superego that makes this deft and open relatedness a live possibility.[96]

At this point, one might wonder what happened to that old "cruel master" that could become a "pure culture of the death drive."[97] It is true that the negative aspects of the superego have thus far been set to the side, a result, to some extent, of Loewald's avoidance of the topic of aggression (an issue that will be taken up in the next chapter and the last). That being said, it is far from "unorthodox" to hold up the superego as, at least in part, a positive agency whose strength coincides not with the "weakness" but with the health of the ego.[98] Without launching into a full defense of Loewald on this point, I want simply to point to two attractive features of his conception of the superego, both of which I will take up in chapter 4: first, the superego is for him less a sublimate of the father than it is that which allows a successful mediation of tendencies traditionally reified in association with mother (union) and father (differentiation). Indeed, it is precisely the excessive distancing from the primordial density that supposedly issues from the father's influence that is *weakened* by the emergence of the superego, inasmuch as it prevents the overbuilding of psychic structure. Second, with regard to the therapeutic task of psychoanalysis: if the superego is a solely negative entity, the enforcer of a crushing guilt that is relieved in the analytic space, then the task of psychoanalysis is "integration," the reduction of the power of the superego as a whole and the absorption of this "grade in the ego" back into the ego itself. If, by contrast, psychic health means a strengthening of the good parts of the superego, then the goal of analysis is to maintain and reinforce a lively "tension" between ego and superego. I believe that the "integration" model, in encouraging a kind of psychic streamlining, lends itself to an ideal of "adaptation" that the "tension" model resists. Despite Loewald's ego psychology credentials, he clearly prefers the latter model to the former,[99] advocating as he does a difficult and dynamic interplay between the "agencies."[100]

The next chapter will examine a theory of a particularly stubborn obstacle on the way to this "inner tension." Its author, coincidentally, claims that it too makes some sense of the "enigmatic signification Freud expressed with the term 'death instinct.'"[101]

"There's no need to be afraid in the hall," she said, "you just have to pretend that you're the ghost who might meet you."
—Anna Freud, *The Ego and the Mechanisms of Defense*

3 Aggressivity in Psychoanalysis (Reprised)

Jacques Lacan and the Genesis of Omnipotence

The visibility of brutality in the twentieth century was cause for much post–World War II theorizing about what Erich Fromm called the "anatomy of human destructiveness." The ethologist Konrad Lorenz famously explained aggression in evolutionary terms, asserting its supposed "life-promoting" function.[1] Damning Lorenz's "biology as ideology" alongside Jean-Paul Sartre's valorization of "creative violence," Hannah Arendt strove to keep the analysis of human violence squarely in the political realm.[2] And weaving his way between these two views, Fromm sought to develop his own characterological analysis that transcended the dichotomy, instinct versus social product.[3]

Different though they were, these authors are united in having taken the time to recognize and dismiss Freud's theory of the death drive on their way to their own respective theories of human aggressiveness.[4] Less willing curtly to reject the instinctual foundation of Freud's later work was the "absolute master" of the postwar French psychoanalytic scene, Jacques Lacan, who, early in his career, saw the death drive at work in his own theory of specular aggressivity (*agressivité*).[5] That this theory, synthesized from a wide range of influences of which Freud was at best a marginal member,[6] had something to do with destructiveness seems to have been the extent to which it "made some sense of" the death drive, and

Lacan would later recognize the tenuousness of the connection in situating the death drive in relation to other concepts in his work.[7] I want nonetheless to explore this early placement of the death drive in the "primitive imaginary of the specular dialectic with the other" because I believe that there is, in fact, an attractive way to connect the two (unsurprisingly, by building on the work of the first two chapters) and, furthermore, that doing so rounds out the developmental model outlined in chapter 2.[8] Loewald deals only with the conflict between what I have called the tension-within and tension-between positions; nowhere does he address destructive drives and the havoc they can wreak in the developmental process.[9] Lacan, by marked contrast, reserves a capital importance for aggressivity, but, I will argue, at the cost of not seeing more basic forces at work in psychic development. Inserting a theory of mimetic aggressivity into Loewald's developmental model, thus pairing the unlikeliest of theoretical bedfellows, will be my primary aim here.

To be clear, however, my proposed integration carries no pretension of symmetry: whereas my hope in the previous chapter was to provide a broad view of Loewald's work, my interest here is *only* in Lacan's theory of specular aggressivity (and not in his understanding of the death drive) and, furthermore, only in this theory inasmuch as it might serve as a point of departure in formulating an understanding of aggressivity that is assimilable to Loewald's developmental model. What follows should thus be understood neither as a comprehensive treatment of Lacanian theory nor as an attempt to fuse the Lacanian and Loewaldian frameworks. As opposed to the first two chapters, in which my primary efforts were focused on following along, the aim here is more constructive: if I dusted off the bones of a developmental model in the first chapter and watched Loewald assemble them in the second, my goal in the present chapter is to fill in the missing pieces.

Working through Lacan's theory in this way comprises my attempt to confront the common understanding of the death drive as a destructive and violent force. As I argued in chapter 1, Freud himself gives us good reason to think of the death drive as a strange appellation for aggressiveness in the works of the later twenties and thirties. If, however, one takes *Beyond the Pleasure Principle* as a point of departure, the death drive is clearly no aggressive drive. Furthermore, when it is first "externalized," it is not sent out into the world as a raging will to seize and dominate. At what point then does a destructive psychic force rear its ugly head? And how precisely does it relate to the death drive?

Aggressivity and the Omnipotent Mother

Offering a captivating image to introduce his theory of the mirror stage,[10] Lacan asks us to think of the "striking spectacle of a nursling in front of a mirror who has not yet mastered walking, or even standing, but who—though held tightly by some prop, human or artificial—overcomes, in a flutter of jubilant activity, the constraints of his prop in order to adopt a slightly leaning-forward position and take in an instantaneous view of the image in order to fix it in his mind."[11] In Lacan's view, infants are drawn to their own image because the sight of this bound sack of flesh gives unity to the chaos of their real bodily situation: "the sight alone of the whole form of the human body gives the subject an imaginary mastery of his body, one which is premature in relation to a real mastery."[12] The identification with this specular other, dubbed the ideal-ego, fuels the formation of the *ego*, the template for which is provided by the image toward which the infant strives (Lacan jokes that, in this sense, "man creates himself in his own image").[13]

Undoubtedly the mirror stage is a positive development in that the *Urbild* of the ego, "out there" and yet representing what is "in here," forms a bridge between "the *Innenwelt* and the *Umwelt*," between "inside" and "outside."[14] This very same development is also, however, one of *alienation*, in that the child's *I*-prototype is an *other* for *it*. In other words, there is a radical disjunction between the ideal organization of the image and the fragmented, disorganized state of the child's actual body, a disjunction that gives rise to aggressivity. *That* aggressivity emerges in this gap between "an original organic chaos" and "a salutary imago," at least in his initial presentation of the theory, is clear[15]—*how* and *why*, however, is less so. At times, Lacan makes it seem as if it is merely the uncanny experience of oneself as doubled that "would trigger uncontrollable anxiety," leading to an "excess of aggressive tension."[16] In this case, aggressivity is simply "correlative to every alienating identification."[17] At others, he seems to situate it in the child's anticipation of "the conquest of his own body's functional unity," giving "rise to an inexhaustible squaring of the ego's audits," in which case aggressivity would be the driving force of the orthopedic quest for completion in the imaginary.[18] Richard Boothby convincingly argues that we should instead understand aggressivity in precisely the opposite fashion: not as aiming at an imagined unity but rather as a "drive toward violation of the imaginary form of the body that models the ego."[19] For the moment, I am interested only in the fact that, in all three of these interpretations, aggressivity is a rage situated in the "rending of the subject from himself" and thus must be understood as an *intrapsychic* force.[20]

Lacan would later clarify, however, that the image must be "ratified" if it is to serve its developmental role:

> Let's recall, then, how the specular relation is found to take its place and how it is found to be dependent on the fact that the subject is constituted in the locus of the Other, constituted by its mark, in the relation to the signifier.
>
> Already, just in the exemplary little image with which the demonstration of the mirror stage begins, the moment that is said to be *jubilatory* when the child, grasping himself in the inaugural experience of recognition in the mirror, comes to terms with himself as a totality functioning as such in his specular image, haven't I always insisted on the movement that the infant makes? This movement is so frequent, constant I'd say, that each and every one of you may have some recollection of it. Namely, he turns round, I noted, to the one supporting him who's there behind him. If we force ourselves to assume the content of the infant's experience and to reconstruct the sense of this movement, we shall say that, with this nutating movement of the head, which turns towards the adult as if to call upon his assent, and then back to the image, he seems to be asking the one supporting him, and who here represents the big Other, to ratify the value of this image.
>
> This is nothing, of course, but an indication concerning the inaugural nexus between this relation to the big Other and the advent of the function of the specular image.[21]

The image is thus only of such interest because the embodiment of the Other—the symbolic order manifested in authority (the law, society, but at first, the parents)—confirms that the child is indeed seeing *itself* in the mirror. It is furthermore this representative that makes the image into an *Urbild*: the mirror stage, as I have indicated, provides only a *prototype* for the ego. The ego itself only comes into being as signifiers (*"girl, blonde, likes chocolate, hates pink, good at drawing, etc."*) are affixed to this imaginary signified.[22] In other words, the ego, as opposed to its

Urbild, is constituted symbolically on an imaginary foundation, and it is the big Other that provides the bricks.

It is no innocent gesture. In an important section of *Seminar IV*, Lacan distinguishes between two sides of the mirror stage:

> There is, on the one hand, the experience of mastery [*maîtrise*], which will make the child's relationship to its own ego essentially one of *splitting*, of a differentiation from oneself that will remain to the end. There is, on the other hand, the encounter with the reality of the master [*maître*]. Insofar as the form of mastery appears to the subject in the form of a totality from which it is alienated, but nonetheless closely related to and dependent on it, there is jubilation; but it is different when, at the moment that form is given, there is also an encounter with the reality of the master. The moment of triumph is also one of defeat. When in the presence of this totality in the form of the mother's body, the subject must find that she does not obey. When the specular structure reflected in the mirror stage comes into play, maternal omnipotence is reflected in the depressive position, and there follows the child's feeling of powerlessness.[23]

As he explains here, the mirror stage results in a *double* alienation, both from ideal ego and also from maternal omnipotence: the emergence of the possibility of mastery thus coincides with the realization of helplessness before the *real* master. In recognizing the child in the mirror ("That's really you!"), the "primitive Other" ratifies the ideal ego (the triumph) while making clear that the child is totally dependent on the Other for that ratification (the defeat).[24]

Since the "I" comes into existence in this way, as terrifyingly heteronomous, the possibility of the mother's absence signifies nothing less than the threat of self-annihilation, thus the overwhelming need to figure out what it is that she desires, what it is that she is lacking, so that the "I" can *be* that "fundamental missing something" (what Lacan calls the "imaginary phallus") and thereby give her no cause for being anywhere else.[25] For this reason, the quest for mastery that is the process of ego formation fuses with the attempt to satisfy a desire "that is, in its essence, unsatisfiable."[26] The signifiers that are affixed to the image are thus accepted as descriptions not of what the child *is* but of what the child *ought to be* in order to fill in maternal lack: "It is precisely inasmuch as [the child] shows its mother that which it is not that it constructs the pathways around which the ego finds its stability."27

As I have said, Lacan typically presents aggressivity as an intrapsychic tension that only erupts as a social problem when the subject "clothes" the other with the "same capacities for destruction as those of which he feels himself the bearer."28 Distinguishing his theory of aggressivity from an intersubjective one, he would even proudly proclaim that it is a "case of Lacan vs. Hegel."29 In binding the process of ego formation to the encounter with maternal omnipotence, however, he has given us good reason to question this view: since the ideal ego is only a "salutary imago" as a result of being invested with phallic significance, one might say that aggressivity is, at the most fundamental level, a rage generated not simply in the gap of oneself from oneself but rather in the ever unsuccessful attempts to please Mother that are *responsible* for the gap of oneself from oneself. The child *is* what it is not *for her* but still fails to be that which is lacking. The "I" plays the "deceptive object" but ultimately does not deceive.30

This move allows us to answer Mikkel Borch-Jacobsen's charge that "if I myself am the rival, there is fundamentally no reason why I should stop competing with 'myself,'" that is, if aggressivity is the product of a completely intrapsychic dialectic of ego formation, then there is no reason why it should ever be "overwritten," as the ego's fundamental connection to otherness is narcissistic.31 At times, Lacan makes it seem as if this is precisely the case and thus that our emergence into the "social" world is only ever a continuation of the imaginary dialectic by other means: as he states quite categorically, "the object relation must always submit to the narcissistic framework and be inscribed in it."32

As I have just attempted to demonstrate, however, the narcissistic pursuit is never *simply* narcissistic: since the process of acquiring an "I" is one and the same as that of failing to seduce the mother, it already points to its failure at its inception, necessarily involving as it does the "narcissistic lesions" that are the "preludes to castration."33 It must be emphasized that castration—the ultimate acceptance that one is not and does not have the phallus—does not involve the subject's further inadequacy before the image, as this kind of acceptance of lack would only widen the gap that generates aggressivity, inciting despair before the further impossibility of the orthopedic venture. Castration means rather that *the ideal ego itself* is lacking, that there is "a part that is missing in the desired image."[34] Although Lacan believes that there certainly are ways of avoiding or dulling this realization (he calls them psychoses), he is also clear that it is implied in the specular dialectic from the start, castration being the telos of the ego.

The Elision of Death and Mastery

Critics of Lacan often fault his developmental theory for privileging the experience in the mirror to the neglect of a more primary affective bond,[35] but, as I have tried to show here, of their inextricability—that is, of the complete dependence of the process of ego formation on maternal recognition and love—Lacan is perfectly clear. One might nonetheless have reservations about the *manner* in which he theorizes this affective tie. For the most part, it is not the mother herself but rather her activity of constituting "a virtual field of symbolic nihilation, from which all objects, each in their turn, will come to derive their symbolic value," which is of fundamental psychic significance.[36] Indeed, he admits that he "can only remain for awhile in the pre-oedipal stages on the sole condition of being guided by the thread that is the fundamental role of the symbolic relation."[37] In this reduction (or perhaps, inflation) of mother to transitory Other, Lacan has precluded the possibility that the child might identify itself not with what she *wants* but with what she *is* (or, at least, with what she is perceived to be). I will return to this point in a moment.

There is another aspect of the mother, however, that transcends her role as protosymbolic: in her all-devouring insatiability, experienced by the child in both horror and attraction, there is also something of the *real*, a something that Lacan attempts to capture in calling the mother "the Thing."[38] In *Seminar VII* he would go so far as to claim that "the whole development at the level of the mother/child interpsychology . . . is nothing more than an immense development of the essential character of the maternal thing, insofar as she occupies the place of that thing, of *das Ding*."[39] As always, Lacan is providing an important corrective to prevailing trends, in this case to the idealization of the mother-infant relationship: "Here is your affective tie," he seems to be saying, "an indissoluble bond of unspeakable horror."

Beyond its corrective function, however, what justifies this claim? Spelling out the logic of *Nachträglichkeit*, Lacan asserts that "what is realized in my history is neither the past definite as what was, since it is no more, nor even the perfect as what has been in what I am, but the future anterior as what I will have been, given that I am in the process of becoming."[40] For this reason, one might say, the "emotional tie," signifying a reversal of the ego's accomplishments, can *only* be experienced retroactively as a source of dread (even if, one might speculate, it was not experienced in this manner in the overwritten past): "What we find in the incest law is located as such at the level of the unconscious in relation to *das Ding*, the Thing. The desire for the mother cannot be satisfied because it is the end, the terminal point, the abolition of the whole world of demand, which is the one that at its deepest level structures man's unconscious."[41] This would all be correct, I believe, *if* the affective tie manifested "afterward" *solely* in the conflictual horror of/attraction to the Thing. If, however, this tie has other "deferred" articulations—the primary of which, for Loewald, is *Eros*—then the theorization of the Thing does not in fact account for all of its vicissitudes.[42]

One might guess where I am going here: in Lacan's all-engulfing mother, the distinction that Loewald makes between dread of union and its precondition, the urge to union, is collapsed. What gets buried under the Thing is the more primary connection to the "other" of the tension-within position, the other not as threat to *one's* being but as co-occupant of the primordial density, of *being itself.* If *this* is the proper domain of the death drive, as I argued in the previous chapter, then we might come to the surprising conclusion that, far from making sense of Freud's "enigmatic signification," Lacan actually *erased* the death drive from his vision of psychic development by negating the kind of bond that is its aim.

I want to pair this insight with a brief analysis of Lacan's attempt in *Seminar II* to derive his theory of the imaginary from the failed *Project for a Scientific Psychology*, where Freud first conceptualizes the defensive and regulatory "barrier-pathway system" that would later be called the ego. Lacan claims there that Freud's account is ultimately "inadequate": this initial theorization fails, in his opinion, to entitle "one to think that the facilitations [*Bahnungen*, the "pathways" constitutive of the regulatory system in the *Project*] will ever have a *functional utility*."[43] It is only when one identifies the barrier-pathway system as a function of the imaginary, that is, as organized visually according to the "gestalt principle," that one can understand how the *Reizschutz* gives rise to this "functional utility" "serviceable for the guidance of behavior."[44] What Freud is pointing toward, but ultimately missing, in other words, is the image: "Freud isn't a Gestaltist—one cannot give him credit for everything—but he does sense the theoretical demands which gave rise to the Gestaltist construction."[45]

Very swiftly then, Lacan translates Freud's concern with how the nervous system deals with the deluge of excitations that threaten to overwhelm it into a proto-gestaltist assertion of the psyche's world-structuring capacity. Mirroring could most certainly be thought of as a form of defense and regulation: being able perceptually to organize the world is a part of dealing with one's place in it.[46] But the problem of the precise relation between the two is not even raised: homed in as he is on the "reflected relations of the living," Lacan turns homeostasis into reflection and coping into mirroring, imagining himself engaged in an exercise in translation rather than transformation.[47]

In this move, the problem of "mastering excitation" that is really at the center of Freud's *Project* is elided and replaced with a picture of psychic development that relies exclusively on specular aggressivity.[48] If Freud can be accused of universalizing an obsessive neurotic view of reality, Lacan could in turn be said to universalize aggressive struggle at the expense of the more basic drive to mastery. And if this preference is viewed in light of his elision of the death drive, an even more substantial critique can be furnished: if Lacan theorizes an excessively "rigid" ego, it is because there is no pull of the primordial density to counter the drive to mastery and thus because there is only, in his view, a drive to an excessive, rigidifying mastery. Both characters in the drama I have investigated in chapters 1 and 2—the death drive and the drive to mastery—are thereby repressed in favor of a single motivating force: specular aggressivity. There is no urge to union, nor is there a slow grappling with a new environment (no *bewältigen*), only the image, the alienation, and the resulting hostility—a tension-between unshackled from a tension-within.

Toward a New Theory of Aggressivity

Rejecting the "hypothesis of a sort of megalomania that projects onto the infant that which is in the mind of the analyst," Lacan is avid that "the structure of omnipotence is not, contrary to what one might believe, in the subject, but in the mother."[49] In the first section of this chapter, I have argued that aggressivity is best understood not as a wholly intrapsychic force but rather as intimately related to this omnipotent mother. In equating this mother with the big Other, however, Lacan has ruled out the possibility of identifying directly with what she *is*, though the essential connection, in some form, of aggressivity to an orthopedic quest for completion seems to betray this preclusion. The pieces are now more or less in place, and we might wonder anew: what precisely is the relationship "between narcissistic identification with omnipotence and submission to omnipotence?"[50] One way of working toward answering this question, primed in the previous section, would be to see aggressivity as conditioned by and emerging out of the dialectic of death and mastery outlined in the first two chapters. It is this possibility that I want to explore in what follows.

According to Loewald, when infants have made their way through the separation process, acquiring mastery from loss, they come to see the very same "other" toward which they bear an urge to union as a dreaded source of engulfment, as a threat to their emergent autonomy.[51] The paradox, of course, is that they gain this mastery through identification, by being the "other": the "other" thereby comes to be dreaded (comes to be the *other*) in being imitated. The entirety of my proposal in this chapter is captured in the possibility that *this development feeds back into the internalization process*; in other words, that the other is imitated not just in its caring capacity but also in its "engulfing" aspect. If our caregivers are truly the bearers of a schizoid projection, then to *be* them is not just to provide the comfort of presence in absence (to internalize the "other" of the tension-within position) but also to be an all-consuming source of dread (to internalize the *other* of the tension-between position).

The seemingly mistaken identification with an outside that is a source of engulfment, *the curious recognition of oneself in the very element that challenges one's autonomy*, would then give rise to a new motivational force (a new drive, if one wishes), distinct from both the death drive and the drive to mastery: neither to reimmerse oneself in the primordial density nor to protect oneself from loss through protective structure building but rather to *engulf others* in the same way that one feels oneself threatened. Parroting the *other*'s aggressive behavior, I become, for the first time, aggressive; that is, a more basic drive to master external threats ("Others are trying to engulf me" and "I want to protect myself against others") is perverted into a drive to aggress ("I want to engulf others"). What Anna Freud called "identification with the aggressor" is here more than just a manifestation of aggressivity or a mechanism of its genesis;[52] it is rather *the* initial appearance of a genuinely aggressive energy.[53]

Aggressivity is thus generated when the death drive, already projected outward and experienced negatively as a property of the *other*, is aped in this confused form; it is, more concisely, an imitation of a revalued projection.[54] Still bearing the urge to eliminate rigid self/other distinction through this chain, the drive is now set on reducing others to nothingness, on engulfing in the same way that the subject feels threatened with engulfment, in order to accomplish this goal. A drive to erase the independence of the other, to bear *omnipotence* over the other, is thereby produced by imitation of this same other in its capacity as dreaded threat, i.e., *qua other*. In turn, just as aggressivity is a vicissitude of the death drive at odds with the death drive itself, so too is it a kind of mastery-subverting drive to mastery: in aiming to shut out otherness, aggressivity does ward off "external" dangers, but at the cost of real engagement with the environment. It thus contributes *too much* to the construction of the psychic *Reizschutz*, leading to a loss of mastery by what Loewald calls ego rigidity.[55]

I cannot help but worry that my proposal here is so minimal that it runs the risk of vanishing into thin air. Perhaps I am only codifying, within Loewald's theoretical framework, an intuition that children, when they are genuinely *aggressive* and not lashing out in frustration, are only mimicking behavior of which they have previously felt themselves to be objects (which is different, of course, from *actually being* those objects, though the two are not mutually exclusive). Psychoanalysis has, however, generally shied away from theorizing aggressivity in these terms: where it is not put forth as an innate drive (arguably, Freud, Klein),[56] it is typically conceived of either as an unintentional expression of motility (Winnicott) or as rage against narcissistic injury (Fairbairn, Kohut).[57] If, as many schools of psychoanalysis recognize, parents are objects of both schizoid projection and imitation, would it not make sense that children receive back part of what they project outward?

In sum, I propose that aggressivity be understood as *neither* constitutional, i.e., inborn aggression, *nor* as a by-product of environmental failure (whether we understand this failure as familial or as the irrationality of the social order) but rather as a necessary developmental misstep. While I would agree with Wilhelm Reich's argument that there is no "innate" aggressive drive and that more neutral drives, inflamed by other conditions, are perverted into an aggressive one, I would disagree that those conditions are *only*, or even *primarily*, "external": given the nature of preoedipal life as both Loewald and Lacan imagine it, parents must inevitably be identified as aggressors.[58] The question, from an "environmental" perspective, is not whether the parent is aggressive or not but whether the parent *confirms* the child's negative projection or lowers the intensity of the feedback loop of aggressivity by parrying the projection with patience and what Bion calls "reverie."[59] I will address this question of managing aggressivity in the final section of this chapter.

Dependence and Omnipotence: On Jessica Benjamin

To help further elucidate the distinctiveness and force of the proposal, I would like to mobilize it toward a critique of two other theories of aggressivity that are strikingly similar to the one developed here: those of Jessica Benjamin and René Girard. Seeking to move away from the classic psychoanalytic preoccupations with intrapsychic structures and drives toward an "intersubjective view,"[60] Benjamin explains aggressivity as emerging within a "struggle for recognition." No less than adults, infants act in the world and seek some kind of direct response to their actions. Many toys ("the mobile that moves when baby jerks the cord tied to her wrist, the bells that ring when she kicks her feet") are designed to provide a "contingent responsiveness," but none can provide the kind of recognition that other subjects do: "The nine-month-old already looks to the parent's face for the shared delight in a sound. The two-year-old says, 'I did it!' showing the peg she has hammered and waiting for the affirmation that she has learned something new, that she has exercised her agency."[61] This need for recognition leads inevitably to paradox: "at the very moment of realizing our own independence, we are dependent upon another to recognize it. At the very moment we come to understand the meaning of 'I, myself,' we are forced to see the limitation of that self."[62] We have already encountered this idea in Lacan: that the moment the "I" comes into existence coincides with the realization of its utter dependence.

This same paradox becomes somewhat unfamiliar, however, when stated in more dramatic terms: "the self is trying to establish himself *as an absolute*, an independent entity, yet he must recognize the other as like himself in order to *be* recognized by him."[63] To be aggressive, for Benjamin, is to seek to dissolve this intersubjective tension by denying the other's subjectivity and attempting to enthrone the omnipotent self. But how did we get from the realization of dependence and limitation to the desire to establish oneself as an absolute? "Hegel" might be a good one-word answer here: like self-conscious individuals proving "themselves and each other through a life-and-death struggle," children confronted with separateness feel they "must raise their certainty of being *for themselves* to truth."[64] Even if we accept the translation, however, we might still wonder why precisely dependence and limitation seem so naturally to elicit omnipotent striving. Are the two this obviously and immediately connected?

In an important note in "The Omnipotent Mother," Benjamin distinguishes omnipotence from a more "immediate, originary state . . . in which the limits of reality are not known and the other is experienced as 'there' without awareness of an opposing center of intentionality" (a perfect description of the tension-within position).[65] In her view, omnipotence is "the reactive effort to recreate [this] presumed state, as if power could be known before the knowledge of powerlessness and difference, which is actually the condition of power. This reconstruction creates omnipotence, which can then be understood as defensive denial, not simple ignorance, of the other's independence."[66] The developmental narrative outlined in this chapter also connects dependence and omnipotence, but contains two crucial middle steps that link what Benjamin calls here the "simple ignorance" of otherness to its "defensive denial": first, when the tension-within position is broken, the child does indeed wish to return to its "wholeness," but to say that this wish involves an aggressive stamping out of otherness is to accord the child at this stage too much volition, too much strategy and control. Wholeness is not aimed at so much as it is assumed, and where it *is* desired, the wish is much better characterized as a blind fleeing, prompted wholly and terrifyingly by the world-shattering experience of separateness. Second, even when separateness becomes something minimally habitable, omnipotence does not immediately follow: coming to gain enough stability so as to provide sufficient "presence in absence" does not lead the "I" to feel entitled to any "grandiose ambitions."[67] It does, however, recast the "other" in the position of dreaded *other*, introducing the dimension of omnipotence, but not yet as a project of the ego. It is only in a final identification with this *other* that children,[68] aping the aggressive imposition to which they themselves have felt victim, become the kinds of beings who take an active and existential satisfaction in the domination of others.

Collapsing these three moves into one, Benjamin equates the coming "to understand the meaning of 'I, myself'" with "the desire to establish oneself as an absolute," leaving us to assume that aggressivity is a natural correlate of an unaccepted dependence and thus that we simply *are* aggressive (rather than cripplingly depressed or terrorized) in the absence of intersubjective tension. If we are to explain rather than merely assert the fact that "minds tend toward an autonomous omnipotence," the "breakdown of tension between self and other" that is the "root of domination" must be understood as a positive *product* of that tension.[69]

In a curious attempt to reconcile intersubjectivity with Freudian drive theory, Benjamin asserts that omnipotence "is a manifestation of Freud's death instinct": "Omnipotence and loss of tension actually refer to the same phenomenon. Omnipotence, whether in the form of merging or aggression, means the complete assimilation of the other and self. It corresponds to the zero point of tension between self and other."[70] As I have argued, it is erroneous to equate the strivings toward a tension-less state characteristic of the urge to union and the omnipotent struggles of aggressivity. The infant attempting to maintain the tension-within position and the child out to subdue an other into nothingness are two very different beings, though they both could be said to be attempting to dissolve self/other tension. Distinguishing between these two is necessary not simply to redeem the innocent neonate from slanderous accusations of omnipotence—more or less standard fare in psychoanalytic theory ever since Freud crowned the infant "His Majesty the Baby"[71]—but, more important, to explain the recourse to omnipotence in the first place.

A False Decision: On René Girard

Further light can be shed on the theory proposed here through a comparison with that of René Girard, for whom all culture is in constant danger of an outbreak of violence due to the simple fact of what he calls the "mimesis of desire." We want, so Girard's thesis goes, as and what others want. This mimesis naturally leads to conflict, which in turn only strengthens the basic operation of human desire; in Girard's words, "the unchanneled mimetic impulse hurls itself blindly against the obstacle of a conflicting desire. It invites its own rebuffs, and these rebuffs will in turn strengthen the mimetic inclination."[72] Due to the self-propagating nature of violence, every society is in need of rites of sacrifice, which "serve to polarize the community's aggressive impulses and redirect them toward victims that may be actual or figurative, animate or inanimate."[73] This "scapegoating" operation, whereby a community finds cohesion in the cessation of violence *by* violence, is, for Girard, the sole purpose and function of religion.

Girard is all too aware that his theory bears uncanny similarities to Freud's but argues that he ultimately succeeds where his double comes up short: rather than following through on the brief passages where he explains conflict in terms of *identification* (i.e., *mimesis*), Freud unfortunately falls back on his Oedipus theory to trace the origins of hostility. The distinction between their respective theories is easily summed up in Girard's claim that "the mimetic process detaches desire from any predetermined object, whereas the Oedipus complex fixes desire on the maternal object."[74] It further lavishes too much attention on the paternal rivalry: in Girard's words, "the father explains nothing. If we hope to get to the root of the matter we must put the father out of our minds and concentrate on the fact that the enormous impression made on the community by the collective murder is not due to the victim's identity per se, but to his role as unifying agent."[75] In short, the mother is not *the* object, and the father is not *the* rival.

Abandoning the basic psychoanalytic insight that the bond we have with our parents is the model for all future relationships, Girard thus emphasizes the essential *substitutability* of affect: for him, everyone is a potential rival, everything a potential object of desire.[76] The story told here, by contrast, does not begin with a world of others to fight and objects to want, recognizing that the boundaries that make possible aggressive drives do not exist at the beginning of life, that we are initially but one part of a "tension-within" *out of which* an external world slowly emerges. Furthermore, the initial confrontation with that world is not one of violent usurpation but of basic coping. In effect, Girard's story, like Lacan's and Benjamin's, begins two steps too late—and with curious consequences.

Girard takes as his "principal complaint against Freud" the latter's view that children *consciously* experience patricidal hate and incestuous desire, and only *then* relegate this experience to the unconscious.[77] He dismisses this idea that children are "fully aware" of their aggressive and libidinal impulses, claiming that they do not really process the "hostile colouring" of their relationships until initiated into the adult world of rivalry.[78] In other words, while children certainly aggress, they do not *mean* to aggress because they have not internalized the cultural logic wherein aggression can be consciously justified. Why would Girard pick out this point as his "principal complaint" instead of resting content with a demonstration of the supposedly superior explanatory power of mimetic desire over the Oedipus complex?[79] In short, why must children be exculpated?

A kind of answer is offered in a follow-up work, *Things Hidden Since the Foundation of the World*, where he reveals his hand, as it were. Girard claims there that the revelations of *Violence and the Sacred* are not just pieces of a theory of culture but rather descriptions of *Satan* himself, the paradoxical source of both order and disorder in society. Although "the three great pillars of primitive religion—myth, sacrifice, and prohibitions—are subverted by the thought of the Prophets," the Old Testament is "inconclusive" in its defeat of Satan because "we never arrive at a concept of the deity that is entirely foreign to violence."[80] Only the Gospels finally refute the "logic of violence" in full. "Christ," Girard contends, "is the only agent capable of escaping from these structures and freeing us from their dominance" and is thus the ideal bearer of the message "to abandon the violent mimesis involved in the relationship of doubles."[81]

In *Violence and the Sacred* we think we are getting a theory of *what is*. In *Things Hidden*, by contrast, we find that we have an option, that it is possible to vanquish "transcendent violence" with "transcendent love."[82] Like Kierkegaard in *Sickness Unto Death*, where the seemingly inescapable vicissitudes of despair are presented as a way of hyping the monumental "or" of faith, Girard backs his audience into corner and demands a decision. Without detracting from the finesse with which he accomplishes this rhetorical move, one cannot help but feel a bit cheated when he claims that it is Jesus who first exposes "the secret of social violence" and who unveils "the possibility of a life refusing mimetic rivalry, and, in consequence, violence."[83] For this possibility, in which Girard believes, is clearly no innocent conclusion: once revealed, it becomes rather transparent that all forms of human sociality have been lumped within the violence/sacrifice circuit (the "either") so as to prepare and package it to be neatly refused for the "or," thus the necessity of clearing the "presocialized" of the allegation that *they too* might consciously aggress.[84]

What ought to be refused, then, is not violence itself but the violence versus peace paradigm. Other stories can be told—the dialectic of death and mastery, for instance—and to more reasonable ends. For Girard, as we have seen, childhood must be clearly demarcated from the adult world of violence. With Freud, it is possible to see more continuity between the two, to see children as the kinds of beings that *mean to dominate*, and who do so for reasons having to do with the nature of preoedipal relations. Perhaps, with Girard, human desire and aggressivity are infinitely malleable—"arbitrary," as he so often repeats—and children are "innocent" of knowledge of their aggressive impulses until initiated into culture at large. Or perhaps, with Freud, the groundwork for "adult" desire and aggressivity are molded from day one, in the course of interactions with the most important people in our lives at a time when we are more or less heteronomous.[85]

Overcoming Aggressivity

In this last section I want to offer a few tentative thoughts about how aggressivity is transcended (partially, at least). For Lacan, as I have already reviewed, aggressivity is overcome with the full initiation into the symbolic that attends castration: as Bruce Fink explains, "the overwriting of the imaginary by the symbolic (the 'normal' or 'ordinary neurotic' path) leads to the suppression or at least the subordination of imaginary relations characterized by rivalry and aggressivity . . . to symbolic relations dominated by concerns with ideals, authority figures, the law, performance, achievement, guilt, and so on."[86] This "subordination of imaginary relations" is, however, only half the story: for, in addition to addressing the narcissistic struggle in the imaginary, the symbolic is also the medium of taming the horrors of the *real*, of repressing the simultaneous attraction to and fear of the maternal "Thing."

The most important act associated with castration is, for Lacan, the acceptance of the infamous *Nom-du-Père*, the signifier of the mother's desire: the *non* (no) of the father prohibits access to *jouissance*, thus relieving the dread of the Thing, while the *nom* (name) of the father offers a reason why the Thing cannot be had, an explanation with a single *noun* (*nom*) of the impossibility of jouissance. With this pivotal nomination tying the question of desire to meaning, the child embarks on a new path: instead of tarrying with the Thing, to seek instead all of "the reasons why I can't have it." As Lionel Bailly explains, "it is far better for the child to 'go with' the paternal metaphor than to be constantly defeated by the inexplicability of Mother's behaviours, or its own inability to impose its will upon the exterior world"; thus, those who are not "duped" by the *Nom-du-Père* "err" in clinging to the possibility of oedipal victory (which is why, as Lacan jokes in *Seminar XXI, les non-dupes errent*).[87] Faced with the lack of the *imaginary phallus*, with the impossibility of maternal seduction, the subject thus turns its attention to the task of living up to the demands of the *ego ideal* (the internalized ideal of the Other), which manifests in the more abstract and noncorporeal features ("charm," "sense of humor," "intelligence," etc.) of the *symbolic phallus*.[88]

One can thus read Lacan, as I have already hinted, as offering a theory of language similar to that of Loewald: the symbolic, in this view, takes over and finds new expression for the real contradiction between the pull and dread of jouissance, which is then allowed to play out in language rather than reality.[89] We would still be left to wonder, however, why some narcissistic worlds are shattered while others are left intact. As Jacob Rogozinski wonders, "by what magic is the subject able to pass from the imaginary to the symbolic, to assume castration as the law of its desire while overcoming the horror that it inspires in him?"[90] It is at this point that allowing in the developmental importance of the relative mainte- nance of the tension-within position—one might say, *the magic*—helps to unburden the symbolic of the great responsibility to socialize infants on its own.

One of the most important tasks in maintaining that level of care, for Donald Winnicott and Wilfred Bion, is to manage aggressivity properly when it manifests itself. According to Winnicott, for a parent to provide an adequate "holding environment" is not just to provide care but also to be able to cope with the frustration at breaks in care continuity, which inevitably lead, in his view, to a destructive lashing out. He speaks of a parent's capacity to "survive" infant attacks: that is, to just *be there* when they happen, to neither respond in kind nor to disappear, to "not retali- ate." For Winnicott, this positive nonretaliation is an important compo- nent in the emergence of reality in the child's world.[91] In my own terms, in being provided with a clear demonstration that the parent is not in fact the dreaded *other* of the tension-between position, even when provoked at the extreme, the child comes to recognize the distinction between its negative projection and the actual other.[92]

Bion proposes a very similar idea to Winnicott's "holding environ- ment" with his theory of containment: the mother, in his view, is a "con- tainer" for the infant's negative affect. When a child is excessively fearful, "an understanding mother is able to experience the feeling of dread, that this baby was striving to deal with by projective identification, and yet retain a balanced outlook."[93] Similarly, when the child lashes out aggres- sively, a good mother recognizes the act, and even experiences herself as an object of the aggressivity, but maintains her composure and feels neither victimized nor retaliatory.

Unlike Winnicott's mother, however, Bion's is charged with an additional task: not only to bear aggressive attacks and maintain her composure but also to translate raw destructive energy (what Bion calls "beta elements") into more usable thoughts ("alpha elements"). The containing mother absorbs a child's enraged actions and returns them in more manageable form: "I know you're mad about such and such, but this isn't going to help anyone. Let's try this instead." Rather than fleeing from or combating destructive energy, she transforms it into words; she changes a situation in which unprocessed psychic energy is being unleashed to one into which thought can enter. If the aggressive strivings of the child are beaten back with equal force, they will only be redoubled in strength and if they find no resistance, they will not be questioned. Only the patient, painstaking translation of nonsymbolized instinctual energy into words can "contain" aggressivity, can prevent it from becoming pathological. Bion calls this work "reverie."[94]

It is not, then, *that* we acquire language that allows the overcoming of narcissistic aggressivity but, according to Bion, *how* we acquire it. No doubt language ties us to others in a particular way conducive to sociability, but it only becomes a vehicle for healthy affective expression with the patience and skill of good others in early life. If, thus, any strict distinction can be drawn between psychosis and neurosis, it should be theorized not along the lines aggressivity suppressed/aggressivity uncontained (*le père ou pire*—the father or worse) but rather in terms of good enough or failed management of aggressivity.[95]

* * *

Having followed preoedipal conflict to a dialectical resolution with Loewald in the last chapter, I have proposed, in the present one, the existence of an unfortunate by-product, a kind of wrench in the gears, an unwelcome fourth in a process that would prefer only three. With some help, I arrived at this conclusion by carrying to its end a logic that Loewald only incompletely develops: if, as he argues, I am a schizoid being that grows by internalization, then I must necessarily become the threat that I have projected onto the *other*. The basic idea here is simply that we are aggressive because we perceive an aggressiveness directed toward us. We impinge upon others because we imagine ourselves to be impinged upon. I do not find this to be a particularly novel idea in itself, but hope to have couched it in a developmental story that frames it as a moment in our emergence from the tension-within position. For this reason, I have portrayed my argument as an attempt to integrate a heavily revised theory of mimetic aggressivity (Lacan) into a dialectic of dependence (Loewald).

One of the primary victims of Lacan's theory of aggressivity is Freud's notion of *bewältigen*, which means literally "to bring in one's violence" (*in seine Gewalt bringen*), a definition that bears some of the ambiguity of the term *mastery* discussed in chapter 1.[96] To bring in one's violence could mean to subject to power, to mastery in the sense of *Bemächtigung*, but it could also mean to bring violence *in*, to tame the chaos of trauma, to exercise control. According to the theory proposed here, the outbreak of a kind of *Gewalt*, of what Lacan calls aggressivity, is a necessary part of psychic development, but it is not *primary*; it is rather an unfortunate consequence of *Bewältigung* that threatens *Bewältigung* itself. This move, it must be emphasized, is not simply a rejection of Lacan's rather bleak view of ego development: there are serious theoretical drawbacks to the assertion of aggressivity as baseline, drawbacks that are remedied in a more comprehensive narrative that takes it to be a derivative, though admittedly inevitable, perversion of more basic human drives.

PART III

Working Through

4   The Psyche in Late Capitalism I

Theodor Adorno, Max Horkheimer, and the Crisis of Internalization

For both Marx and Freud, one might say that the word *religion* was, above all else, an answer to the question: "Why do people accept a society grossly misaligned with their basic drives?" For the Marxists of the Second International who either believed in the evolutionary necessity of communism or else saw revolution on the immediate horizon, this question received a dismissive reply: "Well, they won't for long." For the social theorists of the Frankfurt school, on the other hand, who were charged with making sense of the triumphs of American consumerism, the failures of Russian communism, and the horrors of European fascism, the problem of "religion" gained considerably in urgency, and one could even say that it was *the* central problem of their collective work (there is perhaps no more confused assertion, for a critical theorist, than that capitalist society is becoming increasingly "secular"). Indeed, that the vast majority of people happily submit to such a highly irrational and devastatingly unstable mode of production was a fact so unsettling to the Frankfurters that they believed nothing less than an entirely different way of thinking was necessary to root out the insidious ways in which we have internalized social structure.

For the critical theorists, religion is more than just "false consciousness": if we are really to understand how human beings actively and energetically reproduce conditions that make them passive and depleted, then we must understand modern ideology as a committed *psychic invest-ment* in late capitalist society. Turning to psychoanalysis for help with this task, the Frankfurt School found that some work had already been done to articulate what "highs" capitalism itself offers. There was, for instance, a significant psychoanalytic literature linking the drive to amass wealth with anal erotism.[1] In this view, just as the mastery needed for the retention of feces is a precondition for parental love (nothing makes children feel as aesthetically displeasing, and thus as unworthy of love, as the reaction of their parents to a failure of sphincter control), so too is the mastery needed for the acquisition of money a precondition for the pursuit of objects of desire. Money puts us in the position of getting what we want, with the added bonus that its retention allows us endlessly to defer the task of thinking about what it is, precisely, that we want—in that lies its very real gift.[2]

On its own, however, this psychic allure is not enough to overcome our repulsion to its pursuit, to pacify what Rousseau called "the mortal hatred of sustained work."[3] For that, capitalism needed to enlist the ser-vices of that which once signified a sphere wholly different from com-modity production: *culture*. It is for aid in analyzing the "culture industry" that the Frankfurt School really looked to psychoanalysis, but, in so doing, they found that the culture industry was of just as much help in under-standing psychoanalysis. It is Herbert Marcuse, perhaps, who is best known for his fusion of psychoanalytic and social theory in works like *Eros and Civilization* and *One-Dimensional Man*, but it is not his vision of the psyche in late capitalism with which I will begin.[4] In this chap-ter I would like rather to look at the intriguingly underdeveloped and yet clearly essential psychoanalytic forays of Theodor Adorno and Max Horkheimer, who found in the "structural" theory of id, ego, and super-ego aid in clarifying the nature of subjection in late capitalism and in particular the effects of the rise of a media industry devoted to the pro-duction of mass culture. Unfortunately, and like so many psychoanalysts, they took on a psychic model without trying to make sense of the drive theory that undergirded it. In brief, my hypothesis in this chapter is that integrating Freud's mature drive theory into their work might strengthen their theses about the travails of the psyche in late capitalism and that, more generally, some of the grays in first-generation critical theory might appear green through a more polished version of the psychological lens that they themselves employed.[5]

My route to this end will be more circuitous than this opening implies, as a fair bit of preparatory work is needed to set up my intervention. For Adorno and Horkheimer, the appearance of the culture industry signified not just a new mechanism of power but a fundamental alteration in the psychic constitution of the capitalist subject. Providing a general framework within which to understand this transformation, first through a reading of *Dialectic of Enlightenment* and then through an exposition of Jessica Benjamin's conception of this psychic reorganization, will be the aim of the first two sections of this chapter. With this problematic established, I will then set to work refashioning a concept that will serve as the key to unlocking a new interpretation of the crisis of internalization, one that is explicitly equated in *Dialectic of Enlightenment* with the death drive: *mimesis.*[6] Having smuggled the drive theory developed in the first three chapters into their work, I will finally offer an account of the nature of the psychic gratification provided by the culture industry, how that gratification serves to limit critical capacities, and what there is left to do in the wake of this transformation. As should be clear by now, what follows is less an interpretation of Adorno and Horkheimer's crisis narrative than it is a reconstruction of it. I am interested here less in discovering their "true" intentions, or providing a comprehensive exegesis of their more psychoanalytic writings, than I am in employing their work toward a rethinking of the psyche in late capitalism.

Odyssean Fantasies: The Function of the Culture Industry

I want to begin with a discussion of a text that has come to be representative of the critical thrust of the Frankfurt school as a whole: *Dialectic of Enlightenment*. Of its six sections, surely the most maddening and seemingly out of place is the chapter on Odysseus. Jarringly turned into a transhistorical phenomenon, Enlightenment begins here with a curious self-renunciation in the service of self-preservation: in naming himself "no one" for Polyphemus, or in his resistance to Circe's enchantment,[7] Odysseus demonstrates the basic maneuver from which the subject emerges.[8] As with Freud's living vesicle in *Beyond the Pleasure Principle*, the subject is born—or, rather, is able to survive as more than a temporary blip in the chaos of existence—by paradoxically submitting to a kind of self-deadening in order to live. Hegel had a very good term for this capacity, which inaugurates Western subjectivity: the *cunning of reason*. It is through his cunning—that is, the counterintuitive negation of himself in the service of his own mastery—that Odysseus triumphs, and it is for this reason that he embodies the dawn of Enlightenment.

The triumph of cunning receives, however, only brief celebration: once secured, survival very quickly becomes a source of great anxiety. Having duped the more powerful with a weapon as light as the word, the subject "is driven objectively by the fear that, if he does not constantly uphold the fragile advantage the word has over violence, this advantage will be withdrawn by violence."[9] Mastery, in short, becomes *preemptive* mastery. No longer content with the magic of survival by cunning, Enlightenment, for whom "the mere idea of the 'outside' is a real source of fear," seeks to eliminate unexpected surprises by making of nature something manipulable, organizable, navigable.[10] The cunning through which the subject emerged is made extraneous. Adventure has been left for routine. The subject has "matured": "Everything—including the individual human being, not to mention the animal—becomes a repeatable, replaceable process, a mere example of the conceptual models of the system."[11]

Though his cunning has become obsolete, however, Odysseus is nonetheless clung to in the realm of ideology: "The lone voyager armed with cunning is already *homo oeconomicus*, whom all reasonable people will one day resemble: for this reason the *Odyssey* is already a Robinsonade."[12] Long past the point of needing to submit to true risk, long past the time for true heroics, the subject nonetheless maintains this back-to-nature fantasy.[13] Indeed, the less actual risk, the less the possibility of the return of a real "outside" of the subject's world, the more that risk is embraced as the truth of subjectivity, the more subjects see themselves as bold adventurers blazing new trails through a dangerous world. In reality, they are, as Marx said, traveling well-trodden paths, being little more than physical embodiments of economic roles.[14] Capitalists and workers alike thus have their lives drained of the significance attributed to them in fantasy.

I understand the birth of the culture industry, as it is imagined in the work of Adorno and Horkheimer, to be a response to this particular impasse: what the culture industry offers to subjects increasingly incapable of sustaining a fantasy opposed to their reality are new ways of satisfying the demand for the perils of Odysseus. The culture industry thus

makes accessible risk, danger, individual triumph, cunning, a dangerous
"outside," etc. Its capacity to convince individuals of the existence of the
last of these Odyssean elements—that everything is *not* simply "repeatable, replaceable processes," that there exists real *difference* in the world,
that there is still a dangerous and exotic "outside" to be conquered—is,
for Adorno and Horkheimer, perhaps the most important function of
the culture industry. The problem here, to be clear, is not that that difference does not actually exist but that it is *created by* the culture industry, that differences are introduced in domesticated form: "Something is
provided for everyone so no one can escape; differences are hammered
home and propagated. The hierarchy of serial qualities purveyed to the
public serves only to quantify it more completely. Everyone is supposed
to behave spontaneously according to a 'level' determined by indices and
to select the category of mass product manufactured for their type."[15]
Unassimilable difference is thus foreclosed: yes, variety and distinction are produced, so as to convince ailing subjects that they are *still*
adventurers in a heterogeneous world, but only within the industry's
own "classification, organization, and identification of consumers."[16] In
short, difference within sameness, rather than *real* difference,[17] and with
material consequences: "The more all-embracing the culture industry
has become, the more pitilessly it has forced the outsider into either
bankruptcy or a syndicate."[18]

Framed thus, I find it difficult to accept claims about the supposed
outdatedness of the culture industry thesis. As Shane Gunster has persuasively argued, Adorno and Horkheimer's once horrifying hybrid "culture industry" was formulated in response to the commodification of
culture *in general* and not to the specific organizational structures and
techniques of Fordist production.[19] Most certainly the thesis needs *updating*: since their times, organized capitalism has given way to neoliberal
capitalism, unionized labor to "flexible" labor, mass production to small-
batch production, a culture industry producing mass media to one that
actively cultivates niche markets, all meaning that the conditions that
produced the transformation they theorized have changed. That being
said, it is incorrect to conclude that their theory has been thereby made
irrelevant, given that two things have remained steadfastly constant
amidst the profound economic, political, and technological transformations since the "Fordist-Keynesian" era: a) the predication of economic
growth on the exploitation of living labor and b) the "overcoming of
spirit by commodity fetishism" definitive of the growth of the culture

industry.[20] Statements about the supposed outmodedness of the concepts of "late capitalism"[21] and the "culture industry" will continue to be premature so long as commodity consumers are categorized and catered to by mass media institutions.[22]

In brief, what distinguishes Adorno and Horkheimer's present from other eras of Enlightenment is its cultivation of a domesticated "outside"— a "regression organized by total enlightenment"—as inoculation against the threat of a real outside.[23] Enlightenment thus comes to recognize that it must reintroduce, in innocuous form, that which it means to eliminate if it is not to exhaust itself.[24] It cannot do with routine alone; risk, the founding gesture of subjectivity, must be taken, albeit in a way that the status quo is not endangered. If capitalism harbors dreams it cannot fulfill, a great outdoors made inaccessible within its bounds, then late capitalism is born from the realization that it is more efficacious to the maintenance of capitalism partially to satisfy those dreams, to provide access to a domesticated "outside," than it is to attempt to stamp them out completely.

These partial satisfactions are not, however, "distractions" or "ersatz satisfactions" that merely cover up the continuation of business as usual. The satisfactions made possible by the Odyssean fantasies engineered in the twentieth century are so real, in fact, that they have *fundamentally altered the psyche*. Like the owl of Minerva, Freud theorized the psychic dynamics of the bourgeois subject at a time when it was already beginning to disintegrate. Under the spell of the culture industry, the tensions that held together the bourgeois psyche begin to unravel and a new form of maintaining psychic stability is established. For this reason, late capitalism is defined not only by a reorganization of production, radically heightened capacities of distribution, and a new ideology of consumption but also by a sea change in what Judith Butler calls "the psychic life of power."[25]

The End of Internalization Revisited

In this section I want to examine the interpretation of this psychic transformation proposed by Jessica Benjamin. In a pair of influential articles published in the late seventies, Benjamin attributes to Adorno, Horkheimer, and Marcuse what she calls the "end of internalization" thesis. It goes something like this: in Freud's times the bourgeois individual's psyche was primarily formed through struggles within the family.

When the child finally concedes oedipal defeat, the "moral-paternal law" is internalized in the form of the superego. This ego double then acts throughout the subject's life as an executor of repression, but also as the seat of self-reflection: only by internalizing an external perspective does the subject gain the capacity for real psychic conflict and thus for critical self-evaluation.

With the "rational" dissolution of family authority and the "objective administration" of the individual within a variety of educational and marketing apparatuses, this process of internalization is curbed.[26] Failing to reach the proper oedipal pitch, the child no longer internalizes the father's authority; while thus happily free from the repressive mechanisms of the superego, the subject also now lacks the capacity for self-reflective reason. It thus becomes difficult to say that children become individuals at all,[27] lacking as they are in any mediating authority between themselves and the long tentacles of the culture industry, which has made it possible to avoid oedipal defeat but only by submitting to a more direct domination: "As a result, the possibility for the formation of a revolutionary subject is foreclosed. In the face of this situation the critical theorists look backward to the form of instinctual control which was the basis for ego development and reason in the past—individual internalization—and argued that only it contained a potential for the formation of a critique of domination. This is the impasse which I refer to as the 'end of internalization.'"[28]

In Benjamin's low opinion, the narrative presented here is, in fact, a regressive one, representing a "nostalgic romanticization of paternal authority": if the problem is a failure to reach the proper oedipal conflict that ushers in internalization, then what we need again, to put it bluntly, are strong fathers.[29] By linking "the identification with the *father*, internalization, and the independent conscience," Adorno and Horkheimer imply "that the child has no spontaneous desire to individuate, to become independent, nor the mother to encourage independence—therefore the father's intervention is required to save civilization from regression."[30] She opts for an alternate psychoanalytic framework (the intersubjective) that obviates the need for such a drastic conclusion in according more weight to the child's need to individuate and the mother's role in encouraging independence.[31]

Benjamin also accuses Adorno and Horkheimer of failing to distinguish between preoedipal and oedipal processes of self-formation. As a result of this failure, they "use the concept of internalization confusingly to signify two different but related phenomena, the development of the ego and the super-ego. The identification with parental *authority* as super-ego is collapsed into the identification with parental *competence* or the reality of childhood *autonomy* as ego formation," when "in fact, the claims of the ego and super-ego are more likely to be opposed to one another."[32] One is left to wonder, then, within the bounds of their own work, if it is truly a "decline of paternal *imagoes*" leading to a weakened superego that is the problem or whether some more basic failure of mutuality is at work in the transformation they theorize.

I should first point out the essentially reifying thrust of this critique, which draws attention away from the object of their theory—namely, the impact of the transformations of late capitalism on the psyche—by fault-ing the theory itself. The effect is to make it seem as if there was never any problem there to begin with, only bad psychoanalytic theorists bend-ing the Freudian framework in order to reaffirm and thereby propagate its untruths. Countering the entire psychoanalytic dimension of critical theory with intersubjective theory covers over the problem of the historical situation of the psyche that Adorno and Horkheimer attempt to formu-late. Critical theory thereby reverts to traditional theory. That being said, Benjamin's critique also lays the basis for a different conclusion than she herself makes. Her objections could be taken as strategic moves in the struggle to win favor for the intersubjective framework over the Freudian, but they could also be employed as cues in refashioning a coherent and nonpatrocentric theory of a crisis of internalization.

The first thing to notice in this effort is that her two objections—first, that their theory is patrocentric and, second, that it confuses ego and superego—while warranted and convincing on their own, sit *together* rather uneasily. On one level, the accusation of patrocentrism only holds if it is the superego, the heir of the oedipal struggle, that is weakened in late capitalism, but, as she herself points out, Adorno and Horkheimer are far from clear that it alone is the victim of this psychic transforma-tion. On another level, however, the patrocentrism claim must cede the truth of the idea that our internalized authorities are solely sublimates of the *father*, again a bias that Benjamin calls out. I believe she would be in sympathy with Loewald's view, the one adopted here, that the superego is not a father sublimate but rather that which allows successful navigation of the conflict between tendencies traditionally associated with mother (union) and father (differentiation). The particulars of her critique thus add up to cause not for rejection but for a reconception of the psychoana-lytic basis of their narrative.

Before getting to the "internalization" part of the "end of internalization" thesis, however, I would like to spend a bit of time investigating the supposed "end" it proclaims. As Gillian Rose has persuasively argued, Adorno's claim that society and consciousness have become "completely reified," taken literally, would imply that "no critical consciousness or theory is possible."[33] The trick, as she points out, is that this thesis is inexpressible, for, if it were true, there would be no vantage point from which to understand it as true. Adorno's statement must thus be read as intending to "induce in his reader the development of the latent capacity for non-identity thought," and thus as an "attempt to prevent the complete reification which is imminent."[34]

The end of internalization thesis must be of a similarly paradoxical nature: if it were true that the process of internalization that leads to the capacity for critical self-reflection had been decisively and definitively interrupted by the imposition of the culture industry on the family, it would not be possible to state it. The supposed "end" of internalization can thus really be only a dangerous *diminution* of internalization. Much as I am taken in by the rhetoric of finality, I think it is important to formulate the thesis in these more straightforward and admittedly more boring terms, especially as Benjamin most certainly does not understand the "end of internalization" thesis in the same way that Rose understands Adorno's claim of "complete reification."[35]

I am not, however, out simply to tidy up: for in addition to inviting the all too common charge of philosophical nihilism and generating the kind of confusion that naturally attends hyperbole,[36] declaring an "end" forecloses lines of inquiry that should be relevant to critical theory. Take, for instance, the claim that the family has been *totally* divested of authority. No doubt mass media and state institutions have penetrated the family structure in such a way as to change its dynamics, but this does not mean, to state the obvious, that parents have become helpless patsies in child-rearing. Indeed, it is of the utmost importance for critical theorists to make sense of this altered mediation, and, not coincidentally, this is precisely what Horkheimer attempts to do in "Authoritarianism and the Family Today" through his analysis of the "modern model mother" and "socially conditioned weakness of the father."[37] Benjamin sees Horkheimer there spelling out the demise of the traditional family, but he is crystal clear about the continued importance of the family to present structures of authority.[38]

Even more problematically, the assertion of a real and definitive *end* of internalization would preclude "subjectification," at least as it has traditionally been conceived. In other words, if we have truly become incapable of internalizing structures of authority, then the whole problematic of "subjectification" must be abandoned for one of "direct domination," which, according to Benjamin, is precisely the move one finds in the work of the Frankfurt school. She claims, for instance, that between "Authority and the Family" (1936) and "Authoritarianism and the Family Today" (1949), Horkheimer rejects the idea that instrumental reason is internalized in the form of "subjective reason" for the view that domination has come to work through a direct manipulation of the subject. Adorno similarly speaks of an all-out "replacement" of old forms of internalization for a seizure of the individual by "immediate social power."[39]

In both cases, once again, the accusation is unfair. Nowhere does Horkheimer renounce his earlier claim that "naked coercion" cannot by itself explain power dynamics.[40] If, in "Authoritarianism and the Family Today," he is less concerned with the nature of family mediation, it is because he is more focused there on the nostalgic return to "family values" as a compensatory public fantasy: "The more the family as an essential economic unit loses ground in Western civilization, the more society emphasizes its conventional forms."[41] Adorno, of course, was much more willing than Horkheimer to entertain the possibility of a final "replacement" of old forms of domination, but statements of this nature must, as I have just argued, be understood in the same sense as his claim of "complete reification." In any event, he is insistent in his many confrontations with the culture industry that "it is not enough to consider how mass-media institutions betoken alienation and reification; one must also consider how they preserve the subject, if only through its destruction."[42]

In the end, then, Benjamin's narrative, while laying the framework for a rigorous psychoanalytic interpretation of this transformation, can only be a parody of Adorno and Horkheimer's real position. It is a simple procedure, however, to reframe her thesis as one of diminution: while internalization has not ceased to be an important process of psychic formation, the drama of the family romance has abated with its penetration by the culture industry, resulting in a different, weakened, stunted, etc. form of psychic development. Rounding out this list of adjectives, I believe, is the best way in which to interpret the claim in *Dialectic of Enlightenment* that "in late-industrial society there is a regression to judgment without judging."[43] The capacity to judge is not completely eliminated, but it has been diminished in some way yet to be specified. So in what ways and by what means has the psyche been weakened?

Pre- and Postoedipal Mimesis

To answer this question, it is necessary first to examine a notoriously difficult term employed by Adorno and Horkheimer to a variety of ends: *mimesis*. Simon Jarvis defines mimesis as a "cognitive attempt to be like the object," to which he opposes "thought's attempt to subsume and classify the object."[44] In the first, "primitive" form of thinking, the object is respected as object; in the second, "enlightened" form, it is "violated" in being made to conform to the categories of the subject.

Civilization replaced the organic adaptation to otherness, mimetic behavior proper, firstly, in the magical phase, with the organized manipulation of mimesis, and finally, in the historical phase, with rational praxis, work. Uncontrolled mimesis is proscribed. . . . The severity with which, over the centuries, the rulers have prevented both their own successors and the subjugated masses from relapsing into mimetic behavior—from the religious ban on graven images through the social ostracizing of actors and gypsies to the education which "cures" children of childishness—is the condition of civilization. Social and individual education reinforces the objectifying behavior required by work and prevents people from submerging themselves once more in the ebb and flow of surrounding nature. All distraction, indeed, all devotion has an element of mimicry. The ego has been forged by hardening itself against such behavior.[45]

While mimesis is here what is progressively left behind with the advance of Enlightenment, elsewhere it serves as a kind of regulative ideal: in *Negative Dialectics*, for instance, Adorno asserts that the possibility of a reconciliation of subject and object lies in peeling back the layers subjectivity—by assessing the "'insufficiency' of a conceptual determination with regard to the object to be grasped . . . not as a deficit that can be overcome but as a real result"—so that the object can be freed of the subject's projections and finally experienced as object.[46] This kind of experience, the end point of Adorno's dialectic, what Gerhard Schweppenhäuser calls his "concrete conceptual utopia," is *mimetic*: no longer absorbing the object into its own categories, "Adorno's subject lets the object take the lead."[47]

For all his rage against "ontological returns," then, does Adorno also hope for the recovery of a kind of primitive mentality, for a return "to the things themselves?"[48] I believe that this is the conclusion we are forced to make unless mimesis as "organic adaptation to otherness" is distinguished from mimesis as end point of negative dialectics. To resume the conversation begun in the first three chapters, I propose that primitive, "uncontrolled" mimesis be conceived as the fantasied death drive gratification of what Loewald calls "identification." For Loewald, as I explained in chapter 2, identification precedes and makes possible the work of ego-building internalization: by "being the 'other'" in fantasy so as to cope with the "other's" occasional absence in reality, the preoedipal child directly "attempts to be like the object." Although this immature form of imitative hallucination is an attempt to erase difference, Loewald contends that it leads, by a strange twist of fate not unlike the emergence of a drive to mastery in *Beyond the Pleasure Principle*, to the creation and reinforcement of the psychic structures of the child's own internal world.

Mimesis as a mature experience of the object *qua* object would then involve, by contrast, a postoedipal, nonprojective relationship: as opposed to preoedipal mimesis, this secondary form is achieved not by a regression to the "primordial density," by lapsing back into self/other confusion (as Habermas and Honneth both contend),[49] but rather by cultivating a strong tension between ego and superego, by curbing narcissism with a strong, critical "I"-overseer. Postoedipal mimesis is thus another name for what I called postoedipal *mastery* in chapter 2: an achievement made possible by the "sublation" of the conflict between id and ego into the ego-superego tension. When this tension is acquired, the subject approaches the object "as it is"[50] not by eliminating its distinction—for "the captivating spell of the old undifferentiatedness should be obliterated"—but rather by curbing its conceptual projections onto the object through self-criticality.[51] The experience (*Erfahrung*) of which Adorno bemoaned the loss thus does not *precede* alienation but follows from its critique: "knowledge of the object is brought closer by the act of the subject rending the veil it weaves about the object."[52] Only a psyche at odds with itself, a product of "thinking against itself," can begin to approach "a state of differentiation without domination."[53] What I want to make clear in this distinction between pre- and postoedipal mimesis is that Adorno hoped to recover not "emphatic childlike experience" but rather reflective, *adult* experience.[54]

In the passage I have just quoted, Enlightenment works against the first form of mimesis—"the childishness of children"—by "hardening the ego against such behavior," and it is an overarching theme of the work of the Frankfurt school as a whole that it works against the second by replacing self-reflective reason, "Reason" in the broad sense as it is understood in Horkheimer's *Eclipse of Reason*, with instrumental reason.[55] Even a hardened instrumentalism, however, is a kind of mimesis, a mimesis "of death. The subjective mind which disintegrates the spiritualization of nature masters spiritless nature only by imitating its rigidity."[56] In other words, the subject mimics the deadening imposed on the world by its own struggle for survival. Since, however, it is imitating its own projection, this "mimesis of death" is an antimimetic mimesis, an expression of mimesis that generates narcissism, insulating the subject further and further from any real encounter with the object.

Although Adorno spoke throughout his work of "ego-weakness," he would have done better with a slightly different term for the product of this mimesis of death: passages where he describes a "hardening within the individual" or a "spiritual death by freezing" are very similar in concern and tone to those where Loewald laments a "brittle rigidity" within the ego, a function, for Loewald, of an impoverished secondary process (or, for Lacan, of an uncurbed aggressivity).[57] I thus much prefer Loewald's concept of *ego rigidity* over ego weakness to describe the "coldness" that is the "fundamental principle of bourgeois subjectivity."[58] The problem, in this reformulation, is not how to strengthen the ego, which has today actually become *too* strong, but how to remedy the "loss of inner tension" between ego and superego in order to interrupt the "practice of reifying every feature of an aborted, unformed self, withdrawing it from the process of experience and asserting it as the ultimate That's-the-way-I-am."[59]

Is a mimesis of death, however, the only kind of mimesis allowed by Enlightenment? As I have claimed earlier, late capitalism can be distinguished by its cultivation of a domesticated "outside" as inoculation against the threat of a real outside. Enlightenment comes to realize, in other words, that ego rigidity is not only an utterly miserable condition but also an inherently unstable state, as the mimetic forces that drive toward an erasure of self/other distinction dictate that the psyche is not an inherently defensive and insulated one; thus the necessity of finding some form of gratification for them. The culture industry clearly provides some kind of relief from ego rigidity: as Adorno argues, "mimesis explains the enigmatically empty ecstasy of the fans in mass culture."[60]

But again, relief of what kind? Is it a postoedipal form of limited critical-ity, a superego manufactured to "judge without judging," or is it rather a preoedipal erasure of self/other distinction, a direct administration of the "bliss and pain of consuming oneself in the intensity of being lived by the id?"[61] In other words, does the culture industry soften the ego hard-ened by Enlightenment through the id or the superego? In what man-ner, finally, does it tame the modern subject through its deployment of a domesticated mimesis?

Losing Oneself; or, "A Pure Culture [Industry] of the Death Drive"

"Who can say," wonders Bernard Stiegler, "they have never felt the modest desire, in a dark and listless mood on one of those wistful Sunday afternoons of autumn, to take in a good movie?"[62] Why do we so readily turn to the moving image, that specific technology that coemerged with and defines the culture industry? In most of the essays collected in *The Culture Industry*, Adorno focuses not on the appeal of the products of the culture industry but on their effects: conformity, conventionalism, sameness, normality, immediacy, nonspontaneity, etc. The exception to this rule is "Freudian Theory and the Pattern of Fascist Propaganda," which does the most to articulate how precisely fascist propaganda—equated, for better or worse, with the media of the culture industry—elicits the drives.[63]

Like Lacan, Adorno argues that the image is a powerful vehicle for identification, especially, we might add, when coordinated in motion with sound to create an unprecedented capacity to establish reality. In identifying with the "leader image," in recreating "'the *earliest* expres-sion of an emotional tie with another person,'" the follower gratifies, we are told, "the twofold wish to submit to authority and to be the author-ity himself."[64] With Loewald, we might expand this claim as follows: by identifying with that which it would like to be, the subject is gratifying (or attempting to gratify) the primal wish to *be* the "other," to fabricate a presence in the other's absence, and thereby to be in a longed-for environ-ment in fantasy. The identification with doctors or criminals on television dramas, for instance, allows viewers to have exciting occupations and to be immersed in environments of supposed life-and-death significance. The identification with action heroes and leads of romantic comedies allows moviegoers to occupy roles of stereotyped masculinity and femininity and participate in fantasied gendered worlds. The fascist leader is only a specific case of this general principle: the identification with the "leader image" allows followers to be powerful in a way they are not and also to feel a security that they do not have.[65]

In brief, then, the moving sound image allows coordinated identification, a kind of "pseudo-revolutionary blurring" in which the subject is "carried along in the current," that plays on the *preoedipal mimetic desire to recreate a confusion of subject and object.*[66] As Stiegler convincingly argues, the specific medium of film and television lends itself to making these identifications: any director with a "minimum amount of know-how in the exploitation of video-cinematographic techniques will be able to [make us] adhere to the time of this flowing away [where] we forget ourselves in it."[67] In other words, the capacity made possible by the moving sound image is to give ourselves over to the time of the other, to "lose ourselves" in the narrative for a few "restorative hours": "During the 90 or 52 minutes of this pastime, the time of our consciousness will have entirely passed over into the time of these moving images, linked to one another by noise, sounds, words and voices. 90 or 52 minutes of our life will have passed outside of our real life."[68]

One might say then that the distinguishing appeal of what were for Adorno and Horkheimer the quintessential products of the culture industry—film and television—is the provision of a forum for "giving myself up to the time of the other" and thereby "losing myself" through identificatory fantasy.[69] One does not, of course, actually *escape* anything in temporarily "losing oneself": given the "growing concordance" between the fantasy produced by the culture industry and the reality of everyday life, consumers are not escaping anything but the wish to escape in the first place.[70] "The dreams have no dream," as Adorno says.[71] At the same time, this concordance should not be understood as definitive: indeed, a large part of the reason people so readily imbibe the products of mass culture is their utter boredom and exhaustion in work. The culture industry can only do so much to make over reality. The language of escape is thus perfectly apposite here: in the act of "losing oneself" there is at work a real yearning for "escape from the boredom of mechanized labor," even if what is settled on is only a form of temporary relief that undermines the possibility of actual escape.[72]

While Adorno and Horkheimer could have followed me up to this point, they might have been troubled by the idea that the form of immediate gratification found in this "losing oneself" is truly gratification, though for two related reasons that must be held apart, as they lead to very different consequences. The first is that what is experienced by the subject as *immediate* is anything but: the rhythmic head nodding to a pop song veils the homogenizing process that produced it. In this updated commodity fetishism thesis, the subject's *experience* of gratification is not denied, only that this experience lacks mediating preconditions. But Adorno, in particular, goes much further than this: not only are our experiences mediated, but they are in fact not at all what we think they are. The concertgoer is not, in his view, gaining any independent pleasure from the music or the atmosphere but is rather only "worshipping the money that he himself has paid for the ticket."[73] This is because, as Gunster bluntly puts it, exchange-value has wholly replaced use-value; or, in Adorno's words, "the more inexorably the principle of exchange-value destroys use-values for human beings, the more deeply does exchange-value disguise itself as the object of enjoyment."[74]

We could admit a complete engulfment of use-value by exchange-value, however, without having then to assert, with Gunster, that mass culture "fails to 'deliver the goods,' [i.e., that] hallucinatory pleasures are false agents for gratification" and thus that the "blockbuster film" and the "latest hit CD" "rarely, if ever, do satisfy."[75] The psychoanalytic frame that Adorno employs bristles at the notion of false gratification as it has been conceived here by Gunster (admittedly, as it is often conceived by Adorno himself): is not hallucinated satisfaction still satisfaction? From a psychoanalytic point of view, a form of satisfaction that masks its own mediation, and even that diminishes the possibility of attaining a deeper and more lasting gratification, is *still* satisfaction; to deny that the culture industry "delivers the goods" is both to possess an overly narrow conception of what "the goods" are but also to depose one's opponent in fantasy instead of reality.

It is for this reason that I find it misleading, though not wrong per se, to say that the culture industry provides "ersatz satisfaction" or caters to "false needs." When invoking these phrases, the Frankfurt school thinkers generally emphasize the transience of the gratification and the use of that gratification in ameliorating alienated labor.[76] In other words, the opportunity to "lose oneself" is ultimately only temporary relief from ego rigidity, an anxiety-filled lapse back into the "bliss and pain of being lived by the id" in a world otherwise defined by "spiritual death by freezing"; in the end "the rigidity is not dissolved but hardened even more."[77] This claim that the satisfaction here is impermanent and subjectifying is quite different, however, from the claim that it is *false*, that "goods" are not being delivered. Indeed, the latter claim imperils the grounds for critique laid by the former: to reject the idea that the culture industry provides real satisfaction is to make subjection in late capitalism not condemnable but unintelligible.[78]

Since my proposal involves an atypical understanding of the death drive—in my view, neither an aggressive nor a pathological drive—as well as one of the culture industry—an industry whose efficacy lies in the fulfillment of real psychic needs, I want to be clear about my basic claim in this section, which is twofold: first, that it is the defining task of the culture industry to satisfy our primary drive *not to be ourselves* and, second, that the historically specific individuals "hardened" by economic rationalism and dissatisfying work are especially desirous of its gratifications, and willing to accept them even while admitting to themselves that they are being manipulated, because they are desperate for relief from the stifling rigidity of their own egos.[79] Thus, if "the culture industry is taken more seriously than it might itself wish to be," it is because it fulfills a need that is manipulated under modern social conditions[80]— or, again, because it "answers the psycho-dynamic question of how the subject is able to persevere in the face of a rationality which has itself become irrational."[81]

I have so far discussed only the kind of drive gratification made possible by the moving sound image—the "vanguard" of the culture industry, according to Adorno.[82] It would not be untoward, however, to see this phenomenon of "losing oneself" in all of the various leisure vehicles for Odyssean fantasies,[83] which span the gamut from the "medicinal bath" of "fun" and the "light art" of entertainment to "the bliss induced by narcotics": traveling to exotic lands to lose oneself in native culture, attending rock concerts and going to clubs to lose oneself in the music, drinking and smoking of various kinds to lose oneself in the stupor, sports to lose oneself in the game, or "extreme sports" to lose oneself in the rush.[84] I would even suggest that activities unimagined in Adorno and Horkheimer's time can be made sense of in this way: Internet browsing to lose oneself in a free associationesque "flow" or Internet browsing while also watching television so as to maintain peak levels of self-absence. One might object that the culture industry is only a loose configuration of media apparatuses and that it is a mistake to attribute to it a unified function. One of my aims, however, in recounting the Odyseus section of *Dialectic of Enlightenment* was to demonstrate that, for Adorno and Horkheimer, the culture industry is more than just a new character in the unfolding drama of Enlightenment, that it is instead a particular kind of dialectical *solution* that allows the overcoming of an impasse to its progress. It is thus defined in their work not by the various evolving forms that comprise it but more essentially by the function that it serves.

Living Straight Ahead; or, The Being of "Being-Thus-and-Not-Otherwise"

I have yet, however, to relate how this function of providing outlets for "losing oneself" connects to that upon which the Frankfurt school so obsessed: namely, normalization, conformity, and standardization. Earlier I questioned the precision of Adorno's term "ego-weakness," which was already in circulation before his appropriation of it. In a short paper from 1938, for instance, Otto Fenichel defines a "weak ego" as one too defensive and anxious to tolerate tension and thus, for this reason, incapable of analysis.[85] If this is what is meant by the term, I much prefer "ego rigidity," both descriptively and aesthetically, for its implicit affirmation of openness and receptivity over "strength."[86] But Adorno had an altogether different phenomenon in mind: a weak ego, for him, was one that had given in to the "ever-present temptation of regressing to a state where the basic desires for libidinal gratification—which are never eliminated, only disciplined—once again take control," thus stunting the ego and its capacity for judgment and reality testing.[87] On first glance, something is amiss: if egos have truly been made weak in this way, then subjects in late capitalism would not be the brutally efficient executors of instrumental reason that they are.[88]

Indeed, the problem is not that subjects have become divorced from reality or incapable of judging, deciding, and calculating,[89] but that reality has become static, rigidly "one way," and that the subject's judgments and decisions are themselves not judged and assessed, only applied. It is thus not that society "generates illusions and distortions, presenting a façade that is actively misleading," but rather that it generates a remarkably stubborn adherence to the status quo.[90] In "Notizen zur neuen Anthropologie," Adorno characterizes the "new anthropological type"[91] that emerges in late capitalism as "Vor-Sich-Hinleben," or "living straight ahead."[92] The expression is related to *vor sich hinschauen*, or "looking straight ahead" without looking about to orient oneself to one's surroundings. This quality of living straight ahead, Adorno tells us, is ingrained from an early age in children, who are instructed "ceaselessly to follow goals, stubbornly live for them, their eyes consumed by the gain one is always trying to snatch up, without looking left or right."[93] By being trained to aim straight ahead without looking around, the subject is reduced to the task of applying pregiven codes of judgment.

One could certainly frame this as a problem of "ego weakness," but the fit is not exact: it is not that the ego does not judge for itself— it does, and quite efficiently—but rather that it bears no capacity for self-reflectively assessing its own judgments. For this reason, it makes much more sense to describe this loss as *superego* weakness (keeping in mind again that the superego is not understood here as a father subli- mate):[94] the superego fails to provide the ego with the tension of a real adversary, becoming much more like a motivational coach who only castigates the ego for failing to live up to preestablished norms.[95] The superego thus sees its function *streamlined*: there is self-reflection, a judgment of the ego by the superego that produces a certain tension, but the superego possesses no real force of its own, no capacity for "unco-ordinated judgement."[96] In place of a difficult dialogue between two stubborn agencies, there are preestablished standards of judgment; their only communication concerns the failure or success of the ego in meeting those standards (standards that, as all analysts know, are typi- cally enforced quite harshly).

Jonathan Lear gets at the difference in superego types that I am try- ing to formulate in his distinction between two kinds of reflection, one "pretense-enforcing" and the other "pretense-transcending."[97] The first, which he associates with the typical functioning of the superego, keeps "us on the straight and narrow when it comes to the demands of morality and civilization."[98] The second, which he calls "ironic" reflection, is not about failing to live up to ideals but about questioning "whether there is any longer an ideal to live up to or fail to live up to."[99] The first is a sign that civilization "has its hooks" in us; the second that "civilization has itself become unhooked."[100] I would like to suggest that this first reflec- tive capacity corresponds roughly to that of the diminished superego that guides the subject "straight ahead" and the second to the critical reflection of a strong superego.[101] Like the superego that "judges without judging," pretense-enforcing reflection keeps one "firmly ensconced" in the status quo.[102] Pretense-transcending reflection, by contrast, "disrupt[s] our lives in somewhat unpleasant and unfamiliar ways"; it is, as both Kierkegaard and Adorno assert, a form of "infinite negativity."[103]

As has been well documented, the culture industry is relentless in producing and reinforcing standards of beauty, intelligence, masculinity, femininity, the typical features of what Lear calls the "pretense" of the ego. That we are constantly bombarded by these standards is, perhaps, one explanation for their acceptance; their insistence alone is quite overwhelming. My suspicion, however, is that we are *primed* to accept them in a more complicated way having to do with the energetic balance of the psyche. As I claimed in chapter 2, the superego—the agency that enforces ideals and norms, from which the ego views and judges itself—inherits from the death drive a dedifferentiating force and gives it stable expression. The superego, in short, gains its strength from death drive sublimation.

My proposal here is that what occurs in the confusion of subject and object characteristic of the identifications the culture industry makes possible is a *direct death drive gratification* that siphons the energy once sublimated into the superego by lowering the temperature of oedipal conflict. It is thus not simply that the culture industry's administered form of relief is fleeting but also that it saps of its strength the authority responsible for critical self-reflection.[104] Like capital working on both the demand and the supply of labor,[105] the culture industry gains its efficacy from working on both sides of the ego, *providing id satisfaction as a way of diminishing the superego's capacities*.[106] To Jessica Benjamin's argument that Adorno and Horkheimer confused two levels of psychic functioning, we can thus reply that their "inconsistency" on this matter reflected the fact that both the relations id-ego and ego-superego are transformed by the crisis of internalization. If their theory unintentionally works at two levels, it is because the psyche is doubly transformed.

I have thus far focused on the weakening of the superego as a problem of diminished criticality, but it is no less one of diminished *sociality*: the emergence of the superego marks the entrance of the child into the adult universe, the moment when it becomes possible to identify with others not as "others" (what I have called preoedipal mimesis) but rather as real others (postoedipal mimesis). In other words, on account of the fact that we "lose ourselves" in the machinations of the culture industry, "it is no longer possible to lose oneself *in others*;" that is, the pervasive opportunity for primary identification reduces the possibility for secondary identification.[107] Given what Loewald has said of the temporal orientation of the structural agencies, superego weakness is also a problem of diminished *temporality* and thus ought to be understood as the psychic dimension of what David Harvey calls the "time-space compression" of late capitalism.[108] With the enervation of that which represents "the past as seen from the future," the "category of the future" is slowly replaced by the "the idea of an extended, but manageable and controllable, present."[109]

In sum, to say that the culture industry simply disseminates messages of conformity is to miss its real power.[110] Both increasing feelings of disconnectedness and the "leveling" first theorized by Kierkegaard must be understood as predicated on a more primary psychic satisfaction. Critics of the culture industry have generally focused on its homogenizing and alienating effects without investigating why we willingly and, most of the time, self-consciously fall for the ruse. What I have tried to do here is follow up on Adorno's little hints about the psychic motivation for conformity.

A Superego Substitute: Adorno *Contra* Horkheimer

We thus arrive at the difficult question: out of this "construction of a configuration of reality," what kind of "demand for its [reality's] real change" follows?[111] Horkheimer, for his part, places his hope in "small groups of admirable men" who have managed to escape the fate of being stunted by the culture industry, who still have enough of their wits about them to perceive and combat the irrationalities of modern life.[112] He calls these privileged few "resistant individuals."

> The resistant individual will oppose any pragmatic attempt to reconcile the demands of truth and the irrationalities of existence. Rather than to sacrifice truth by conforming to prevailing standards, he will insist on expressing in his life as much truth as he can, both in theory and in practice. His will be a life of conflict; he must be ready to run the risk of utter loneliness. The irrational hostility that would incline him to project his inner difficulties upon the world is overcome by a passion to realize what his father represented in his childish imagination, namely, truth. This type of youth—if it is a type—takes seriously what he has been taught. He at least is successful in the process of internalization to the extent of turning against outside authority and the blind cult of so-called reality.

He does not shrink from persistently confronting reality with truth, from unveiling the antagonism between ideals and actualities. His criticism itself, theoretical and practical, is a negative reassertion of the positive faith he had as a child.[113]

Unlike "submissive" individuals, resistant individuals neither repress the world of "childish imagination," nor do they carry immaturity into adult life. They instead *sublimate* their infantile desires and cultivate the "positive faith" of childhood in the secondary process. Loewald hints at the effects of the division and fragmentation of the modern world on psychic health, but does not come all of the way around to Horkheimer's conclusion: that the culture industry forces the healthy into an isolated unhealth and thus that "resistant individuals" must relentlessly fight against and expose the untruth of prevailing standards from a place of utter loneliness.

This controversial "privileged few" justification, to which Adorno himself ascribed at times, is, to my mind, one of the worst inheritances that we have received from the Frankfurt school and an idea that ought to be happily and decisively abandoned. Although it is not, strictly speaking, incompatible with critical theory,[114] it is fairly remarkable that someone who charged *himself* with making sense of the possibility of his own theorizing should come to the conclusion that it is on account of "a stroke of undeserved luck" that he and a few others who closely resemble him are "not quite adjusted to the prevailing norms,"[115] and thus capable of making "the moral and, as it were, representative effort to say what most of those for whom they say it cannot see or, to do justice to reality, will not allow themselves to see."[116] Marx and Durkheim could have made the same move, but they instead, being good critical theorists, accounted for the possibility of their own work within the historical dynamic analyzed in that work. To his credit, Adorno, like Freud, typically supplied the resources for a critique of his own position. In what follows, I will attempt to situate critical theory within the crisis of internalization narrative that I have just outlined and in so doing offer not simply "reasons for the right of criticism" but also a description of a possibility for that criticism unique to subjects of late capitalism.[117]

Adorno emphasized throughout his work, and often against his own assertions, that it is rather delusory to think that anyone could escape the culture industry's long reach: nobody can claim to see through the haze of the present any more than a theory can claim to be free of the marketplace.[118] Whereas Horkheimer clung to the special privilege of membership in his vaunted group of "admirable men," Adorno took seriously their claim in *Dialectic of Enlightenment* that "the whole world is passed through the filter of the culture industry."[119] Just as it would be impossible, for Kant, to throw off the categories of understanding, so too is it impossible, for Adorno, to step outside the culture industry today. It has reshaped the world and consciousness both (though not "completely," as I have argued), endangering the very process that gives rise to the resistant individual's "truth." To be even more precise, if the process of internalization has been compromised in late capitalism, it is more likely that the "truth" of the resistant individual is not the product of successful sublimation but rather the omnipotent dream of the regressed narcissist.[120] When "there is no peeping out," we ought to be suspicious of those who claim to have found a peephole.[121]

Since no one escapes the desublimation of the culture industry, both the kind of psychic health envisioned by Loewald and the kind of resistance encouraged by Horkheimer can only be desperate clinging to ideals whose real basis has been eroded. This is not to say, however, that Adorno gave up on the ideal of a critical capacity able to resist the fictions of the culture industry and approach the object *qua* object in mimetic rapport, only that he precluded the possibility of attaining this goal *directly*. In a world where everything is passed through the filter of the culture industry, the kind of nondominating relationship characteristic of postoedipal mimesis most certainly cannot be practiced: "we are *not yet* able to think the priority of the object."[122] The question, then, is how we begin to reestablish the kind of psychic tension that holds at bay an aggressive narcissism and makes superfluous the real need for administered breaks from oneself.[123]

Robert Hullot-Kentor has suggested recently that the only way out of direct domination today is *through* the new anthropological type; that is, through the use of "what new powers this new type of being might have, among which [Adorno] mentions the following: a cold readiness for sacrifice, a cleverness in the struggle with meta-organizations, a speechless preparedness to do what is decisive."[124] Robbed of the capacity of making pliable its own ego, the new anthropological type is coldly instrumental to the core and thus capable, despite "system-immanent" thinking, of a particular kind of blunt resistance. Thus, "if regression is the tendency of the new type of human being, this not only makes us vulnerable to the slightest manipulation of the most primitive impulses; it can also become the ability to find the no less requisitely primitive impulse to stand up and say 'Enough!'"[125]

While Hullot-Kentor is correct to emphasize that "there is nothing to return to," if he means by this that the kind of psychic tension that held together the old anthropological type is a thing of the past, he conceives of the transition to the new anthropological type as complete, the very move I have been attempting to parry here. As Rose argues, it is because we are able to conclude that everything cannot be completely reified if we understand the thesis of complete reification that there is still hope. Or, as Adorno himself argues, it is in the gap between the people that the culture industry attempts to fashion and the people that we are that it is possible to "glimpse a chance of maturity."[126] Thus the "possibility that, by the standards of a truly emancipated humanity, [is] visible in our present situation, however faintly or negatively," lies not in the (extremely limited and questionable) capacities of the new anthropological type but rather in the incompleteness of the transformation.[127] But what distinct possibility opens up while straddling these two anthropological types?

My proposal is the following: that, while heading toward that much worse fate of direct domination, we can turn around and assess the form of authority from which we are departing and redeploy it on our own terms. In other words, the relentless critique of the "schema of mass culture" is not only a way of unveiling its source of appeal and loosening entanglement in the tight circuit of interpellation and projection that is its filter *but also a practical training in the exercise of a critical capacity that takes over from the old superego the task of limiting the ego.* A critique of the culture industry is also a making conscious of the manipulation of one's drives. Thus the confrontation of the intolerability of life without the fleeting gratifications of the culture industry is also an illumination of primary process life and a taking within one's conscious control an old way of mitigating ego rigidity: the lasting satisfaction that comes with "criticism of that unyielding, inexorable something that sets itself up in us" (i.e., the ego).[128]

Adorno's devotion to "unfruitful negativity" would be, in this view, not simply a form of resistance aimed at attaining a kind of "sober-mindedness" about the present but also a way—a way, again, that is *made possible* by late capitalism—of recultivating the kind of psychic conflict that would allow for a noncoercive mimesis; that is, of reclaiming the *experiential satisfaction* of living outside one's own conceptual projections.[129] This move frees Adorno of the charge made by Rose that negative dialectics is ultimately a "morality (*Moralität*), in the limited sense which Hegel criticized: a general prescription not located in the social relations which underlie it."[130] Negative dialectics is no "morality of method": "not to be at home in one's home" is a direct response to the diminution of internalization wrought by the culture industry and only a way of achieving mimetic rapport for a being who has been partially loosened from the old superego.[131]

One might still, however, follow Jessica Benjamin in accusing Adorno of a nostalgia for the repressed bourgeois subject,[132] and it is important to clarify that, despite their hope for the return of an interest in forming autonomous subjects, neither he nor Horkheimer had anything but criticism for the bourgeois superego.[133] Indeed, Adorno did not desire a return of repression so much as he saw the possibility of something else to fill the vacuum left by its demise: "we must have a conscience, but may not insist on our own conscience," which is nothing but "self-assertion . . . pretending to be the moral."[134] To offer a *real* "replacement of the appropriate super-ego," we must reinvent a mostly unconscious "authority" crippled by the culture industry as a conscious agent of "autonomy."[135] *Where the bourgeois superego guided by an individualistic ethics was, so shall a conscious critical capacity guided by a dialectical social theory be.*[136] The moment of possibility engendered by the culture industry is thus located not, as later cultural critics would have it, in its new modes of creativity and innovation but rather in the fact that it partially "frees" us of an old form of internalized authority,[137] leading both to the danger of "direct domination" by "immediate social power" but also to the possibility of consciously directed ego curbing.[138]

Bewältigung, Gewalt, Verwaltung

If the term *culture industry* is to be more than a reminder of the manufacturedness of culture, then we must be able to name the *function* that unites the diverse set of media and practices that comprise it, which means not simply asserting the *effects* of the culture industry—conformity, conventionalism, etc.—but rather shedding light on the kind of satisfactions provided by it and how those satisfactions work on the psyche. Addressing these latter problems—that is, a) naming the reason that we all so willingly devour the machinations of an industry that most of us understand to be manipulative and b) theorizing how the consumption of those products changes the nature of our psychic lives—is absolutely necessary if the term *culture industry* is to bear any weight. To the first question, I have answered that the culture industry provides the subject hardened by economic rationalism administered breaks from its own ego, opportunities to "lose oneself," to lapse back into indifference, if only for an afternoon at the movies. To the second, I have said that this direct death drive gratification weakens the superego, which, in this diminished state, more easily accepts codes of judgment upon which it does not itself cast judgment. It is only because we are able so regularly and easily to "lose ourselves" that we accept "living straight ahead."

This reformulation of Adorno and Horkheimer's understanding of the culture industry's effect on the psyche not only articulates a more rigorous psychoanalytic frame for the project of critical theory but also historically situates it, thereby accounting for its very possibility but also the possibility it engenders.[139] From this perspective, it is because we are "straddling" anthropological types, loosened from the bourgeois superego but not yet reduced to products of immediate social power, that it is possible to engage in a particular kind of critical self-reflection: namely, of consciously appropriating the superego function of judging the ego and thereby limiting its narcissistic "rigidity." Of the numerous pessimists scattered throughout the history of philosophy, Adorno certainly ranks among the greats; but, for all the suffocating bleakness that emanates from his work, his theory of a crisis of internalization contains within it this objective possibility of transforming an old form of psychic authority that unconsciously disciplined the ego into a critical capacity that consciously limits the ego.[140] This transformation is, as I have argued here, less a return to the superego than it is a reinvention of it. Perhaps this hoped-for reconstruction is another way of expressing Freud's wish that psychoanalysis replace religion.

In this view, critical theory is more than just theory that is able to account for its own possibility: if Adorno's critical method has an end point (postoedipal mimesis), then he must view critical practice not simply as a way of bucking ideology and coming to a sober view of the world but also as a way of recreating a kind of experiential satisfaction, one in which one's conceptual projections onto the object have been curbed and in which thereby the object is experienced "as such." I take this view to account not for the objective or ethical necessity of critical theory but for its *pleasure*, for its *appeal*, and thus, perhaps, for the rather uncritical pervasiveness of the word *critical* in academia today: as

opposed to the temporary self-forgetting propagated by the culture industry, critical reflection bears the possibility of the happiness of real self-
transcendence. Thus, when Adorno claims that "thought is happiness,
even where unhappiness prevails," he means that critical thinking allows
a *self*-overcoming—in admittedly small realizations that we have been
repressed or deluded—that is cause for the real drive gratification that
attends knowledge of the world, even though that knowledge reveals the
world to be one structured in such a way as to maintain repression and
delusion and thus one to be transcended.[141]

Since this possibility—that of creating the kind of psychic tension necessary for nonprojective relationships to others and the world and thus
for "autonomy"[142]—is one open to *individuals* engaged in critical practice, one might wonder: does this position consign Adorno to advocating
for individual redemption in a fallen world? Despite his own political
involvements,[143] I do not believe Adorno could, under the constraints of
his own theory, support "political action" in any straightforward sense.[144]
To promote movement in a people confined to their narcissism is, for
him, the best way to ensure the maintenance of domination.[145] He did,
however, hold out possibility for one particular form of collective struggle, which he called "education to maturity" (*Erziehung zur Mündigkeit*)
(reminiscent of Freud's "education to reality" [*Erziehung zur Realität*]).[146]
I agree with Iain Macdonald that "when Adorno speaks of an 'education
in maturity,' he does not have in mind merely *self*-education, but actual
reforms of the educational system that would allow critical thought, and
therefore autonomy, to be cultivated across the board in society."[147] It is
this education that would then create the kind of community necessary
for "*substantial autonomy*," an "autonomy integrated into the very fabric
of society," as opposed, one might say, to the "formal autonomy" available
to those without the requisite ethical substance.[148] If Adorno thus had a
politics, it was one that was simultaneously an education that developed
the capacities for autonomy necessary for political action—a politics that
made politics possible.

In the previous chapter, I analyzed the relation between what Freud
calls *Bewältigung*, the fundamental capacity of the psyche to "master"
stimuli and achieve a degree of equilibrium, and the outbreak of a kind
of violence (*Gewalt*) that Lacan calls aggressivity. In the theory proposed
there, *Gewalt* is not the primary force that is "brought in" by *Bewältigung*
but rather a secondary effect,[149] an unfortunate but understandable consequence of the dialectic of dependence that defines our preoedipal lives.

In Lacanian theory, aggressivity is supposed to be overcome with the resolution of imaginary conflict in symbolic identification (what Freud would call the "dissolution of the Oedipus complex"). In this chapter I identified, with Adorno and Horkheimer, a particular threat to this process of overcoming. By providing direct relief from defensive rigidity, the culture industry lowers the pitch of oedipal conflict, thus diminishing the power of the superego and allowing a more direct administration (*Verwaltung*) of the subject in late capitalism. The possibility of attaining postoedipal psychic *Bewältigung*—defined by a strong tension between ego and superego—is thereby diminished, leaving the subject grasping at the administered relief from the cold confines of its own narcissism. The very same movement, however, also engenders the possibility of consciously achieving that mastery, and it is this achievement that I have portrayed as the end of philosophy for Adorno.

It is not true that the human mind has undergone no development since the earliest times and that, in contrast to the advances of science and technology, it is the same to-day as it was at the beginning of history.
—Sigmund Freud, The Future of an Illusion

5 The Psyche in Late Capitalism II

Herbert Marcuse and the Technological Lure

In this chapter I aim to analyze technology as I did the culture industry in chapter 4: namely, to specify the nature of the psychic gratification that it provides and to articulate how that gratification changes the psyche as a whole. So much has been written about the effects of technological advance on society and the individual, and while we are less likely today to hear talk of the relation between technology and the *psyche* (as we did not that long ago in the work of Siegfried Giedion, Lewis Mumford, or Jacques Ellul),[1] the idea that technological advance is today constantly revolutionizing our practices and modes of perception is commonplace. Much more interesting to me than the question of how technology is changing the world and us, however, is that of why we have invested ourselves in the world-changing capacities of technology in the first place.[2] What about the fruit of technological advance is so irresistibly attractive, and why are technological aspirations so unthinkingly affirmed?

There is, of course, the answer that technology makes life better: perhaps it is still "questionable if all the mechanical inventions yet made have lightened the day's toil of any human being,"[3] but they *have* lengthened the human life span, connected us in new ways, and further extended the mastery of the human race. One might counter that they have also imperiled our mastery, displaced and separated us, and introduced ultimate threats to the continued existence of life on earth,[4] but the platitude that technology makes life better can never really be refuted, especially in a culture where the answer to the woes of technological advance is "More technology!" In any event, it is impossible for the modern subject to avoid all those little things that testify, not in thought but in practice, to the belief that technology makes life better.

My suspicion is simply that there is more to *why* we think technology makes life better than technology making life better, that technology gratifies a *psychic* need before it does material ones. Good arguments could be made that contemporary technological fascination is strictly a problem of social theory: for instance, that the technological advance demanded by the pursuit of relative surplus value is reified and transformed into a cultural value in late capitalism or, with Foucault, that the organizing role of life in the modern episteme dictates that its technological extension is revered as an unquestionable good. We can affirm both arguments, however, while also admitting that there may be a distinctly psychological motivation to technological aspiration as well.

My point of departure in this final investigation will be the work of Herbert Marcuse. In many ways, this book could not have come to fruition without his influence, which can be seen in every chapter.[5] That being said, I am wary, like so many today, of the overall framework of his thought, from his casual equation of material scarcity with Freud's Ananke to his conception of liberation as an anamnestic return to an "original" libidinal state. For all intents and purposes, I agree with Joel Whitebook that Marcuse's "pursuit of 'integral satisfaction' that disavows the incomplete and conflictual nature of human existence brings us into the register of omnipotence and therewith raises the specter of totalitarianism."[6] Thus, instead of looking to Marcuse's thought as a whole,[7] I will focus in this chapter on an intriguing and only partially developed cluster of insights that huddle around the topic of technology. Perhaps more than any of his colleagues, Marcuse was highly sensitive to the ways in which technological advance works not only on the world but also on the psyche. Through an examination and critique of Marcuse's varied thoughts on the matter, I hope to articulate a theory of what kind of psychic gratification is provided by ever increasing technical control, one that centers on the concept of "aggressive sublimation."

Aggressive Sublimation

Throughout his corpus Marcuse returns time and again to the idea that "organized capitalism has sublimated and turned to socially productive use" a "primary aggressiveness" by channeling it toward the employment and development of technology.[8] In "Aggressiveness in Advanced Industrial Societies" he proposes a theory of "technological aggression and satisfaction" in which "the act of aggression is physically carried out by a mechanism with a high degree of automatism, of far greater power than the individual human being who sets it in motion."[9] Human aggression, transferred from subject to object in this fashion, finds "sublimated" expression in being transformed to serve "socially useful" ends. Marcuse claims here simply to be following Freud: "Now the (more or less sublimated) transformation of destructive into socially useful aggressive (and thereby constructive) energy is, according to Freud (on whose instinct-theory I base my interpretation) a normal and indispensable process."[10]

Freud himself has the following to say on the matter: "The instinct of destruction, moderated and tamed, and, as it were, inhibited in its aim, must, when it is directed towards objects, provide the ego with the satisfaction of its vital needs and with control over nature."[11] Although he does not go so far as to say here that the "instinct of destruction" can be *sublimated*, Freud would tentatively endorse the possibility of the "sublimation of the aggressive or destructive instinct" in a letter to Marie Bonaparte in 1937 (to my knowledge, the idea is never invoked in his published work).[12] Though the channeling of aggressive impulses toward technological mastery seems intuitively to fit the bill, I want to get clear in what follows about the conditions under which aggressive energy might find sublimated expression and how precisely technological mastery qualifies as an instance thereof.

First, with regard to the idea of sublimation itself: in "On Narcissism" sublimation is defined as a "process that concerns object-libido and consists in the instinct's directing itself towards an aim other than, and remote from, that of sexual satisfaction."[13] Freud would later add that "sublimation of instinct is an especially conspicuous feature of cultural development; it is what makes it possible for higher psychical activities, scientific, artistic or ideological, to play such an important part in civilized life."[14] Combining these two claims, we can say that sexual energy is "sublimated" when it takes a *socially beneficial* and *nonsexual* aim. For reasons that will soon become apparent, I want to stress the importance of this latter criterion: since direct sexual gratification can also be "socially productive,"[15] the libido should only be considered truly *sublimated* when it has taken a nonsexual aim in addition to a socially useful one. With this in mind, if we want to take seriously Freud's suggestion to Marie Bonaparte, it would have to be possible for an aggressive drive to find a socially useful outlet that *itself involves no necessary aggression*.

Many of Freud's immediate heirs, greatly expanding the concept of sublimation to include "every successful defence effort not producing symptoms or necessitating counter-cathetic energy expense," saw no impediments to this possibility.[16] Ernest Jones, for one, speculated that "a child . . . who has conquered a sadistic love of cruelty may, when he grows up, be a successful butcher or a distinguished surgeon, according to his capacities and opportunities."[17] The model is simpleminded, but the idea acceptable enough: when channeled in the proper manner, aggression could indeed take a new, socially useful form. Later generations of psychoanalysts nonetheless developed a marked resistance to speaking of sublimation proper when it came to the aggressive drives. F. J. Hacker succinctly summarizes this opinion: while the aggressive drives "can be expressed in very different ways and forms, directly and symbolically, internally and externally, destructively and productively," they unfortunately "cannot be sublimated."[18] Why? Because even in the cases where it is put to productive use (butcher, surgeon), where it is directed internally (masochism, asceticism) or where it is symbolic (derision, humiliation), *it retains an aggressive aim* (hacking at a dead animal, cutting open a human being, self-torture, "symbolic violence," etc.).

Surprisingly, and despite his frequent invocation of the idea of aggressive sublimation, Marcuse is at one with the predominant Anglophone psychoanalytic opinion of his time in rejecting the idea that aggressiveness truly finds its aim *changed* in supposedly "sublimated" forms of expression.[19] In *Eros and Civilization*, for instance, he proposes the notion of "destructive sublimation" only immediately to recoil from it: "The development of technics and technological rationality absorbs to a great extent the 'modified' destructive instincts. . . . Is the destructiveness sublimated in these activities sufficiently subdued and diverted to assure the work of Eros? . . . To be sure, the diversion of destructiveness from the ego to the external world secured the growth of civilization. However, extroverted destruction remains destruction."[20] Marcuse thus finds no psychic transformation, only new avenues for different expressions of one and the same drive. In "Aggressiveness in Advanced Industrial Societies" he takes this argument a step further: not only does destruction remain destruction, but the attempt to sublimate it technologically results, in fact, in a "supersublimation," a sublimation that does not actually gratify the original impulse, and thus one that leads to "repetition and escalation: increasing violence, speed, enlarged scope, etc."[21] Technology only pushes aggressive energy around, finding new ways to redirect, diffuse, and, in the process, inflame it.

Marcuse was thus far from endorsing the "normal and indispensable process" of aggressive sublimation that he touted, even further from it than the person to whom he credits its initial formulation. Indeed, he lays down a formidable challenge to its possibility: Is not socially useful aggression—as found, for instance, in the mastery of nature—*still aggression?* In artistic creation, the paradigmatic case of libidinal sublimation, sexuality takes a decidedly nonsexual aim. In the productive consumption of nature, by contrast, aren't we *still* destroying, albeit in an inhibited and controlled fashion?[22]

On behalf of an idea that Freud himself only tentatively proposed, I want to take up Lacan's distinction between aggressivity and the aggression it conditions in order to attempt to formulate what a "non-aggressive aggression" might look like. In chapter 3 I defined aggressivity as a *drive to subjective omnipotence*, a drive to the reduction of self/other tension to zero through a silencing engulfment of the other and the establishment of the "I" as self-sufficient. In childhood this drive most certainly manifests in physical acts of domination and aggression, but it is nonetheless theoretically separable from those acts. Might technological mastery involve the satisfaction not only of aggression but rather, and at a more basic level, of *aggressivity?*

Freud himself, in a memorable passage from *Civilization and Its Discontents*, appears to answer in the affirmative: "Man has, as it were, become a kind of prosthetic God. When he puts on all his auxiliary organs he is truly magnificent."[23] The aim of donning our "auxiliary organs," he tells us, is to be as "magnificent" as our father and thus to occupy his place. It is not exactly *aggression* that he is talking about, but one could certainly say that the kind of power described here is a manifestation of a drive toward omnipotent control, a drive to be like the *other*, that I have argued is definitive of *aggressivity*.[24] For Freud, then, while the use and development of technology often provides a *means* of directly satisfying aggression, *it is itself a form of sublimated aggressivity*, inasmuch as it provides gratification of urges for controlling dominance at a socially useful level, and, in theory, regardless of whether or not the kind of activity enabled serves as a channel for aggression.

No doubt Marcuse had good reason to think technology satisfied aggression in a *direct* rather than a sublimated manner: for him, as for most thinkers of his generation, technology signified, above all, *the bomb*. The variety of networked personal computing devices that is the natural referent of the word today was still a distant possibility. But with the practices enabled by the various technological innovations of the last fifty or so years in mind—walking down the street and making plans on one's cell phone, scrolling through songs on one's iPod, hurtling down the highway at eighty miles per hour, accessing information from around the world on the Internet, etc.—it seems reasonable to say that technology does allow for an increased potency that transcends the simple aim of mastery and that does not lead *necessarily* to the negative consequences about which Marcuse is concerned.[25] This thesis is, admittedly, a difficult one to maintain: if one wants to find violence in something, one will find it. It nonetheless seems like a stretch to say that the abovementioned activities are "violent" in the same way that butchering an animal, torturing oneself, humiliating others, or dropping the bomb are violent. If we are willing to admit this, then it is possible to affirm the proposal that the "magnificence" of donning auxiliary organs offers a socially productive gratification of *aggressivity* acquired without necessary aggression or violence, thereby salvaging the notion of aggressive sublimation.[26]

Technics and Technology

Marcuse addresses the problem of technology throughout his work, but his most sustained effort appears in *One-Dimensional Man*, where he contends that advanced capitalist society is governed by a "technological rationality" wherein "rationality assumes the form of methodical construction; organization and handling of matter as the mere stuff of control, as instrumentality which lends itself to all purposes and ends—instrumentality *per se*, 'in itself.'"[27] This purportedly "value-free" rationality is in fact a historically specific "*capitalist* rationality" and is thus employed toward the creation of "ever more efficient instruments of social control" (for example, the dehumanizing mechanization of the labor process) as well as the intensification of the typical hazards of capitalist production ("waste, planned obsolescence, superfluous luxury items and poisonous chemicals which pollute the environment and destroy human beings").[28] What is truly horrifying about technological rationality, however, is its erosion of the promise of liberal modernity: namely, authentic, creative individuality. In a social situation that demands that its subjects become efficient users of a rationality detached from human needs, "it is no longer possible for something like an individual psyche with its own demands and decisions to develop."[29]

At the same time, however, technological rationality develops the productive forces and our technical capacities in such a way as to make liberation possible, even while its progress continues to increase domination.[30] It is for this reason that Marcuse finds it important strictly to separate technics and technology:

> Technology is taken as a social process in which technics proper (that is, the technical apparatus of industry, transportation, communication) is but a partial factor. . . . Technology as a mode of production, as the totality of instruments, devices, and contrivances which characterize the machine age is thus at the same time a mode of organizing and perpetuating (or changing) social relationships, a manifestation of prevalent thought and behavior patterns, an instrument for control and domination. Technics by itself can promote authoritarianism as well as liberty, scarcity as well as abundance, the extension as well as the abolition of toil.[31]

Our technical mastery over the world *needn't* involve a technological domination of it, and in fact "contains a tremendous potential which, if released, could create a free society:"[32]

> Technical progress is life protecting and life enlarging to the degree to which the destructive energy here at work is "contained" and guided by libidinal energy. This ascendancy of Eros in technical progress would become manifest in the progressive alleviation and pacification of the struggle for existence, in the growth of refined erotic needs and satisfaction. In other words, technical progress would be accompanied by a lasting *desublimation* that, far from reverting mankind to anarchic and primitive stages, would bring about a less repressive and yet higher stage of civilization.[33]

Guided by Eros, technical progress can alleviate the human being's struggle for existence, the very thing that forces a sublimation of antisocial drives in the first place. As this struggle wanes, so does the need for sublimation, leading to the possibility of a nonrepressive desublimation in which we become attuned again to human needs. A "romantic regression behind technology" would reintroduce Ananke;[34] only a society with a developed means of production could allow libidinal energy to return to the psyche in a "lasting desublimation," as opposed to the "repressive desublimation" in which the alienated subject "blows off steam" before returning to the fold.[35]

Marcuse is not claiming here, importantly, that the technical capacities and objects developed in capitalism are simply "neutral" and can be repurposed to different ends. Indeed, what is historically "new" for Marcuse about "technological rationality" is that "domination perpetuates and extends itself not only through technology, but *as* technology."[36] The automobile, for instance, necessitates a system of infrastructure that prioritizes *private* transportation; implied in the technology *itself* is an ideology.[37] This is not to say that it is *just* ideology: the combustion engine *works*, it makes possible a form of travel hitherto unknown.[38] As Andrew Feenberg summarizes, in technology "neutrality and bias can and do in fact coexist;" thus, in freeing ourselves from the pursuit of surplus value, inherited "technology would not be thrown out, nor would it simply be put to new uses in a different social context, but rather it would be employed to produce new technological means, fully adapted to the requirements of a socialist society."[39]

Technology might thus not itself be entirely neutral, but there is a technical aspect of it that need not be employed in the service of domination and, properly repurposed, that could serve as the foundation of a free society. Passé as Marcuse has become since his heyday as champion of the New Left, this vision for technology remains remarkably contemporary, a fact well illustrated in the works of prominent philosophers of technology like Feenberg and Bernard Stiegler. Feenberg, for one, contends that "dystopian critiques" of technology like those of Heidegger and Ellul focus exclusively on the negative and destructive side of technical "de-worlding" to the neglect of the tactical "struggles and innovations of users engaged in appropriating" technology toward unleashing its "democratic potential."[40] Stiegler similarly holds onto the possibility of technology creating "new associative environments" even while leading to dissociation and stupidity.[41] As much as these thinkers admit the existence of domination not through technology but *as* technology, they nonetheless reserve for the simple pursuit of technical mastery a necessary neutrality, i.e., an under-determination that can be appropriated in the service of both domination and liberation, deworlding and reworlding, dissociation and association. Both would agree with Adorno and Horkheimer that instrumental reason represses dialectical potentiality, and thus that its *sole* pursuit reinforces present domination, but the simple desire *that* things work for us at all *must* be a neutral one, i.e., one free from the interests of domination, for their shared project to be viable.

Here we can see what is (or should be) so devastating in Freud's admit-tedly fleeting assertion of an intimate relation between technical mastery and dreams of omnipotence, one grounded in a transhistorical developmen-tal need: to increase one's "likeness to God" the *other*. Technical mastery is never *simply* mastery, i.e., always already technical *aggressivity*,[42] because it is bound up in an orthopedic quest to complete a being whose entrance into the world is defined by separation and lack (which is the same thing as saying: a quest to avoid oedipal defeat).[43] In articulating this idea in the previous section, I was attempting to formulate a coherent version of the, in truth, rather old idea that technology might serve as a medium of aggres-sive sublimation,[44] one with which Marcuse tarries in dismissal.

Within the context of his work on technology that I have just briefly out-lined, one can see the source of neurotic misery: the viability of Marcuse's theory of liberation depends upon technical mastery being a mere *chan-nel* for aggressive energy, that through which it *passes*, and not itself a sublimated manner of pursuing omnipotence. If the technical is always already technological, then no "neutral" condition of liberation exists, and, even more problematically, claims about "instinctual renewal"—for instance, that it is possible today for "an ever larger part of the instinctual energy that had to be withdrawn for alienated labor to return to its origi-nal form"—look themselves like manifestations of a technological drive.[45] What becomes clear in these theoretically ruinous consequences is that Marcuse's varied confrontations with the possibility of aggressive subli-mation were not secondary subplots in his works but rather compulsive returns to a traumatic notion that threatened to undo his entire project.

In the late work, *Counterrevolution and Revolt*, Marcuse would implic-itly call into question his own technics/technology distinction through a critique of Marx:

Marx's notion of a human appropriation of nature retains some-thing of the *hubris* of domination. "Appropriation," no matter how human, remains appropriation of a (living) object by a subject.

It offends that which is essentially other than the appropriating subject, and which exists precisely as object in its own right—that is,
as subject! The latter may well be hostile to man, in which case the
relation would be one of struggle; but the struggle may also subside
and make room for peace, tranquility, fulfillment. In this case, not
appropriation but rather its negation would be the nonexploitative
relation: surrender, "letting-be," acceptance . . . [46]

Not just labor as the production of surplus value but even labor as the
production of *use-value*, the kind of labor previously held responsible
not for technological domination but mere technical mastery, is revealed
here be a form of domination.[47] Even while advocating the "use of the
achievements of technological civilization for freeing man and nature
from the destructive abuse of science and technology in the service of
exploitation," the late Marcuse thus gives us reason to believe, against his
own persistent assertion to the contrary, that there is no form of technical
mastery uncolored by urges for domination.[48]

Do We Identify with Machines?

With this unacknowledged self-subversion in mind, perhaps it
is no surprise that Marcuse's separation of technical and technological,
and thus technical and human,[49] is combined, in a strange return of
the repressed, with claims about direct identifications with machines.
Extending Marx's theory of commodity fetishism to the late capitalist era,
where machines become the primary bearers of this fantastic quality, he
writes:

The relationships among men are increasingly mediated by the
machine process. But the mechanical contrivances which facilitate intercourse among individuals also intercept and absorb their
libido, by diverting it from the all too dangerous realm in which
the individual is free of society. The average man hardly cares for
any living being with the intensity and persistence he shows for his
automobile. The machine that is adored is no longer dead matter
but becomes something like a human being. And it gives back to
man what it possesses: the life of the social apparatus to which it
belongs.[50]

Machines might not serve as vehicles of aggressive sublimation, but they can become *libidinal* objects: through the "projection" of human qualities onto machines, they "appear as autonomous figures endowed with a life of their own."[51] The machine also has something to contribute to the relationship: bearing the spiritual quality of social production, it returns to its adorers the relations alienated from them in the production process.

It is one thing if all Marcuse wishes to provide here is an update to the theory of commodity fetishism; it is another, however, to claim that the machine is an object of *identification*, that it usurps the important developmental role played by other people. In his talk of an "automatization" of the superego, it is clear, unfortunately, that Marcuse has the latter in mind.[52] In claiming that the superego is not merely diminished but that it becomes mechanical, that the superego, raised amidst "depersonalized images," becomes a mechanized reinforcer of the status quo, Marcuse thus offers his own psychological explanation of the irresistibility of technology: if we cannot but affirm our technological culture, it is because the psychic agency that keeps us on the straight and narrow is just a series of "unconscious automatic reactions" and thus itself thoroughly technological.[53]

Insistent as care providers today might be to subcontract their duties to devices, the identifications primary to psyche formation are, according to Loewald's developmental model and indeed to all psychoanalytic theory, *identifications with those care providers*, and thus the medium of the internalized products of those identifications—the superego, for one—is unavoidably one of *human perspective*. Marcuse grossly overestimates the degree to which technology can replace personal relationships with impersonal images. The television in particular introduced a powerful new way to inculcate capitalist values and ideals without the mediation of the family, but to say that it "automatizes" the superego is to misunderstand the nature of its insidious effects. Rather than in positing a direct identification with technologies, the better path toward an explanation of technological fascination lies in the more traditional theory of identification with other people. One of the answers today to the question "What does the other want?" is, invariably, "To be looking at a screen" (or else, following the logic of the previous chapter, "Those same things that the people on the screen want"). Our objects of identification are not machines but people who *interface with* machines,[54] and thus the superego imperative today is not itself machinic but rather encourages us to *be* machinic, to be *users*, to be efficient executors of devices.

Where technology does have an influence on superego development, it is thus a mistake to say that it leads to "automatization." The superego is not a "mechanism," but the internalization of an identification from which the ego looks upon itself. It is thus not the television itself but the people who watch and talk incessantly of television and the characters and roles presented on its screen that siphon libidinal energy. Claiming a direct identification with machines is, in fact, a way of denying that technological fascination is a *learned* behavior: in the assertion that the appeal of various devices lies in their "spiritualized qualities," and not in the fact that we are constantly talking about and using them, fetishism is reinforced, not penetrated.

Marcuse is ultimately more of a "topographical" than a "structural" thinker (part of the reason I prefer Adorno and Horkheimer's more unfinished psychoanalytic work to Marcuse's).[55] In his vision of an "objective administration," there is no drama of conflicting internalized objects, only the elicitation of unconscious impulses and the increasing control and direction of consciousness. His belief, along with Stiegler's, that "hyperindustrial capitalism hijacks infantile libido, which is normally invested in parents, directing it toward commodities, thus destroying the processes of primary and secondary identification, i.e., the psyche itself" is thus both exaggerated and theoretically regressive.[56] Part of overcoming Marcuse's technological neurosis is to reject this simplistic topographical model, as Freud did, for one centered on real psychic dynamism, which means, amongst other things, admitting that it is not *just* the machine but *we* who propagate an unconscious technological fascination.

To sum up: the rejection of the possibility of aggressive sublimation leads Marcuse to argue for two opposing positions, one more optimistic and the other deeply fatalistic, both of which should be avoided today: on the one hand, that there is an aspect of technological development—the technical—free, at least analytically, from "human motivations"; on the other, that technological development has led to the "mechanization" of psychic processes, that our minds are being "automated." Although it bears a tendency to stubborn repetition, the human psyche is not, and will never be, mechanized in the way Marcuse worried, given the nature of its formation.[57] This is not to say, however, that technical development does not alter the instinctual economy. With the concept of aggressive sublimation proposed here, I am trying to take seriously this possibility without then going so far as to say that the superego is itself being "automated."

The Language of Thanatos

In chapter 2 I followed Loewald in arguing that Eros (whose genesis I have attributed to the sublimation of the death drive) is evinced by the use of words to reveal either a latent "thing" that unconsciously structures language use or else a "deficient word" that works to conceal its lack of referent. Sublimation, in this view, is the cathexis of language, the attempt to find drive satisfaction not *with* language but *in* language (I take this view of sublimation to meet the two criteria described in the first section). In this chapter I have entertained the possibility of a sublimation of aggressivity and must now confront the obvious conclusion that it is primarily in language that we see the effects of aggressive sublimation, in other words, that there is an intimate relation between technological development and linguistic practice.[58] Following through the logic of sublimation unpacked in chapter 2, we can tentatively envision this translation as follows: if, in death drive sublimation, the urge to union of subject and object is sought in the union of word and thing, then, in aggressive sublimation, the drive to subjective omnipotence and objective destitution characteristic of aggressivity similarly finds expression in a kind of dominance of word over thing.

In this view, Eros and sublimated aggressivity—perhaps the word *Thanatos* could be incorporated here—share the aim of seeking a secondary "wholeness," just as the urge to union and aggressivity both seek a kind of tensionless repose, but, whereas Eros aims to find words for things and things for words, Thanatos aims to render whole by closing off investigation into unnamed things and deficient words, repressing anything that might threaten the cohesion of the present. It draws a circle around *what is* and claims it sufficient, everything else being extraneous or hostile to the current configuration of the ego.[59] What is being entertained here is the following: that language is a medium not only to bring about better communication between unreconciled entities (its communicative function) and not only to gain further mastery over one's environment (its instrumental function) but also *to silence*, to engulf the other, whether it is a conversation partner or one's own id, into nothingness (its aggressive function).[60]

Marcuse himself devoted a large number of pages to precisely this problem: that technological rationality enacts a "closure of discourse."[61] To describe this "language of one-dimensional thought," he employs three adjectives that adequately cover the effects of aggressive sublimation: "functionalized, abridged, and unified."[62]

1. *Functionalization:* The language of Eros, in seeking words for unnamed things and things for deficient words, necessarily transcends function and is thus seen from the functional perspective as strictly useless. The language of Thanatos, by contrast, is a language that serves the ego in pursuit of preestablished ends and thus one that *works at the cost of investigating the purpose of working.* It is the language of the subject oriented "straight ahead," only reflective in its capacity to measure success or failure in living up to goals.

2. *Abridgment:* Similarly, whereas the language of Eros is *drawn out,* dwelling on words that have been condensed and deemed outmoded, and blindnesses where words fail, the language of Thanatos is stingily economic. Marcuse focuses his energy on a *spatial* abridgment: in the acronym NATO, for instance, one can see how the "language of total administration" serves to "repress undesired questions:" "NATO does not suggest what North Atlantic Treaty Organization says, namely, a treaty among the nations of the North-Atlantic—in which case one might ask questions about the membership of Greece and Turkey."[63] I might add to Marcuse's understanding of abridgment another feature: a *temporal* abridgment, an increasingly shortened half-life of words, captured in the pervasive term *updating* (which, as Christoph Türcke argues, has come "to be perceived as the essence of dealing with reality").[64] In this dual spatial and temporal abridgment, language's dialectical potential is subdued, as words both *mean less* and *mean for a shorter amount of time.*[65]

3. *Unification:* Finally, while the language of Eros recognizes a noncorrespondence between words and things, the language of Thanatos stresses unification, by which Marcuse means not a dialectical reconciliation but the imposition of a false totality. One of the ways in which this unification is accomplished is by prepackaging phrases so that they already contain their own judgment: contradictions that were once inimical to logical thought are reified in constructions like "clean bomb" and "harmless fall-out";[66] words are given a false familiarity through personalization ("It is 'your' congressman, 'your' highway, 'your' favorite drugstore, 'your' newspaper, it is brought to 'you,' it invites 'you,' etc.").[67] The space for assessment is closed once the object is already characterized as "clean" or "harmless" or "mine;" things are "pre-judged," already processed for consumption, requiring no work to be metastasized by the subject. A unified

language gives answers to "questions in advance of their being posed."[68] What is eliminated in this transformation is the space between the "is" and the "ought" designated by concepts, and thus the possibility of dialectical movement. In Marcuse's words, technological rationality "leaves no space for distinction, development, differentiation of meaning: it moves and lives only as a whole."[69]

These three features combine in Thanatos to rein in the self-undermining thrust of language, to rob language of its capacity to point beyond itself.[70] While Eros, working through the superego, challenges the ego to push beyond the fragile boundaries of its own world, Thanatos presents the ego with a clear path to anxiously pursue and a unified world whose loose ends have been neatly tied off, thus leading to the "affirmation and intellectual duplication of what exists anyway."[71]

In this view, language is not a medium with an "inherent telos" but the site of a struggle between competing instinctual interests.[72] Whatever "resources" it contains for rendering ourselves "communicatively fluid" are always in competition with other resources that work against that fluidity.[73] It is a widely accepted point amongst critical theorists after the communicative turn that the first-generation Frankfurt school thinkers generally confused reified language for language as such.[74] Given the fact that they preempted quite explicitly the turn to intersubjectivity and ordinary language philosophy,[75] it might be better to see them as asserting that the dialectical possibility implied in all language use is something that can *go away* and, in fact, *is* going away. Distinguishing between the languages of Eros and Thanatos is one way to codify theoretically the great alarm and urgency with which they greeted this eclipse. For the Frankfurt school, the ultimate question concerning language is the same one that Freud asks of civilization: not "What is its value?" but rather "With what success will Eros combat Thanatos?"[76]

* * *

My primary claim in this chapter is that the advance of technical mastery—the proliferation of "prosthetic" devices and organizational forms both in and out of the workplace and the ever greater role those devices and forms play in mediating and structuring the environment—allows increasingly for an expression of aggressivity that may be considered "sublimated." Technological development is thus driven not only by a desire for technical mastery and the socially determined meanings attributed to that mastery but also by a distinctively *psychic* investment, the possibility of which is the absent center around which Marcuse's thoughts on the relation between technology and the drives circulates. Undoubtedly, technical mastery is indeed mastery; but inherent in the evolution of technical skills is the fantasy of mastering Ananke once and for all, of completing the subject and thus rendering need of the object superfluous. In short, technical control always already bears technological aspirations.

What is perhaps most remarkable about late capitalist society is its provision of the means, on the one hand, to sublimate aggressivity, to technologically shore up the self and silence the other, and, on the other, to gratify the death drive in fantasy, to "lose oneself" in a confusion of subject and object. Though it is by no means the only experience wherein one finds a conjunction of self-erasure and omnipotence, I have in mind the paradigmatic case of using a smart phone, the technology that is for our current regime of capital accumulation what the automobile was for the Fordist-Keynesian era.[77] On a smart phone, I feel capable of doing just about anything with a touch of a button, and yet, at the same time, the activity enabled by smart phone use gives rise to experiences distinctly lacking in self-presence. Either I am in control or I am absent: this oscillation between "the two alternatives of no-self and all-self," characteristic of what Isaac Balbus calls the "infancy of modernity," defines subjection in late capitalism.[78]

Although I have tied technical development to aggressivity in a way that Marcuse doggedly avoided, I am not denying that increased technical mastery creates new possibilities that can be exploited to varying ends, only that that exploitation could ever be liberating without first working over our investments in that mastery. In itself, the view that technics is always already technological is no more pessimistic than the idea that art is not the product of a free creator but a libidinal sublimate or that the way in which we love is unavoidably structured by past relationships. That we are driven in a particular way does not preclude the possibility of coming to a greater consciousness about that determination, partially freeing ourselves of its influence and even harnessing it toward different ends.

Mystified and mystifying as he may have been at the end, I believe Heidegger was thus on the right path in claiming that what is needed today is neither the liberation of technical progress nor mass technical slowdown but rather the acquisition of what he calls a "free relation" to technology: an understanding of the unconscious motivations that drive us to an obsessive and unthinking affirmation of it.[79] Along with an understanding of the nature of the drive gratification provided by the culture industry, seeking this relation is part and parcel of what it means to acquire psychoanalytic insight into the nature of our selves in late capitalism.

Our very mastery seems to escape our mastery.
—Michel Serres, Conversations on Science, Culture, and Time

Conclusion

In parts 1 and 2 of this book, I investigated certain portions of the works of Freud, Loewald, and Lacan in order to fashion a drive theory hinted at by all but arrived at by none. In part 3 that drive theory was both historically situated and further developed in dialogue with Adorno, Horkheimer, and Marcuse. I would like finally to drop the scaffolding and guide the reader along the contours of the new edifice.

With a great deal of help from Loewald, I have argued here that the death drive is best understood as a drive against self-individuation to recreate the kind of care structure characteristic of early life in which self/other boundaries are fluid. The aim of the death drive, put otherwise, is *not to be ourselves*, to annul the fact that we are separate individuals. This separateness is made particularly harsh in early life by the total and terrifying dependence on the "other"—the other of what I have called the tension-within position, a position wherein infants feel themselves to be one component of a more global situation that includes the "other" in it. One might object that *death* is not really the right word for that toward which the infant strives (Loewald himself calls it union), and this is no doubt true in the sense that the infant has not an inkling of what death really means for adults (but, then, the same goes for love and murder as well). It needs to be emphasized, nonetheless, that it is an *end of one's existence as a separate individual* that is desired and thus that the death drive is, in this sense, a perfectly apposite phrase.

So if I am born as a creature that does not wish to be itself, how do I grow to become *self-interested,* to become someone who cares and strives for individuality? For Loewald, the first step in this direction lies with a peculiar manifestation of the death drive that comes to resist the death drive itself: the infant wants so immoderately to keep intact the primordial density that, even when the parent is absent, the child fabricates parental presence in fantasy—a process termed "identification." "I may not share a world with this much-needed 'other,' but *I* can directly *be* the 'other,' and thus *not be myself in fantasy* when I am forced to reckon with myself in reality."

While this imitation is, in itself, only an instantiation of the death drive, it also serves as the foundation of a process of *mourning:* the fantasy may shatter with little force, but it serves its purpose if it has mitigated even slightly the pain of absence, if it has provided a "presence in absence." Over time, identifications are made and remade, only to fail and fail again, but the effort is not for nothing, as those identifications never really disappear but rather quietly morph into *internalizations,* into pieces of the infant's own growing psychic structures. In other words, the fantasy "I am the 'other'" is paradoxically the source of the subject that is posited within it; having *been* the "other," the "other" comes to be one part of *me.* Which might also be to say: I will always be my parents, at least in part.

The "I" may only be a precipitate of various past identifications, but it nonetheless, in its emerging cohesiveness, comes to be a source of some pride. "I can do this. I prefer that. And, most importantly, I, unlike others, never leave myself." This is not to say that the infant has yet achieved anything like independence, only that a tension has begun to grow between the demand to cultivate a *growing* independence and the still frequent need for union; in other words, between the ego and the id, between the drive to mastery and the death drive.

Caretakers must inevitably suffer under the weight of these contradictory imperatives, and in a very particular way. Their efforts come to be seen in a schizoid manner: on the one hand, they are the sources of nurture and care, the other half in the primordial bond. On the other, they threaten engulfment of the prized and fledgling ego. The pull of the tension-within position is too strong, and the "I" simultaneously wishes and fears to be swept away in it. This fundamental and inevitable conflict is what Freud gendered in naming the Oedipus complex: mother as bond, father as separation. While, at certain points in history, this gendering of the conflict resonated with familial reality, the conflict itself only seizes upon gender divisions and does not depend on them.[1]

It is tempting, with Loewald, to make sense of *aggression* in terms of disappointment: by separating from my parents, I "kill" them—or at least their early psychic representatives. But there is another possibility implied within his model, which I developed with help from Jacques Lacan in chapter 3: if parents are the objects of a schizoid projection—that is, seen by the child as both caring and engulfing—and they are *also* the primary objects of identification, the projection must invariably feed back into the identification. In other words, children come to attempt to *engulf* others, to express an *omnipotence* over them, because they themselves have felt engulfed in the same way: "identification with the aggressor," only with the twist that the aggressor need not be what we would consider a real aggressor. This is to deny neither that children often suffer under *actual* aggression nor that that aggression shapes development. When children lash out, and they are met not with patience and a capacity for what Wilfred Bion calls "reverie" but rather with an equally or excessively strong and violent force, their belief that their parents threaten the ego is confirmed rather than disproven.

In sum, the death drive, the drive to mastery, and aggressivity are the three drives that govern preoedipal life, and their contradictory demands force the child to the oedipal breaking point. The great solution to this crisis, for both Loewald and Lacan, lies with *language*. In my capacity to speak and communicate, I find the possibility of partially satisfying the demand to break down my own ego boundaries—namely, by pushing beyond my present reality through a reconnection of "words" and "things"—in such a way that the conflict between this demand and those of the ego is transformed into the more manageable tension between ego and superego. Put differently, the ego reconciles with the id by finding a place for it within itself.

The death drive is not, however, the only preoedipal force that finds sublimated expression in the superego. Especially if it has not been skillfully managed with parental "reverie," aggressivity—the drive to engulf the other into nothingness—imposes itself by joining the death drive in attaching itself to language. Whereas the sublimated expression of the latter (I have called this *Eros*) pushes the ego beyond itself, having transformed a drive to ego destruction into one of ego transcendence, the sublimated expression of the former (*Thanatos*) moves in the opposite direction, insulating the ego further and further from destabilizing otherness.

I have been unable to resist the temptation to depict the final stage of this developmental sequence as a figure. Like all visual representations, it veils as much as it reveals, but hopefully some light is shed on the relations between the different elements upon which I have been working.

Though I have remained homed in on a psychoanalytic logic throughout, the concern driving this project—namely, how precisely we ought to understand the particular manner in which subjects in late capitalism are alienated—stems from critical social theory. One might say that, for this book, Freud is the secondary process, Marx the primary (an idea so strikingly depicted in the famous image from Jean-Luc Godard's *Le Gai Savoir* included here).[2] In chapters 4 and 5 I turned to the Frankfurt school's shared belief that they were witnessing a fundamental change in the psyche that somehow simultaneously weakened and strengthened the force of the superego. I have made sense of this theory of psychic transformation in claiming that a) Eros's sway over the superego is weakened by the direct death drive gratification provided by the products of the culture industry and b) Thanatos's claim on the superego is strengthened by the aggressive sublimation involved in technological advance.[3] Certainly the energetic sapping of Eros and emboldening of Thanatos makes for no rosy prospects, but it does, as I argued in chapter 4, open a distinct possibility of resistance for late capitalist subjects: freed from the strict

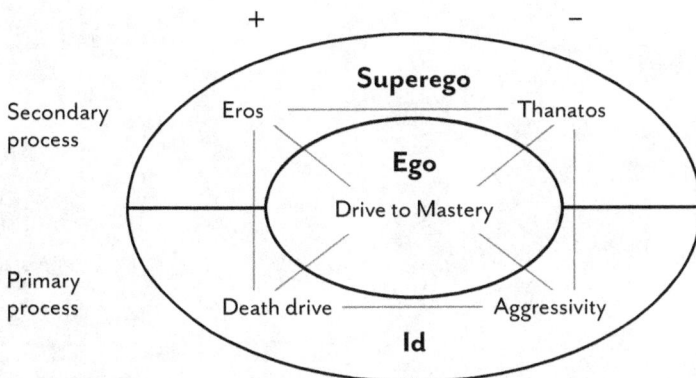

FIGURE C.1.   Completed figure.

moral codes of bourgeois individualism, it becomes possible to assess the nature and the function of the superego and redeploy this function on our own terms. In a short paper published in the same year as *The Future of an Illusion*, Freud admitted that "we have still a great deal to learn about the nature of the super-ego."[4] I understand this claim in the imperative.

Where's the Sex?

Like Freud's metapsychology papers, the psychoanalytically focused chapters of this book have been dense and formal, and one might wonder what happened to that ethereal and unceremonious rudiment of psychoanalytic theory: sexuality. I have not, of course, managed completely to eliminate sexuality: orality is so closely tied to fantasies of engulfment and anality to the activity of mastery that this book could well be rewritten as *The Mouth and the Anus*. It is true, nonetheless, that I have somewhat methodically avoided the sexual, and it behooves me to offer some evidence that repression is not at work (or, at least, that repression is at work in an interesting way).

FIGURE C.2.   From Jean-Luc Godard's *Le Gai Savoir*.

In Freud, sexuality is a notoriously slippery term. For my present purposes, I take it to pertain to the variety of pleasures that one can experience with one's body, and I take its importance to derive from the limitations imposed on those pleasures in the course of maturation.[5] In the introduction I argued that the kinds of bodies that we have play an important role in the formation of drives,[6] but I did not "flesh" out this claim a) because the book is focused on the developmental logic in which drives themselves are formed and transformed and b) because I understand the question of how that developmental logic is both informed by our bodily capacities and experienced at a bodily level to be one that deserves a book of its own, one that I hope to write as an unwieldy addendum to *Death and Mastery*. Whereas the present book deals with the difficult journey from utter dependence to partial independence (and its implications for the historically specific people that we are), the next one will confront a different but related problem—namely, the kinds of bodies that we have and what we do with them. For better or worse, then, I have chosen to uphold Freud's distinction between metapsychological theory, which exists at a level of abstraction from psychoanalytic experience, and the nonmetapsychological psychoanalytic theory rooted in close observation (though between these two levels there is undoubtedly some conceptual bleed).

Part of the reason I find it necessary to relegate the whole question of sexuality to a separate book is that I believe psychoanalytic theory since Freud has generally shied away from investigating the body as Freud himself did, for a variety of reasons: the swift reification of the "oral, anal, genital" triad, which immediately opened the question of erogenous zones to caricature; the desire of emigrant analysts for a scientific respectability naturally threatened by too much speculation about cloaca and the like; the focus on speech and language, rather than the body, as the locus of analytic knowledge. For a similarly strange confluence of altogether different reasons, including the twin influence of phenomenology and neuroscience and the realization that psychoanalytic theory has privileged the relational aspects of therapeutic work to the neglect of others, the body has increasingly become a topic of interest for contemporary psychoanalysts, but the body that has "returned" to analytic theory is not the body in which I am interested. *This* body is not the body that reveals the affective attunements of the intersubjectivists, nor is it the body that is the seat of an expanded conception of sensation (as in Leo Bersani's proposed "soma-analysis").[7] It is rather the body that has feet, a neck, hair, blood, and, yes, a mouth, an anus, and genitals; it is the body composed of parts the pleasures, significances, and possibilities of which transcend their functions. It is this body that I hope to investigate in a future work.

Administration Today

In the conclusion of *One-Dimensional Man* Marcuse poses a question that could very well serve as *the* fundamental question of critical theory: "how can administered individuals who have made their mutilation into their own liberties and satisfactions, and thus reproduce it on an enlarged scale—liberate themselves *from themselves* as well as from their masters?"[8] As Claus Offe rightly notes, Marcuse identifies here "a dilemma that he himself cannot overcome."[9] I have attempted in chapter 4 to make some advance in this regard by articulating a model of liberation from one's own ego latent in Adorno and Horkheimer's theorization of a crisis of internalization, though it would obviously be laughable to claim that any resolution on this matter has been achieved.

An even more basic question, however, confronts us today: where do we see the *need* for this self-liberation? Marcuse thought signs of general discontent abounded, both "in the 'catalyst groups' of the counter-culture (the student movement, women's movement, in grass roots democracy, etc.), but also in the working class itself: spontaneous sabotage, absenteeism, the demand to reduce the working day."[10] Where today, by contrast, do we see evinced the need to overcome not simply the egregious dictators and profiteers of the world but the performance principle itself?

Contrary to those who would argue that the impetus for critical theory has disappeared with the adaptation of the individual to the structures and strictures of late capitalism, I believe this need is as evident as in Marcuse's times, though the increasing strategic adroitness of administrative society has turned the evidence from positive to negative. One finds alienation today not only in protest but also in the great triad of industries devoted to subduing human explosiveness in late capitalist society: the culture industry, the technology industry, and the psychopharmaceutical industry (the last of these, though untreated in this book, has been lurking in the background throughout). What better evidence could there be of the general alienation of the vast majority of subjects than that, in order to devote most of their time to performing preestablished functions for apparatuses they do not control and to existing disconnectedly alongside positively displeasing people, they do not simply want but *need* to lose themselves in flickering images, to possess the latest devices, and to adjust their neurochemical balances? In this, Marcuse was absolutely right that the absence of these industries "would plunge the individual into a traumatic void," being far more psychically "unbearable" than the possibility of "radioactive fallout."[11]

It is incorrect to conclude, however, that late capitalist society is therefore *incompatible* with human drives, given that that society is constantly doing a great deal to pacify and manage our instinctual lives. Individual and society can actually be fairly well reconciled in late capitalist society, though not in the way we would like. Furthermore, dissatisfaction with that administered reconciliation is most certainly no source of resistance: I can perfectly well know that I am anesthetizing myself to a world that creates ego rigidity through direct death drive gratification or aggressive sublimation while quite happily enjoying my "heart-warmers in the commercial cold."[12] As I argued in chapter 4, there are historically specific *possibilities* for resistance today, but they are only possibilities—and, furthermore, possibilities that are opened up by the same developments that threaten to close them off forever.

I thus cannot claim to have done anything here to ameliorate the pessimism of the first-generation critical theorists, but then I do not believe that it is something that needs to be ameliorated.[13] Whenever I hear mention of this common characterization of the Frankfurt school, I cannot help but feel that theories are not being faulted in such a way as to overcome pessimism, but rather that the need to overcome pessimism is fueling a desire to find faulty logics.[14] Indeed, this is the only way I can make sense of claims about the culture industry thesis or the theory of technological rationality being wrong or dated at a time when the commodification of culture and obedience to blind instrumentalism are so pervasive as to be invisible in their obviousness.[15]

Although I am certainly open to Shane Gunster's claim that "deep pessimism offers a necessary first step in building a visceral awareness that culture need not be the way it is today," I am not making a claim about the value of pessimism, only affirming Freud's plea that we not confuse the disagreeable and the untrue.[16] The triumphant procession of Thanatos is indeed quite worrisome, but we should not cover over the problem with repressively confident assertions of theoretical progress. "Eternal Eros" still has a fighting chance "in the struggle with his equally immortal adversary," but not if we blind ourselves to the power of that adversary.[17]

Notes

Introduction

1. More recently, thinkers like Jacques Derrida and Roberto Esposito have drawn attention to the violence that follows from an "immunological crisis" of more basic coping responses; see Jacques Derrida, "Autoimmunity: Real and Symbolic Suicides—a Dialogue with Jacques Derrida," trans. Pascale-Anne Brault and Michael Naas, in *Philosophy in a Time of Terror*, ed. Giovanna Borradori (Chicago: University of Chicago Press, 2003); Jacques Derrida, *Rogues: Two Essays on Reason*, trans. Pascale-Anne Brault and Michael Naas (Stanford: Stanford University Press, 2005); Roberto Esposito, *Immunitas: The Protection and Negation of Life*, trans. Zakiya Hanafi (Cambridge: Polity, 2011).

2. Karl Marx, *The Marx-Engels Reader*, ed. Robert Tucker (New York: Norton, 1978), 150.

3. Cf. Karl Marx, *Capital Volume One: A Critique of Political Economy*, trans. Ben Fowkes (London: Penguin, 1976), 799.

4. According to Leszek Kolakowski, "human beings are what their behavior shows them to be: they are, first and foremost, the totality of the actions whereby they reproduce their own material existence." Leszek Kolakowski, *Main Currents of Marxism: Its Rise, Growth, and Dissolution*, trans. P. S. Falla, 3 vols. (Oxford: Oxford University Press, 1978), 1:156. What is essential about human beings, on this view, is their capacity to provide material stability for themselves with their inventive tool-making and organizational abilities—in short, their capacity to *master* their environment.

Marx himself often spoke of mastery (admittedly as neither *Bewältigung* nor *Bemächtigung*) in a positive sense: he claims, in *The German Ideology*, that the "natural form of the world historical co-operation of individuals will be transformed by this communist revolution into the control and conscious mastery [*Beherrschung*] of these powers," and, in the *Grundrisse*, that communism will mark "the advent of real mastery [*Herrschaft*] over . . . the forces of nature" (Marx, *The Marx-Engels Reader*, 164, 246). Running with a passage from the Paris manuscripts that describes communism as a "fully-developed naturalism," a *"genuine* resolution of the conflict between man and nature," Ernst Bloch understands this mastery as involving a "humanization of nature": "the abolition of alienation in man and nature, between man and nature or the harmony of the unreified object with the manifested subject, of the unreified subject with the manifested object." Ibid., 84; Ernst Bloch, *The Principle of Hope*, trans. Neville Plaice, Stephen Plaice, and Paul Knight, 3 vols. (Cambridge: MIT Press, 1996), 1:240. Although I agree with Isaac Balbus that Marx's proposed "resurrection of nature" might have been "merely another name for its effective domination," I prefer in this one instance to side with Bloch and thus to think that, by "mastery of the forces of nature," Marx meant a deft and noninstrumental relation to the world. Isaac D. Balbus, *Marxism and Domination: A Neo-Hegelian, Feminist, Psychoanalytic Theory of Sexual, Political, and Technological Liberation* (Princeton: Princeton University Press, 1982), 275.

5. See Sigmund Freud, *The Standard Edition of the Complete Psychological Works of Sigmund Freud*, ed. and trans. James Strachey, 24 vols. (London: Hogarth and the Institute of Psycho-Analysis, 1966), 21:112–13.

6. I would hope this way of framing my project prevents it from being seen as "an expression of an orthodoxy hostile to experimentation." Axel Honneth, "The Work of Negativity," in *Recognition, Work, Politics: New Directions in French Critical Theory*, ed. Jean-Philippe Deranty, Danielle Petherbridge, John Rundell, and Robert Sinnerbrink (Leiden: Brill, 2007), 128.

7. Horkheimer and Adorno were already interested in psychoanalysis by the time Fromm came to the Frankfurt Psychoanalytic Institute (Adorno wrote his 1927 *Habilitationsschrift* on Freud and Kant), but it was largely Fromm that set the agenda for a synthesis of psychoanalysis and social theory. Martin Jay, *The Dialectical Imagination: A History of the Frankfurt School and the Institute of Social Research, 1923–1950* (Berkeley: University of California Press, 1996), 88.

8. Erich Fromm, "The Method and Function of an Analytic Social Psychology: Notes on Psychoanalysis and Historical Materialism," in *The Essential Frankfurt School Reader*, ed. Andrew Arato and Eike Gebhardt (New York: Continuum, 2005), 523.

9. Herbert Marcuse, *Eros and Civilization: A Philosophical Inquiry into Freud* (Boston: Beacon, 1966), 134. Horkheimer would similarly disagree with Freud's understanding of the death drive, at the same time agreeing with the pessimism that underlay it, attacking Fromm while nonetheless retaining his beliefs; see Jay, *The Dialectical Imagination*, 102.

10. The phrase comes from Joel Whitebook, "The Marriage of Marx and Freud: Critical Theory and Psychoanalysis," in *The Cambridge Companion to Critical Theory*, ed. Fred Rush (Cambridge: Cambridge University Press, 2004), 74–102. Beginning perhaps with Fredric Jameson's *Late Marxism*, the importance of psychoanalysis to critical theory (attributed notably by Martin Jay) has been called into question: Freud was important, of course, but his categories were never "centrally organizing" as, say, Weber's, or Lukács's, or Nietzsche's were. Fredric Jameson, *Late Marxism: Adorno, or the Persistence of the Dialectic* (London: Verso, 1990), 26. This claim of exaggerated importance, combined with a retreat from the purportedly "patrocentric" implications of the critical theorists' conception of the decline of the family (as articulated by Jessica Benjamin), has made for a dearth of studies devoted to the psychological component of critical theory, despite the fact that Horkheimer himself claimed that Freud's "thought is one of the foundation stones without which our philosophy would not be what it is" (quoted in Jay, *The Dialectical Imagination*, 102). The only book-length exceptions, to my knowledge, are C. Fred Alford, *Narcissism: Socrates, the Frankfurt School, and Psychoanalytic Theory* (New Haven: Yale University Press, 1988); Joel Whitebook, *Perversion and Utopia: A Study in Psychoanalysis and Critical Theory* (Cambridge: MIT Press, 1996); and Yvonne Sherrat, *Adorno's Positive Dialectic* (Cambridge: Cambridge University Press, 2002). It is thus not surprising that many works addressing the connection between psyche and society make little or no mention of the Frankfurt school: see, for instance, Paul-Laurent Assoun, *Freud et les sciences sociales: Psychanalyse et théorie de la Culture* (Paris: Armand Colin, 1993); Kanakis Leledakis, *Society and Psyche: Social Theory and the Unconscious Dimension of the Social* (Oxford: Berg, 1995); Neil J. Smelser, *The Social Edges of Psychoanalysis* (Berkeley: University of California Press, 1998); Fred Weinstein, *Freud, Psychoanalysis, Social Theory: The Unfulfilled Promise* (Albany: SUNY Press, 2001); Kelly Oliver and Steve Edwin, eds., *Between the Psyche and the Social: Psychoanalytic Social Theory* (Lanham: Rowman and Littlefield, 2002).

11. Akeel Bilgrami offers a pithy critique of the "It's too late" charge in *Secularism, Identity, and Enchantment* (Cambridge: Harvard University Press, 2014), 203.

12. As a representative smattering, see Frank Sulloway, *Freud, Biologist of the Mind: Beyond the Psychoanalytic Legend* (New York: Basic Books, 1979); François Roustang, *Dire Mastery: Discipleship from Freud to Lacan* (Arlington: American Psychiatric, 1986); Richard Webster, *Why Freud was Wrong: Sin, Science, and Psychoanalysis* (New York: Basic Books, 1996); John Forrester, *Dispatches from the Freud Wars: Psychoanalysis and Its Passions* (Cambridge: Harvard University Press, 1997); Frederick Crews, ed., *Unauthorized Freud: Doubters Confront a Legend* (London: Penguin, 1999); and, above all, Catherine Meyer, ed., *Le Livre noir de la psychanalyse* (Paris: Les Arènes, 2005).

13. Hans Loewald, *Papers on Psychoanalysis* (New Haven: Yale University Press, 1980), 120.

14. Loewald calls it the "apparatus model" (ibid., 119).

15. Freud, *Standard Edition*, 2:305.

16. In what follows, I am interested less in what "really" happened than I am in two fundamentally different ways in which we can understand the Wolfman case as Freud himself describes it. It is for this reason that I do not engage Nicolas Abraham and Maria Torok's polyglottal reconstruction of the case, Jeffrey Moussaieff Masson's revelation that Pankejeff had been "anally seduced" as a child (subsequently qualified by Kurt Eissler), or the many attempts to divine the precise nature of Freud's personal overinvestment in the case. Nicolas Abraham and Maria Torok, *The Wolf Man's Magic Word: A Cryptonomy,* trans. Nicholas Rand (Minneapolis: University of Minnesota Press, 1986); Jeffrey Moussaieff Masson, *The Assault on Truth: Freud's Suppression of the Seduction Theory* (New York: Ballantine, 2003), xvii; K. R. Eissler, "Comments on Erroneous Interpretations of Freud's Seduction Theory," *Journal of the American Psychoanalytic Association* 41, no. 2 (1993): 575–76; Mark Kanzer, "Further Comments on the Wolf Man: The Search for a Primal Scene," in *Freud and His Patients,* ed. Mark Kanzer and Jules Glenn (New York: Jason Aronson, 1980); William Offenkrantz, "Problems of the Therapeutic Alliance: Freud and the Wolf Man," *International Journal of Psychoanalysis* 54 (1973): 76; Patrick J. Mahony, *Cries of the Wolf Man* (New York: International Universities Press, 1984), 176. I only turn to the Obholzer interviews in the third section of this introduction to argue that the complete fabrication of the primal scene does not preclude the possibility that its articulation had some therapeutic value.

17. Freud, *Standard Edition,* 17:67; Harold P. Blum, "The Borderline Childhood of the Wolf Man," in *Freud and His Patients,* 352.

18. The Wolfman's analysis ended in 1914, but the war delayed publication of case until 1918.

19. Freud, *Standard Edition,* 17:3.

20. Ibid., 17:44.

21. Grubrich-Simitis connects the Wolfman case and the metapsychology papers in Ilse Grubrich-Simitis, "Trauma or Drive—Drive and Trauma: A Reading of Sigmund Freud's Phylogenetic Fantasy of 1915," *Psychoanalytic Study of the Child* 43 (1988): 13.

22. The following is a brief history of what drive substantially *is,* as opposed to Freud's own history of what the drives individually *are* in chapter 6 of *Civilization and Its Discontents* (see Freud, *Standard Edition,* 21:117–19).

23. "Instincts and their Vicissitudes," "Repression," "The Unconscious," "A Metapsychological Supplement to the Theory of Dreams," and "Mourning and Melancholia" (all collected in the fourteenth volume of the *Standard Edition*). Freud would destroy the other seven papers (ibid., 14:105), though a draft of the twelfth paper (meant to conclude the book) was discovered with the Freud/Ferenczi correspondence and published as *A Phylogenetic Fantasy: Overview of the Transference Neuroses,* ed. Ilse Grubrich-Simitis, trans. Axel and Peter Hoffer (Cambridge: Belknap, 1987).

24. See Loewald, *Papers on Psychoanalysis,* 119–24.

25. Freud, *Standard Edition,* 14:118, 121.

26. Strachey generously chalks up the contradiction to an "ambiguity in the concept itself—a frontier-concept between the physical and the mental," though it is clear from the discussion that precedes this conclusion that he thought the confusion real (ibid., 14:113).

27. Ibid., 14:136 (my emphasis).

28. Sigmund Freud and Karl Abraham, *A Psycho-Analytic Dialogue: The Letters of Sigmund Freud and Karl Abraham, 1907–1926,* ed. Hilda C. Abraham and Ernst L. Freud, trans. Bernard Marsh and Hilda C. Abraham (New York: Basic Books, 1965), 228.

29. Grubrich-Simitis goes so far as to claim that "in Freud's later friendships it is the mutuality with Ferenczi that matches the intimacy and inspiring intensity of his relationship with Fliess" ("Trauma or Drive," 7).

30. Sigmund Freud and Sándor Ferenczi, *The Correspondence of Sigmund Freud and Sándor Ferenczi,* ed. Ernst Falzeder and Eva Brabant, trans. Peter T. Hoffer (Cambridge: Belknap, 1996), 2:263.

31. Ibid., 2:51.

32. Ibid., 2:263.

33. Ibid., 2:51.

34. See chapter 1 for a survey of the reception of the death drive.

35. Loewald, *Papers on Psychoanalysis,* 119–120.

36. Ibid., 122.

37. Ibid., 123 (my emphasis).

38. As opposed to *somatic* forces that do "not arise from the external world," as he had postulated in "Instincts and Their Vicissitudes" (Freud, *Standard Edition,* 14:118).

39. Freud and Abraham, *A Psycho-Analytic Dialogue,* 261, quoted in Sulloway, *Freud, Biologist of the Mind,* 275.

40. William Morton Wheeler, "On Instincts," *Journal of Abnormal Psychology* 15 (1917): 316, quoted in Sulloway, *Freud, Biologist of the Mind,* 4.

41. John Fletcher makes a similar point in *Freud and the Scene of Trauma* (New York: Fordham University Press, 2013), 310.

42. The claim that drives are formed in relation to the environment need not contradict Freud's assertion that they are, once formed, "objectless": drives might be formed in relation to objects, but they persist even when that relation changes and the original object is renounced. As Adam Phillips explains, when "Freud proposed that the object was merely 'soldered' on to the instinct, that our primary commitment was to our desire and not to its target," "he was implying that we are not attached to each other in the ways we like to think." Adam Phillips, *Terrors and Experts* (Cambridge: Harvard University Press, 1995), 78. As Phillips makes clear, he was *not* implying that we are simply not attached to each other.

43. Part of the reason that Freud—the late Freud, anyways—is mistakenly read as speaking of biological instincts rather than environmentally formed drives is a lack of attendance to the history I have outlined here, but the more glaring cause is the simple fact that the German term for "drive," *Trieb,* is rendered

by translators James and Alix Strachey in *The Standard Edition* as "instinct." Contemporary psychoanalytic theorists nearly universally lament this choice and the misunderstandings it has produced, and I imagine that the revised standard edition of Freud's works, edited by Mark Solms, will correct this mistake; but, before history buries another controversy, a limited defense of the poor Stracheys seems in order, if only because one of the most important lessons of psychoanalysis is that we should be wary of the aggressively obvious.

The first thing that must be said on their behalf is that Freud himself, whose English was nearly flawless, personally signed off on their specific translations of key words, and thus most certainly would have himself been aware of the fact that *Trieb* was being translated as "instinct." One might chalk this up to his desire to gain a better scientific reception, but this interpretation does not alter the fact that Freud, who was quite sensitive to the implications of words, approved the translation "instinct." Second, despite the fact that drives, unlike instincts, are neither innate nor determinately satisfied (hunger is only satisfied in eating, sexuality, on the other hand . . .), they are nonetheless *experienced by the subject with the force of an instinct*. Drives may be formed in the child's relation to the environment, but once those drives are formed they bear their own autonomous and uncompromising force. Sexuality, for instance, might be a product of early development and not a constitutional given, but we are not therefore free to ignore its demands. Thus, while "instinct" is most certainly the wrong translation for *Trieb*, it does capture its real unmanageability, unlike the word "drive." In the sentence "he has a *drive* to succeed," for instance, we hear that this person is a hard-working go-getter, not that he is dealing with forces beyond his control.

Finally, there is, for Freud, some connection between *Trieb* and "instinct" (*Instinkt*), even if it is not one of identity. In the *Three Essays on a Theory of Sexuality* he offers the following well-known example: "Our study of thumb-sucking or sensual sucking has already given us the three essential characteristics of an infantile sexual manifestation. At its origin it attaches itself to one of the vital somatic functions; it has as yet no sexual object, and is thus auto-erotic; and its sexual aim is dominated by an erotogenic zone" (Freud, *Standard Edition*, 7:182–83). In other words, the sexual act of sucking, the gaining of pleasure from the act of biologically pointless sucking, depends upon, or "props" itself upon, the vital function of eating, but it also becomes detached from that function, thus transforming into what Freud calls a "component instinct" or "part drive" (*Partialtrieb*), a part of what comes to be our basic drives. Thus the acts involved in oral pleasure, as well as their associated fantasies (engulfing, devouring, consuming, etc.), come to play an important part in the constitution of the drives more generally.

In sum: to say that drives are environmentally formed does not mean that we can reduce drive to environmental influence because a) once drives are formed, they are no more easily ignored than biological instincts for having been acquired and can be just as much a source of resistance to the environment as they can be of complicity; and b) there are constitutional factors that go into the formation of drives. Adrian Johnston, who also believes that "the complete denial of all features pertaining to instinct . . . might be too extreme, too sweeping," offers a helpful comparison of *Trieb* and *Instinkt* in *Time Driven: Metapsychology and the Splitting of the Drive* (Evanston: Northwestern University Press, 2005), 156–69; as does Laplanche in *Freud and the Sexual: Essays, 2000–2006*, ed. John Fletcher, trans. John Fletcher et al. (New York: International Psychoanalytic, 2011), chapter 1.

44. Though it is true that those structures do come to oppose the drives, they are no longer understood to be primarily opposed to them or separate from them.

45. Part of my claim here is that it is more accurate to say that psychic reality is a product of unconscious drive rather than the unconscious *tout court*, given that it is the drives that make the unconscious an effective force. Imagine a man who, at the age of six, lost his mother to cancer: if this man should have no memory of his mother—if, in other words, his memories of her had been banished by the guardian of consciousness to the depths of the unconscious—there is nothing about this act *in itself* that is cause for neurosis or unhealth. With Nietzsche's assertion of the naturally fortifying effect of forgetfulness in mind, we might even say that this man is better off with no memory of his mother. *That* we repress, that *there is* an unconscious, in other words, could be just as much occasion for happiness, cheerfulness, hope, pride, and presence as it is for misery, gloominess, despair, self-hatred, and absence, or, for that matter, nothing whatsoever; cf. Friedrich Nieztsche, *On the Genealogy of Morals*, trans. Walter Kaufmann and R. J. Hollingdale (New York: Vintage, 1989), 58. What makes the man's repression of the memories of his mother effective, what makes the unconscious an active force in his life, is the fact that the drives that were formed and elicited in his early relationship with his mother remain after the memories of that relationship have been repressed. It is the drives, in short, that make the descriptively unconscious *dynamically* unconscious.

46. Freud, *Standard Edition*, 19:176.

47. Psychic reality is, unfortunately, more often than not thought to be composed simply of the complexes, fantasies, and scenes themselves (as in the Wolfman case, the conclusion of *Totem and Taboo*, or the whole of *Moses and Monotheism*). To his detractors, these essays seem typical of Freud's delusion. His defenders, on the other hand, laud him for asserting in these instances the "reality of fiction"; see Peter Brooks, "Fictions of the Wolfman: Freud and Narrative Understanding," *Diacritics* 9, no. 1 (1979): 78; Jonathan Culler, *The Pursuit of Signs: Semiotics, Literature, Deconstruction* (London: Routledge, 1981), 202. Too much energy, to my mind, has been spent trying to justify or deny the reality of the fantasies Freud offers up under the name *primal scene*. Although I agree, for what it's worth, that they are indeed *real*, what I dislike in this conversation is that it shifts emphasis away from the reality of the drives that undergird them. When the debate is over whether the Wolfman *actually* witnessed his parents having sex at the young age of eighteen months instead of whether the Wolfman had *drives* that operated without his volition or control, it is easy for the question of psychic reality to turn into a parody.

48. Freud, *Standard Edition*, 23:255–70.

49. Ibid., 23:266.

50. Loewald, *Papers on Psychoanalysis*, 105.

51. No doubt realization (bringing the unconscious to consciousness) also involves a kind of transformation. What I mean to emphasize here is that in the late view, analysis is less about robbing an overwhelming scene or thought of its unconscious power and more about an expansion of subjectivity.

52. I am deeply indebted here to Jonathan Lear's argument in *Love and Its Place in Nature* that a psychoanalytic interpretation not only expresses "archaic mental activity" in "higher level thinking" but also *transforms* it. Jonathan Lear, *Love and Its Place in Nature* (New York: Farrar, Straus and Giroux, 1990), 7. Though Freud, in the image of a scientist discovering an independent reality, tended to present himself as "uncovering a hidden thought," what he was actually doing in helping minds to better understand themselves was, on Lear's account, aiding a developmental process wherein nonconceptual, "primitive mental activity" raises itself to the level of concepts and judgments in overcoming "myriad inhibiting forces, which freeze much of the mind's activity at archaic levels" (ibid., 8). Although I obviously agree with the general spirit of this intervention, I do worry that to speak of a developmental process pushing forward toward concepts and judgments instead of objectless and conflicting drives latching on to expression is to see teleology where Freud saw contingency. I also, and much more tentatively, wonder if this understanding of interpretation does justice to the retroactivity of meaning: an interpretation might not be picking out a previously existent reality in the "scientific" way that Freud imagined, but in finding expression for a meaningless psychic undercurrent it comes to have been the case that something like the event it recounts did happen (Freud names this phenomenon with the term *Nachträglichkeit*). In other words, in articulating the Wolfman's primal scene, Freud does something like "uncover a hidden thought," even if the hidden thought did not preexist the uncovering.

53. Albeit in such a way that that which is created appears to have been there all along—such is the strange temporality of psychoanalysis.

54. Freud, *Standard Edition*, 17:49.

55. See, for instance, Masson's well-known attack on Freud's "suppression" of his early seduction hypothesis in *Assault on Truth*. In his theory of "general seduction," Jean Laplanche attempts to recover the early seduction thesis, but within the psychoanalytic framework. Jean Laplanche, *Nouveaux Fondements pour la psychanalyse* (Paris: Presse Universitaires de France, 1987).

56. Freud, *Standard Edition*, 17:60.

57. He would come to doubt this conclusion in 1919, when he convinced Pankejeff to reenter analysis on account of "a small residue of unanalyzed material." Muriel Gardiner, ed., *The Wolf-Man: With the Case of the Wolf-Man by Sigmund Freud* (New York: Basic Books, 1971), 111. In Freud's defense, Pankejeff himself always felt that he had been helped by the first four years of analysis (though he felt nearly the opposite about everything that transpired after 1919). Mikkel Borch-Jacobsen and Sonu Shamdasani, *The Freud Files: An Inquiry Into the History of Psychoanalysis* (Cambridge: Cambridge University Press, 2012), 229; James L. Rice, *Freud's Russia: National Identity in the Evolution of Psychoanalysis* (New Brunswick, NJ: Transaction, 1993), 108.

58. Freud, *Standard Edition*, 17:70–71.

59. Karin Obholzer, *The Wolf-Man: Conversations with Freud's Patient—Sixty Years Later*, trans. Michael Shaw (New York: Continuum, 1982), 36.

60. That these interviews would constitute an attack on Freud and psychoanalysis was determined from the outset: Muriel Gardiner, the editor of the Wolfman's memoirs, who had concluded in that work that "the positive results of the Wolf-Man's analysis are impressive indeed," had forbidden Mr. Pankejeff from conducting any interviews, thus preventing the publication of Obholzer's book until after his death in 1979 (ibid., 22). Obholzer's annoyance at this restriction and psychoanalytic orthodoxy more generally comes across very clearly in the interviews, but the axe grinding does not detract from a set of fascinating conversations.

61. Ibid., 172, 138; Borch-Jacobsen and Shamdasani, *The Freud Files*, 229.

62. Obholzer, *The Wolf-Man*, 118, 110, 104.

63. See Mahony, *Cries of the Wolf Man*, 150.

64. I thus find little basis for concluding either that Pankejeff was simply "one of those tragic individuals who remain forever inside a gaping wound" or that debunking the "analytic myth of his 'cure'" reveals Freud's total failure (ibid., 151; Frank J. Sulloway, "Exemplary Botches," in Crews, *Unauthorized Freud*, 184). The former assumes an overly rosy picture of human life, and the latter does the same for the therapeutic process.

65. My reluctance stems from the term's being at the center of a now dated culture war described by Ian Hacking in *The Social Construction of What?* (Cambridge: Harvard University Press, 1999). By social constructionism, I simply mean a mode of explaining human behavior that privileges society and culture over agency and biology. To be clear, in none of what follows do I mean to dismiss any of these modes of explanation. In a comprehensive vision of why human beings do what they do, agency, biology, and society all have a place. My point here is only to reserve a distinct space for a theory that the present moment has conspired to collapse.

66. See ibid., 6.

67. "The term 'theo-logy' implies, as such, a mediation, namely, between mystery, which is *theos*, and the understanding, which is *logos*." Paul Tillich, *The Protestant Era*, trans. James Luther Adams (Chicago: University of Chicago Press, 1948), xiii.

68. Here I am following Frederick Neuhouser's understanding of theodicy, which cannot "reconcile us to present reality—cannot guarantee that the promise of good that is hidden in the evils of our actual circumstances is or ever will be realized," but that can still offer a kind of reconciliation: "affirmation of the world in its basic structure." Frederick Neuhouser, *Rousseau's Theodicy of Self-Love: Evil, Recognition, and the Drive for Recognition* (Oxford: Oxford University Press, 2008), 6. The questions that lead to Freud's introduction of the death drive, like the questions of theodicy, ask about the root of human evils: Why do we irrationally aggress other beings? Why do we tend toward lifeless repetition? Why are we constantly attempting to shed our own existences? And his answer

to these questions, in addition to involving the postulation of a new drive opposition, is essentially narrative.

69. Nikolas Rose, *Inventing Our Selves: Psychology, Power, and Personhood* (Cambridge: Cambridge University Press, 1996), 23.

70. Ibid., 9.

71. Ibid., 9.

72. I readily adopt Jan Goldstein's "minimalist position toward the self" articulated in *The Post-Revolutionary Self: Politics and Psyche in France, 1750–1850* (Cambridge: Harvard University Press, 2005), 2.

73. Rose, *Inventing Our Selves*, 6.

74. From a more methodological angle, I am, like both Theodor Adorno and Gillian Rose, skeptical of the reduction of the psychological to the sociological because it leads to "simplistic correlations between the individual and society." Gillian Rose, *The Melancholy Science: An Introduction to the Thought of Theodor W. Adorno* (New York: Columbia University Press, 1978), 92. Rejecting the possibility of unifying sociology and psychology, Adorno writes: "Our psychological analyses lead us the deeper into a social sense the more they abstain from any reference to obvious and rational socio-economic factors. We will rediscover the social element at the very bottom of our psychological categories, though not by prematurely bringing into play economic and sociological surface causations where we have to deal with the unconscious, which is related to society in a much more indirect and complicated way" (quoted in Jay, *The Dialectical Imagination*, 230). In Adorno's view, we learn more about society through psychology than we do through a sociology that cavalierly subsumes psychology; see also Theodor W. Adorno, "Sociology and Psychology, Part 1," *New Left Review* 1, no. 46 (November-December 1967): 74.

75. Moishe Postone, "Critique and Historical Transformation," *Historical Materialism* 12, no. 3 (2004): 63.

76. Peter Gay, *Freud for Historians* (Oxford: Oxford University Press, 1985), 88.

77. Mark Poster makes this point about dependence in *Critical Theory of the Family* (New York: Seabury, 1978), 15.

78. I am responding here, in part, to Leonore Tiefer's claim that sexual drives are constituted by culture: "Your orgasm is not the same as George Washington's, premarital sex in Peru is not premarital sex in Peoria, abortion in Rome at the time of Caesar is not abortion in Rome at the time of John Paul II." Leonore Tiefer, *Sex Is Not a Natural Act and Other Essays* (Boulder: Westview, 2004), 4.

79. I am in agreement with Peter Gay both that "the reputation of psychoanalysis as responsible for a static and undifferentiated model of human nature . . . is wholly undeserved" and that the "need for years of care and tuition . . . makes the modern historian, the ancient Egyptian, the Kwakiutl Indian . . . into cousins," but do not believe this agreement entails an affirmation of his defense of the concept of human nature, which he finds less problematic than I. Gay, *Freud for Historians*, 158, 89. The universality of our "preconditions" does not entail a universality of *what we are*.

80. I might add, as a slightly different point against the reduction of drive to environment, that the external influence that does go into the formation of drives is typically conflictual (and I might even say inevitably conflictual), making impossible any one-to-one correspondence between interpellation and psychic structure. The experiences in response to which drives initially form—those of receiving a response to one's vocalizations, of being held, of the vibrations of voice, etc., while certainly subject to social influence (adherence to the "cry it out" method, for instance), are not the same as those typically later (developmentally) ones that foster adjustment to the status quo—those of enforced individuation, of adherence to clock time, of the rules and norms of "good behavior," etc. The "modern model mother" might be teaching her children the basic habits of good capitalist subjectivity, but in the care environment, established even before birth, she is also ingraining in them a model of gratification that is at odds with the cold alienation of living in a world dominated by economic rationalism. In other words, there is no contradiction between Christopher Lasch's family as "haven in a heartless world" and Wilhelm Reich's family as "factory of ideology"; thankfully, the family is still *both*; see Christopher Lasch, *Haven in a Heartless World: The Family Besieged* (New York: Norton, 1995); Wilhelm Reich, *The Sexual Revolution: Toward a Self-Governing Character Structure* (New York: Farrar, Straus and Giroux, 1963), 38.

81. Rahel Jaeggi, *Alienation,* ed. Frederick Neuhouser, trans. Frederick Neuhouser and Alan E. Smith (New York: Columbia University Press, 2014), 30. I thus disagree with Jaeggi that alienation critique can only be culturally specific, only an "element of the critical, evaluative self-interpretation of a modern culture that has made freedom and self-determination its core values" (ibid., 41).

82. According to Terry Eagleton, the fact that "transhistorical truths are always culturally specific, always variably instantiated, is no argument against their transhistoricality." Terry Eagleton, *The Ideology of the Aesthetic* (Malden, MA: Blackwell, 1990), 410.

83. Freud, *Standard Edition,* 22:95.

84. For instance, in *The Future of an Illusion,* where he entertains the possibility that psychoanalysis itself is an illusion.

1. Death, Mastery, and the Origins of Life

1. I emphasize, with Samuel Weber, the narrative aspect of the late metapsychology both to indicate that it is the plot of a story as much as the basics of a theory that is being outlined in what follows, but also because the "structural" elements of id, ego, and superego, too often described topographically or schematically simply as components of the mind, must be understood as parts of a developmental story. That Freud himself thought of the structural model as a natural outgrowth of his drive theory is to me without question: indeed, he refers to *The Ego and the Id* as a "sequel" and a "continuation of 'Beyond.'" Sigmund Freud

and Sándor Ferenczi, *The Correspondence of Sigmund Freud and Sándor Ferenczi*, ed. Ernst Falzeder and Eva Brabant, trans. Peter T. Hoffer, 3 vols. (Cambridge: Belknap, 1996), 3:29, 84. Cf. Samuel Weber, *The Legend of Freud* (Minneapolis: University of Minnesota Press, 1995), 138–40.

2. Paul Ricoeur hints at this idea of a "nonpathological aspect of the death instinct" in the form of "mastery over the negative," but does not develop the thought. Paul Ricoeur, *Freud and Philosophy: An Essay on Interpretation*, trans. Denis Savage (New Haven: Yale University Press, 1970), 286.

3. I thus disagree with Peter Gay that, with the introduction of the death drive, "the desire for mastery, along with other candidates for the status of a primitive drive with which Freud had experimented over the years, now fade into relative insignificance." Peter Gay, *Freud: A Life for Our Time* (New York: Norton, 1988), 401.

4. Dominique Scarfone, *Jean Laplanche* (Paris: Press Universitaires de France, 1997), 56.

5. Precursors, both avowed and unavowed by Freud, nonetheless abound: the fragments of Empedocles on love and strife, Aristophanes' myth from Plato's *Symposium*, Friedrich Hufeland's *On Sympathy*, F. W. J. Schelling's *Ages of the World*, Arthur Schopenhauer's *The World as Will and Representation*, Friedrich Nietzsche's *Beyond Good and Evil*, Gustav Fechner's psycho-physics, Sándor Ferenczi's biological work, Wilhelm Stekel's invocation of *Thanatos* in 1909, Sabina Spielrein's "Destruction as a Cause of Coming Into Being." Most of these predecessors are discussed in Todd Dufresne, *Tales from the Freudian Crypt: The Death Drive in Text and Context* (Stanford: Stanford University Press, 2000), 13–88; see also George Makari, *Revolution in Mind: The Creation of Psychoanalysis* (New York: HarperCollins, 2008), 306–19. Sarah Kofman explores the Empedocles connection in *Freud and Fiction*, trans. Sarah Wykes (Cambridge: Polity, 1991), 21–52. Peter Sloterdijk does the same for Hufeland in *Bubbles*, trans. Wieland Hoban (Los Angeles: Semiotext(e), 2011), 239–51. The import of Schelling's work for psychoanalysis is drawn out by Slavoj Žižek in *The Indivisible Remainder* (London: Verso, 1996), 13–91. John Kerr debunks the Spielrein influence in "Beyond the Pleasure Principle and Back Again: Freud, Jung, and Sabina Spielrein," in *Freud: Appraisals and Reappraisals*, ed. Paul E. Stepansky, 3 vols. (Hillsdale: Analytic, 1988), 3:39. Though he is usually not mentioned as a precursor, Jung expresses the idea that "death is no external enemy, but a deep personal longing for quiet and for the profound peace of non-existence" in *Psychology of the Unconscious: A Study of the Transformations and Symbolisms of the Libido*, trans. Beatrice M. Hinkle (New York: Moffat, Yard, 1917), 390. Henri Ellenberger trots out more obscure predecessors, including the German Romantics Von Schubert and Novalis, the Russian psychiatrist Tokarsky, and the Russian zoologist Metchnikoff in *The Discovery of the Unconscious: The History and Evolution of Dynamic Psychiatry* (New York: Basic Books, 1970), 514.

6. Importantly, the repetition compulsion is tied *directly* to the drive to mastery and only *indirectly* to the death drive. Paul Denis offers a more in-depth history of the term *Bemächtigung* in Freud in "Emprise et théorie des pulsions,"

Revue Française de Psychanalyse 56, no. 5 (1992): 1299–312. However, whereas Denis sees a slow abandonment of the term after the *Three Essays*, I see instead a decisive conceptual transformation in *Beyond the Pleasure Principle* (ibid., 1312).

7. Overreacting to Ives Hendrick's "glorification of repressive productivity," Marcuse argues that "the assumption of a special 'mastery instinct' . . . destroys the entire structure and dynamic of the 'mental apparatus' which Freud has built." Herbert Marcuse, *Eros and Civilization* (Boston: Beacon, 1966), 219. As I will demonstrate here, mastery was a preoccupation of Freud's throughout his career.

8. Sigmund Freud, *The Standard Edition of the Complete Psychological Works of Sigmund Freud*, ed. and trans. James Strachey, 24 vols. (London: Hogarth and the Institute of Psycho-Analysis, 1966), 3:111; Sigmund Freud, *Gesammelte Werke: Chronologisch Geordnet*, 18 vols. (London: Imago, 1991), 1:337.

9. Freud, *Standard Edition*, 14:85; Freud, *Gesammelte Werke*, 10:151.

10. Freud, *Standard Edition*, 17:54; Freud, *Gesammelte Werke*, 12:82.

11. Freud, *Standard Edition*, 14:120.

12. Ibid., 7:188.

13. Ibid., 7:194.

14. In his article on Jensen's *Gradiva* (1907), in "The Disposition to Obsessional Neurosis" (1913), and in the *Introductory Lectures* (1916) (ibid., 9:88; ibid., 12:322 and 324; ibid., 16:327–28). The term *Bemächtigungsdranges* (urge for mastery) appears in "Triebe und Triebschicksale" (Freud, *Gesammelte Werke,* 10:231).

15. Kristin White, "Notes on 'Bemächtigungstrieb' and Strachey's Translation as 'Instinct for Mastery,'" *International Journal of Psychoanalysis* 91, no. 4 (May 2010): 813.

16. The game wherein he threw a "wooden reel with a piece of string tied around it" "over the edge of his curtained cot, so that it disappeared into it" (an action accompanied by an expression that Freud takes to "represent the German word *'fort'* ['gone'])," and then "pulled the reel out of the cot again by the string and hailed its reappearance with a joyful 'da' ['there']" (Freud, *Standard Edition*, 18:14–15). Freud understands the game as a symbolic expression of "the child's great cultural achievement—the instinctual renunciation . . . which he had made in allowing his mother to go away without protesting" (ibid., 18:15).

17. Ibid., 18:16.

18. Freud, *Gesammelte Werke*, 13:36. I believe that Leo Bersani's interpretation of the compulsion to repeat as a "permanent tendency on the part of the ego to resexualize its structure," to open itself to the "shattering effects of sexuality," collapses the distinction that Freud was attempting to make between the compulsion to repeat and the death drive, the latter being at the root of the former but nonetheless a wholly separate phenomenon. Leo Bersani, *The Freudian Body: Psychoanalysis and Art* (New York: Columbia University Press, 1986), 61, 63. Bersani might accept this charge, it being evidence that he resists Freud's "project of domesticating and rationalizing" his own discoveries; but to follow him down this path, one would have to be certain that domestication is the *only* *thing* that Freud is up to in his late work, and of this, I am thoroughly unconvinced (ibid., 102).

19. Jean Laplanche and Jean-Bertrand Pontalis, *The Language of Psychoanalysis*, trans. Donald Nicholson-Smith (London: Hogarth and the Institute of Psycho-Analysis, 1973), 218.

20. Ibid. Jacques Derrida, in his reading of *Beyond the Pleasure Principle* in *The Post Card*, also connects *Bewältigung* and *Bemächtigung* but imagines them both to denote a "violent exercise of power." Jacques Derrida, *The Post Card: From Socrates to Freud and Beyond*, trans. Alan Bass (Chicago: University of Chicago Press, 1987), 404. As I have shown here, Freud never uses the term *Bewältigung* to mean anything like a "violent exercise of power," and one can only assume that this misrecognition is a function of "reading Freud with one hand" and Hegel with the other (ibid., 394). A profound dexterity, to be sure, that I will not attempt to master here.

21. Freud himself, however, never seems to have used the phrase *Bewältigungstrieb*; Ives Hendrick incorrectly claims that he does in "The Discussion of the 'Instinct to Master,'" *Psychoanalytic Quarterly* 12 (1943): 563. The passage that he refers to uses the term *Bemächtigungstrieb*. Siegfried Bernfeld might be the first person to use the phrase in *Psychologie des Säuglings* (Vienna: Springer, 1925), 207.

22. This translation is further justified by Freud's own policy of switching back and forth between the two words around the time of *Beyond the Pleasure Principle*: for instance, in *The Ego and the Id*, when he discusses mastery of the Oedipus complex (*Bewältigung des eigentlichen Ödipuskomplexes* and *das Ich des Ödipuskomplexes bemächtigt*). Freud, *Gesammelte Werke*, 13:264–65.

23. Freud, *Standard Edition*, 19:163. Paul-Laurent Assoun compares Freud's *Bemächtigungstrieb* (translated as "drive to expropriate") and Nietzsche's *Wille zur Macht* in *Freud and Nietzsche*, trans. Richard L. Collier (London: Continuum, 2002), 152–55.

24. The uses of mastery in *Civilization and Its Discontents*, "Why War?", and the *New Introductory Lectures* continue to suffer from a lack of terminological clarity.

25. To my knowledge, the only authors who have attempted to pick up this thread are Ives Hendrick and Paul Denis. In "Work and the Pleasure Principle" Hendrick offers a useful definition of mastery, in the sense of *Bewältigung*, as aiming "to control or alter a piece of the environment, an ego-alien situation, by the skillful use of perceptual, intellectual, and motor techniques in order to control or alter a piece of the environment." Ives Hendrick, "Work and the Pleasure Principle," *Psychoanalytic Quarterly* 12 (1943): 314. Though I am obviously in agreement with Hendrick about the importance of the drive to mastery, I concur with Marcuse's assessment that his "work principle" glorifies "repressive productivity as human self-realization" (Marcuse, *Eros and Civilization*, 219). In "Emprise et théorie des pulsions" Denis proposes an elaborate and comprehensive reconstruction of psychoanalytic metapsychology centering on a notion of drive as having two distinct vectors, one of mastery, the other of satisfaction (Denis, "Emprise et théorie des pulsions," 1318). Unfortunately, rather than attempt to work out his theory in relation to the Eros/death drive dualism, Denis aims to "remove the ambiguities of the concept of mastery" by "dissociating it from any reference

to the death drive" (ibid., 1316). Roger Dorey also focuses on the term *mastery*, making important connections between *Bemächtigung* and *Bewältigung* in their relation to *Todestrieb*, but prefers to speak of a "relationship of mastery" instead of a "drive to mastery," distinguishing his own work from that of Denis precisely on this point. Roger Dorey, "The Relationship of Mastery," trans. Philip Slotkin, *International Review of Psychoanalysis* 13 (1986): 323–32; Roger Dorey, "Le désir d'emprise," *Revue Française de Psychanalyse* 56, no. 5 (1992): 1426.

26. Laplanche and Pontalis, *The Language of Psychoanalysis*, 97.

27. Freud, *Standard Edition*, 21:119.

28. See Sándor Ferenczi, *Thalassa: A Theory of Genitality* (London: Karnac, 1989).

29. Franz Alexander flirted with the existence of the death drive, but would later decide it better to speak of a "disintegration of mature behavior into its elementary parts." Franz Alexander, "The Need for Punishment and the Death-Instinct," *International Journal of Psycho-Analysis* 10 (1929): 256–69; Franz Alexander, *Fundamentals of Psychoanalysis* (New York: Norton, 1963), 75. Ernest Jones also claims that Max Eitingon was a supporter of the death drive theory. Ernest Jones, *Sigmund Freud: Life and Work*, 3 vols.(London: Hogarth, 1957), 3:298.

30. Gay, *Freud*, 552.

31. Fritz Wittels, *Sigmund Freud: His Personality, His Teaching, and His School* (London: Allen and Unwin, 1924), 251; Gay, *Freud*, 395.

32. Otto Fenichel, *The Psychoanalytic Theory of Neurosis* (London: Routledge and Kegan Paul, 1946), 60.

33. Heinz Hartmann, "Comments on the Psychoanalytic Theory of Instinctual Drives," *Psychoanalytic Quarterly* 17 (1948): 370.

34. Wilhelm Reich, *Reich Speaks of Freud*, ed. Mary Higgins and Chester Raphael (New York: Farrar, Straus and Giroux, 1967), 90.

35. To name just a few others: in a suggestive response to *Civilization and Its Discontents*, Karen Horney felt "obliged to reject the thesis of the death instinct and an innate destructive instinct, as well as the thesis of an innate evil in man." Karen Horney, "Der Kampf in Der Kultur [Culture and Aggression]: Einige Gedanken und Bedenken zu Freud's Todestrieb Und Destruktionstrieb," trans. Bella S. Van Bark, *American Journal of Psychoanalysis* 20 (1960): 136; Erich Fromm argued that while the death drive "takes into consideration the full weight of destructive tendencies," it "fails to take into account sufficiently of the fact that the amount of destructiveness varies enormously among individuals and social groups." Erich Fromm, *Escape from Freedom* (New York: Holt, 1969), 180–81; Donald Winnicott found "the term 'death' instinct unacceptable in describing the root of destructiveness." Donald Winnicott, "The Theory of the Parent-Infant Relationship," *International Journal of Psychoanalysis* 41 (1960): 591; and, finally, Heinz Kohut thought that the "concepts of Eros and Thanatos do not belong to a psychological theory." Heinz Kohut, "Introspection, Empathy, and Psychoanalysis—an Examination of the Relationship Between Mode of Observation and Theory," *Journal of the American Psychoanalytic Association* 7 (1959): 478.

36. There have, of course, been many rogue analytic writers who have attempted to salvage the death drive in some form, Karl Menninger perhaps being among the most prominent of them; see *Man Against Himself* (New York: Harcourt Brace, 1938). A wide-ranging bibliography can be found at "Death Drive," *Psychology Wiki*, http://psychology.wikia.com/wiki/Death_drive.

37. Although it was undoubtedly part of Klein's intention to have *gained* legitimacy in relating her theories to those of Freud, this endorsement only indicated her lack of scientific rigor to many analysts, resulting in the initial marginalization of her "school" from the Anglo-American "mainstream."

38. I am following many commentators here, including Hanna Segal, who argues that Klein was first interested in aggressive impulses in children and only later came to associate these impulses with Freud's death drive, which she employed as synonymous with aggression. Hanna Segal, *Melanie Klein* (New York: Penguin, 1979), 57. Todd Dufresne similarly argues that Klein was interested in "not so much the death drive itself, but its representative, the destructive impulse, *Destruktionstrieb*" (Dufresne, *Tales from the Freudian Crypt*, 69). Michael Eigen also finds the essentials of Klein's interest in the death drive in her discussion of a "primary anxiety of being annihilated by a destructive force within." Melanie Klein, *Envy and Gratitude and Other Works, 1946–1963* (New York: Free Press, 1975), 5; see Michael Eigen, *Psychic Deadness* (London: Karnac, 2004), 28.

39. Jean Laplanche, "The So-Called 'Death Drive,'" in *The Death Drive: New Life for a Dead Subject?*, ed. Rob Weatherill (London: Rebus, 1999), 45 (my emphasis).

40. The obvious reason for this change of heart would be outside pressure from his colleagues to abandon his speculative hypothesis, but I do not think that the elder Freud was that susceptible to external forces, especially where it concerned his major theoretical structures. The better explanation, to my mind, is that Freud offered only partially formed reflections in *Beyond the Pleasure Principle* that he himself did not know what to make of, and then, by working through the "economic problems" involved in his proposal as well as introducing the structural model into psychoanalysis, came to interpret his reflections as essentially related to aggression.

41. Pearl King and Riccardo Steiner, eds., *The Freud-Klein Controversies, 1941–45* (London: Routledge, 1992).

42. Lacan was one of the illustrious figures in attendance at Alexandre Kojève's celebrated lectures on Hegel, which stressed the importance of the "master/slave" dialectic for understanding Hegel's *Phenomenology*.

43. It is noteworthy that none of the participants in undoubtedly the most important colloquium ever convened on the topic of the death drive make any specific links between the death drive and primary aggressivity. Jean-François Rabain, "Compte rendu du colloque sur la pulsion de mort," *Revue Française de Psychanalyse* 53, no. 2 (1989): 767.

44. Jean Laplanche, "La pulsion de mort dans la théorie de la pulsion sexuelle," in *La Pulsion de Mort* (Paris: Presses Universitaires de France, 1986), 17.

45. Pierre Marty, *Les mouvements individuels de vie et de mort: Essay d'économie psychosomatique* (Paris: Payot, 1976), 120.

46. Piera Aulagnier, *The Violence of Interpretation: From Pictogram to Statement*, trans. Alan Sheridan (Hove: Brunner-Routledge, 2001), 20.

47. Julia Kristeva, *Revolution in Poetic Language*, trans. Margaret Waller (New York: Columbia University Press, 1984), 241.

48. Serge Leclaire, *A Child Is Being Killed: On Primary Narcissism and the Death Drive*, trans. Marie-Claude Hays (Stanford: Stanford University Press, 1998), 32–33.

49. André Green, *Life Narcissism, Death Narcissism*, trans. Andrew Weller (London: Free Association Books, 2001), 222.

50. Jacques Derrida, "Différance," in *Speech and Phenomena and Other Essays on Husserl's Theory of Signs*, trans. David B. Allison (Evanston: Northwestern University Press, 1973), 150.

51. Jacques Derrida, *Archive Fever: A Freudian Impression*, trans. Eric Prenowitz (Chicago: University of Chicago Press, 1996), 10.

52. Gilles Deleuze and Félix Guattari, *Anti-Oedipus: Capitalism and Schizophrenia*, trans. Robert Hurley et al. (Minneapolis: University of Minnesota Press, 1983), 329.

53. Slavoj Žižek, *The Parallax View* (Cambridge: MIT Press, 2006), 62.

54. Weber makes a similar argument against the Lacanian and Deleuzean appropriations of the death drive in *The Legend of Freud*, 121–22.

55. By "organic" and "inorganic," Freud means roughly "living" and "not-living." For attempts to translate Freud's theory into contemporary biological terms, see Rob Weatherill, *The Sovereignty of Death* (London: Rebus, 1998), chapter 5, and Thomas Hoffman, "Revival of the Death Instinct: A View from Contemporary Biology," *Neuropsychoanalysis* 6 (2004): 63–75.

56. Freud, *Standard Edition*, 18:38.

57. As Weber argues, without this addition (a *Da!* to complement his original *Fort!*), Freud's story could not have gotten off the ground: "Life, and with it the speculative theory of the death drive, would have imploded by virtue of its very immanence and intensity. It would have vanished into its nucleus. And nothing would ever have happened" (Weber, *The Legend of Freud*, 138).

58. Freud, *Standard Edition*, 18:26–27.

59. Ibid., 18:27 (my emphasis). In *The Post Card* Derrida erroneously claims that there is no mention of death in the text until Freud defines the term *instinct*: "Dead silence about death. It has not yet been mentioned. Almost half the book" (Derrida, *The Post Card,* 353). Freud's definition of an instinct comes on page 36 of the *Standard Edition* text. The passage given here is on page 27. Before an objection can be lodged, the discussion quickly turns to Heidegger and Freud on death (ibid., 358). Two hands!

60. *Reiz*, as James Strachey notes in *Civilization and Its Discontents*, "means 'stimulus' as well as 'charm' or 'attraction'" (Freud, *Standard Edition*, 21:83). What Freud is proposing, then, with this remarkable phrase, is that life itself depends on building a shield against that which the living being finds attractive, that by which the living being is charmed; to live, in other words, one must be protected from that toward which one is attracted, which is also to say that one must be protected from oneself.

61. Benno Rosenberg, *Masochisme mortifère et masochisme gardien de la vie* (Paris: Presses Universitaires de France, 1991), 157.

62. Weber describes this process as a kind of self "scorching" (Weber, *The Legend of Freud*, 142).

63. Freud, *Standard Edition*, 18:29.

64. Though I take the "tension-between" position to be roughly equivalent to Klein's paranoid-schizoid position (save for the fact that in the tension-between position, aggressive imposition is met not with aggression but the drive to mastery [see *n*69]), the "tension-within" position finds a similar correlate not in the depressive position but rather in what Thomas Ogden calls the "autistic-contiguous" position, which he imagines to be "before" yet constitutive of the "experience of bounded surfaces." Thomas Ogden, *Subjects of Analysis* (Lanham, MD: Rowman and Littlefield, 1977), 36.

65. Marcuse notices this same confusion of internal and external in Freud, but comes to conclude that it is the external influences that take priority (Marcuse, *Eros and Civilization*, 136–37). It is the externality of the external, however, that is called into question by Freud's narrative; see Jacqueline Rose, *Why War?—Psychoanalysis, Politics, and the Return to Melanie Klein* (Oxford: Blackwell, 1993), 94.

66. Freud, *Standard Edition*, 18:29.

67. Ibid., 18:30. Without distinguishing between the death drive and the drive to mastery, Pentti Ikonen and Eero Rechardt are forced to posit a "paradoxical double function of the death drive." Pentti Ikonen and Eero Rechardt, *Thanatos, Shame, and Other Essays: On the Psychology of Destructiveness* (London: Karnac, 2010), 100. While I am generally in sympathy with their "view that psychoanalytic aggression theory should not be limited to relate only to aggressive and destructive behaviour . . . but should be restored to its original scope, so as to make it again a theory of the death drive," I find that their own theory blurs rather than clarifies the distinctions between binding, mastery, aggression, etc. and disagree with their normative definition of the death drive as a "striving towards a state of peace," preferring to reserve the term *peace* for the postoedipal mimesis discussed in chapter 4 (ibid., 94).

68. Adrian Johnston presents a convincing case that all drives should be understood on the model of the death drive, i.e., as inherently split, "*designed to sabotage themselves.*" Adrian Johnston, *Time Driven: Metapsychology and the Splitting of the Drive* (Evanston: Northwestern University Press, 2005), 183. Though I agree that the death drive should indeed be conceived of as self-subverting, I would stress its specificity (that it is not simply a feature of drive in general) and that its being "self-defeating" is in fact *life-promoting* (ibid., 151). I would further take issue with his notion of *inherent* conflict: as I have articulated the developmental logic here, the death drive must *necessarily* come into conflict with itself, but this is something different than saying that it is *inherently* conflictual. In positing a "*temporal conflict*" internal to drive itself, Johnston avoids the actual sequence within which drive turns against itself and, for this reason, can only chalk up Freud's articulation of the reasons for the organism's "prolonging its own life" to confusion (ibid., 146, 127). The inclination to posit an "essential affinity of every drive with the zone

of death" comes from Lacan, who, like Johnston after him, attempts doggedly to square the pre- and post-1920 conceptions of drive, a task that I have explicitly renounced in the introduction. Jacques Lacan, *Seminar XI: The Four Fundamental Concepts of Psychoanalysis*, trans. Alan Sheridan (New York: Norton, 1981), 199; Johnston, *Time Driven*, 175.

69. Klein proposes this idea in "On the Development of Mental Functioning," but considers aggression rather than simple mastery to be the response to aggressive imposition: "Part of the death instinct is projected into the object, the object thereby becoming a persecutor; while that part of the death instinct which is retained in the ego causes aggression to be turned against that persecutory object" (Klein, *Envy and Gratitude*, 238). Rosenberg claims that the death drive is that which is primordially "expulsed-projected" in *Masochisme mortifère*, 156.

70. Freud, *Standard Edition*, 18:54.

71. See the discussion of libido in the next section.

72. Freud, *Standard Edition*, 18:51–52.

73. Ibid., 18:26.

74. Miriam Bratu Hansen, "Benjamin and Cinema: Not a One-Way Street," *Critical Inquiry* 25 (Winter 1999): 317.

75. Dorey, "The Relationship of Mastery," 329.

76. Freud, *Standard Edition*, 18:29.

77. Jean Laplanche, *Life and Death in Psychoanalysis*, trans. Jeffrey Mehlman (Baltimore: Johns Hopkins University Press, 1976), 57.

78. Freud, *Standard Edition*, 19:159–60. Freud had attempted to solve some of these issues in *The Ego and the Id*, though there he still equated the constancy principle with the pleasure principle. "The Economic Problem of Masochism" represents a decisive step forward in the acceptance of his new dual instinct theory insofar as he abandons the conception of pleasure that he had maintained for at least thirty years. For this reason, I believe it is somewhat misleading to speak of the "pleasure principle" after "The Economic Problem of Masochism."

79. Ibid., 19:160.

80. Ibid. Given what has been demonstrated thus far, I find Catherine Malabou's claim that there is ultimately no beyond of the pleasure principle in Freud (a point she uses to justify the claim that her "new wounded" cannot be understood within the confines of psychoanalytic theory) to be false. Catherine Malabou, *The New Wounded: From Neurosis to Brain Damage*, trans. Steven Miller (New York: Fordham University Press, 2002), 214.

81. Freud, *Standard Edition*, 14:148.

82. In the well-known joke about the broken kettle, A. defends himself against B.'s charges with the following: "First, I never borrowed a kettle from B. at all; secondly, the kettle had a hole in it already when I got it from him; and thirdly, I gave him back the kettle undamaged" (ibid., 8:62). Of course, any one of A.'s defenses would have worked on its own, but taken together they belie their own intent. The pleasure principle and the drive to mastery, along with their cooperation in the service of the libido, might be read in a similar fashion, as asserted over and against an unsettling fact to which the structure of their relations nonetheless attests. There is not self-mastery, there is other-mastery.

There is not zero principle, there is pleasure principle. There is not death drive, there is life drive.

83. Ibid., 19:160.

84. Ibid., 19:163.

85. On the priority of the death drive to Eros, see Louis Beirnaert, "La pulsion de mort chez Freud," *Études* 342 (March 1975): 401; J. B. Pontalis, "On Death-Work in Freud, in the Self, in Culture," in *Psychoanalysis, Creativity, and Literature: A French-American Inquiry*, ed. Alan Roland (New York: Columbia University Press, 1978), 86; Fátima Caropreso and Richard Theisen Simanke, "Life and Death in Freudian Metapsychology," in *On Freud's "Beyond the Pleasure Principle*," ed. Salman Akhtar and Mary Kay O'Neil (London: Karnac, 2011), 101–2.

86. This is my own way of making sense of the fact that Freud defended both an instinctual dualism and an energetic monism (I develop this idea further in the second section of the following chapter). Laplanche comes to the nearly opposed conclusion that libido is the sole psychic energy (noting that "destrudo" "did not survive a single day") and that the death drive is its "constitutive principle" (Laplanche, *Life and Death in Psychoanalysis*, 124).

87. Derrida, as I have already mentioned, devotes an entire section of *The Post Card* to the text of *Beyond the Pleasure Principle*, of which he offers an "athetic" reading, in recognition of "the essential impossibility of holding onto any thesis within it" (Derrida, *The Post Card*, 261). Relating Freud's speculative efforts not only to the death of his daughter Sophie (as Wittels had long ago done) but also to Freud's own position as authoritative "grandfather" (PP) of the psychoanalytic movement, Derrida argues that Freud himself is engaged in a "*Fort-Da*" in the text, with himself and with his theory of the death drive (ibid., 301). Freud is waffling, unable to decide, and this indecision is built into both the content and the form of *Beyond the Pleasure Principle*: "Freud does with (without) the object of his text exactly what Ernst does with (without) his spool" (ibid., 320). While Derrida's reading highlights a number of previously uninvestigated relations between *Beyond the Pleasure Principle*, the events of Freud's life, his philosophical struggles, and the crisis of his own authority that he creates in the text, his reading also suffers from this breadth, and I have offered, in the notes to this chapter, a few examples of how Derrida is much too libidinal to actually remain with the text.

88. Georges Bataille, *Theory of Religion*, trans. Robert Hurley (New York: Zone, 1989), 19. Françoise Dolto picks up on this idea in *La Vague et L'Océan*:

> Let's take the ocean to be the human species. Each wave is an individual who reaches the maximum of its possibilities of expression before, at the peak of its force, returning to the non-differentiation of the ocean's mass. In returning to this indifferentiation, the wave would represent, at the moment when it begins to fall, the experience of the death drives. Due to the momentum of the wave to maximally individualize itself at the moment of its breaking, there is a decrease in the very drive that formed the wave—is this not called "entropy?"—and a return to being a specimen of the human species; in other words, a return to the "it," until the moment when a new "I" will speak.

Françoise Dolto, *La Vague et l'océan: Séminaire sur les pulsions de mort* (Paris: Gallimard, 2003), 34.

89. Freud, *Standard Edition*, 18:26.

90. Roberto Esposito, *Immunitas: The Protection and Negation of Life*, trans. Zakiya Hanafi (Cambridge: Polity, 2011), 8–9.

91. Catherine Malabou highlights the normativity inherent in this conception of psychic health: "In the same way that the sculptor can only work upon a material that has a consistency somewhere between polymorphism and rigidity, the psychoanalyst is helpless to do anything with the material—that of the psyche—which is either too 'hard' or too 'soft'" (Malabou, *The New Wounded*, 175).

2. Between Need and Dread

The translation of the epigraph comes from William James, who was working from the French. William James, *Varieties of Religious Experience: A Study in Human Nature* (London: Routledge, 2002), 122. A direct translation reads: "I grew sick of life; some irresistible force was leading me to somehow get rid of it. It was not that I wanted to kill myself. The force that was leading me away from life was more powerful, more absolute, more all-encompassing than any desire. The thought of suicide came to me naturally then as the thought of improving life had come to me before." Leo Tolstoy, *Confession*, trans. David Patterson (New York: Norton, 1983), 28.

1. A self-professed ego-psychologist and by-the-book Freudian, Loewald was a clinical professor in psychiatry at Yale. Before emigrating to America in the forties, he had studied philosophy, his "first love," with Martin Heidegger (and even furnished extensive transcripts for his teacher's Marburg lecture course in 1924–25). James W. Jones, "Hans Loewald: The Psychoanalyst as Mystic," *Psychoanalytic Review* 88 (2001): 793; Theodore Kisiel, *The Genesis of Heidegger's "Being and Time"* (Berkeley: University of California Press, 1993), 540. When Loewald began publishing his own work in 1951, his work immediately resounded with the psychoanalytic establishment and yet seemed to point beyond its narrow dogmatism. He was an early supporter of Heinz Kohut's self-psychology "heresy," and in turn was accorded the title of "proto-postmodern" when self-psychologists turned "relationalists." Although his work has experienced a renaissance within American analytic circles in the last decade or two, it is still, unfortunately, largely unknown outside of them.

2. In "On Motivation and Instinct Theory," Loewald argues that "insofar as the death instinct can be equated with the constancy-inertia-unpleasure principle, the death instinct is nothing startlingly new in Freud's theory. . . . What *is* new in Freud's new instinct theory and in the structural theory is the life instinct as an intrinsic motive force of the psyche paired with the death instinct." Hans Loewald, *Papers on Psychoanalysis* (New Haven: Yale University Press, 1980), 124. The question as to why Loewald downplays the significance of the death drive, as well as avoids any systematic confrontation with it, is an open one. My suspicion

is that he felt perfectly comfortable to explore the basic themes of Freud's later metapsychology in his own language, without having unnecessarily to raise the hackles of his dogmatic colleagues in his chosen profession.

3. Ibid., 68. The Hans W. Loewald Papers collection at Yale offers bits of evidence for this claim of the secret (repressed?) importance of Freud's late metapsychology to Loewald. To take two examples: 1. In a letter to Paul Federn, Loewald writes, "Last night, in the Almanach der Psychoanalyse for 1951, I read your paper on 'Die Wirklichkeit des Todestrieb.' It reminded me of the fact that I had wanted to send you the enclosed paper which I had read last spring before the Baltimore Psychoanalytic Society. In this paper ["Ego and Reality"] I have not dared to concern myself with the problems of the death instinct, but with some, to me, less difficult and complex theoretical problems." Hans Loewald, "Loewald to Paul Federn," October 5, 1949, letter, Hans W. Loewald Papers, Manuscripts and Archives, Yale University Library, box 1, folder 2. 2. In the unpublished manuscript "Interpretation, Instinct, Personal Motivation" (the first four chapters of which were shortened into chapter 8 of *Papers on Psychoanalysis*, "On Motivation and Instinct Theory"), Loewald crosses out the following revealing passage: "At this point I must make a confession: to find my way through the tangle of speculative considerations put forth in 'Beyond the Pleasure Principle' in regard to instincts is beyond my present capacity or willingness. I will permit myself to cut through this gordic knot without attempting to untangle it." Hans Loewald, "Interpretation, Instinct, Personal Motivation," unpublished MS, Hans W. Loewald Papers, Manuscripts and Archives, Yale University Library, box 4, folder 73.

4. Cf. Stephen Mitchell, "From Ghosts to Ancestors: The Psychoanalytic Vision of Hans Loewald," *Psychoanalytic Dialogues* 8 (1998): 825–55; Jonathan Lear, "The Introduction of Eros: Reflections on the Work of Hans Loewald," *Journal of the American Psychoanalytic Association* 44 (1996): 673–98; Nancy Chodorow, "The Psychoanalytic Vision of Hans Loewald," *International Journal of Psychoanalysis* 84 (2003): 897–913; Alan Bass, *Difference and Disavowal: The Trauma of Eros* (Stanford: Stanford University Press, 2000), chapter 3.

5. As a word of warning for both this chapter and the next: like many "classic" psychoanalytic theorists, Loewald attributes a great amount of importance to the role of the mother for the life of a child that is, more often than not, imagined as male. For Loewald, the concept "mother" is formed in relation to a specific set of experiences—breastfeeding, holding, vibrations of the voice—where boundaries are diffuse (in contrast to "father," where the same experiences of closeness are supposedly absent). Since he most certainly has the biological mother in mind when employing this term (invoking things like in utero experiences and endocrine coordination), I do not find it appropriate to change *his* language, which I quote extensively; but since he is in fact speaking of a psychic representative and not a biological reality, when developing his ideas in my own words here I will use the gender-neutral terms *parent* or *caretaker* to mean the one who holds close, who feeds, who nurtures, who is the implied party in Winnicott's statement "There is no such thing as a baby." We can thus read Loewald as using the term

mother, like Bowlby, to indicate a primary caretaker or caretakers and affirm that many other persons, of different genders and in a variety of combinations, could serve this role besides the infant's biological mother. John Bowlby, "Separation Anxiety," *International Journal of Psycho-Analysis* 41 (1960): 101. I do not, however, simply mean to swap out problematic terms: I intend also to show, in the last section, that Loewald's developmental theory can be interpreted in such a way as to avoid the mistakes for which feminist theorists have rightly criticized certain psychoanalytic categories.

6. Loewald, *Papers on Psychoanalysis,* 4.

7. Loewald mentions the "biologistic" sections of *Beyond the Pleasure Principle* and the first chapter of *Civilization and Its Discontents* as the primary sources of this other narrative.

8. Loewald, *Papers on Psychoanalysis,* 5. A brief methodological note: in this chapter I will be treating Loewald's first publication, "Ego and Reality," as the core of his thought, and the rest of his work (encapsulated in his collection of essays titled *Papers on Psychoanalysis* and his two books, *Psychoanalysis and the History of the Individual* and *Sublimation*) as filling in the details of this initial articulation of his vision. Particular attention will be paid to his essays "Primary Process, Secondary Process, and Language" and "Internalization, Separation, Mourning, and the Superego" in their relation to "Ego and Reality," as the connections between these three pieces first inspired the writing of this chapter. While recognizing that Loewald's work followed an internal dynamic that led him to new positions over the years, I do not believe those developments prevent one from viewing it as a more or less consistent whole; that is, as offering a unified developmental theory.

9. I have refrained from using the category of narcissism in reference to what Loewald calls the "primordial density," though he himself is prone to employ it on occasion. The myth of Narcissus concerns the perils of identification with a specular other, which assumes at least a minimum of psychic differentiation; I will thus deal with the term *narcissism* in the next chapter on Lacan's mirror stage. While Freud's ambiguous speculations on primary narcissism have proven irresistible to many authors, I think it is a theoretical mistake to use the term to describe a psychic state lacking in clear self/other distinction.

10. Loewald, *Papers on Psychoanalysis,* 6.

11. This connection between the death drive and the mother is made by many others, including thinkers as divergent as Lacan, Marcuse, Goux, and Green and is thus in itself nothing novel. See Jacques Lacan, "Les complexes familiaux dans la formation de l'individu," in *Autres Écrits* (Paris: Seuil, 2001), 35; Herbert Marcuse, *Five Lectures: Psychoanalysis, Politics, and Utopia,* trans. Jeremy J. Shapiro and Shierry M. Weber (Boston: Beacon, 1970), 25; Jean-Joseph Goux, *Symbolic Economies: After Marx and Freud,* trans. Jennifer Curtiss Gage (Ithaca: Cornell University Press, 1990), 237; André Green, *Life Narcissism, Death Narcissism,* trans. Andrew Weller (London: Free Association, 2001), 83–84.

12. Loewald, *Papers on Psychoanalysis,* 11. Claude Le Guen similarly argues that the energy of the death drive is best situated as "a function of the originary id

(in other words, in that which precedes the distinction ego-id)." Claude Le Guen, "Du bon usage de la pulsion de mort," *Revue Française de Psychanalyse* 53, no. 2 (1989): 550.

13. Loewald, *Papers on Psychoanalysis*, 8.

14. Judith Butler, "The Pleasures of Repetition," in *Pleasure Beyond the Pleasure Principle*, ed. Robert A. Glick and Stanley Bone (New Haven: Yale University Press, 1990), 274.

15. See Karen Horney, "Observations on a Specific Difference in the Dread Felt by Men and by Women Respectively for the Opposite Sex," *International Journal of Psycho-Analysis* 13 (1932): 348–60; Dorothy Dinnerstein, *The Mermaid and the Minotaur* (New York: Other Press, 1999), chapter 7.

16. Loewald, *Papers on Psychoanalysis*, 16.

17. Loewald relies on the early Fliess papers to elaborate his conception of fantasy: "[Freud] speaks there of *phantasies* as 'psychical façades constructed in order to bar the way to these memories'—memories, that is, of what he calls 'primal scenes.' . . . In a letter to Fliess of the same date, he describes phantasies as 'protective structures [*Schutzbauten*].' . . . At another point in the same letter he speaks of phantasies as *Schutzdichtungen*, protective fictions." Hans Loewald, *Sublimation: Inquiries Into Theoretical Psychoanalysis* (New Haven: Yale University Press, 1988), 1–2. Although Loewald prefers to render the German *Phantasie* as "phantasy," I will use the more common term *fantasy*, as I remain unconvinced that a technical term is needed here.

18. Loewald, *Papers on Psychoanalysis*, 83. According to Adam Phillips, "one mothers oneself, or rather foster-mothers one's self, with one's mind." Adam Phillips, *Kissing, Tickling, and Being Bored: Psychoanalytic Essays on the Unexamined Life* (Cambridge: Harvard University Press, 1993), 44.

19. Eugenio Gaddini, "On Imitation," *International Journal of Psychoanalysis* 50 (1969): 476.

20. Loewald, *Papers on Psychoanalysis*, 83.

21. "Mourning has acquired the status of a quasi-religious concept in psychoanalysis," at the center of contemporary psychoanalytic theory's understanding of the genesis of the psyche. Adam Phillips, "Keeping it Moving," in Judith Butler, *The Psychic Life of Power* (Stanford: Stanford University Press, 1997), 153. Loewald's place at the beginning of this emergence has not been appreciated.

22. Loewald, *Papers on Psychoanalysis*, 263.

23. Ibid., 263.

24. According to Joel Whitebook, "Loewald introduces a distinction between 'mastery' as 'domination,' that is, domination of inner nature by the imperious subject (cf. Freud's image of the draining of the Zuider Zee), and mastery as 'coming to grips with.' One assumes that, in 'coming to grips with,' the imperious subject is itself civilized, which is to say, simultaneously decentered and naturalized." Joel Whitebook, *Perversion and Utopia: A Study in Psychoanalysis and Critical Theory* (Cambridge: MIT Press, 1995), 253. In this chapter, I am using *mastery* in this second sense of "coming to grips with," which I have identified in the previous chapter with *Bewältigung*.

25. Phillips, *Kissing, Tickling, and Being Bored*, 24.

26. Loewald, *Papers on Psychoanalysis*, 14.

27. Though Loewald was critical of Jung's religious leanings, in this positive appraisal of what I am calling the tension-within position, they were aligned: according to Jung, the "temporary withdrawal into one's self, which, as we have already seen, signifies a regression to the childish bond to the parent, seems to act favorably, within certain limits, in its effect upon the psychologic condition of the individual." C. G. Jung, *Psychology of the Unconscious: A Study of the Transformations and Symbolisms of the Libido*, trans. Beatrice M. Hinkle (New York: Moffat, Yard, 1917), 201.

28. Wherein "there is some prior condition" that is disrupted, leading to "a kind of redemptive hope that we can recover a sense of that prior condition." Jonathan Lear, "The Slippery Middle," in Axel Honneth, *Reification: A New Look at an Old Idea* (Oxford: Oxford University Press, 2008), 131–32. The "occupational hazard" here is not the simple assumption of a prior condition but the "tendency . . . to build too much goodness into the prior condition" (ibid., 132).

29. A brief point on historical specificity: I believe the clarity of the distinctions between, on the one hand, the "other" and tension-within reality and, on the other hand, the *other* and tension-between reality, is what distinguishes the bourgeois/ modern psyche from its prebourgeois counterpart. In constraining the number of identifications made by the child—and in turn the diffusiveness of emotional connection—within the nuclear family, the "other"/*other* takes on a role of heightened importance in psychic development.

30. Bass's understandable but ultimately misplaced claim that Loewald does not deal with "internalization anxiety," and thus that he makes it seem as if "an intrinsic drive toward integration will take care of itself," must be understood as an effect of the absence of any discussion on his part of the need/dread of union in relation to the two realities (Bass, *Difference and Disavowal*, 114). I agree that Loewald does indeed present an overly tidy picture of psychic development (see chapter 3), but on the perils of internalization he is perfectly clear.

31. In Bass's words, "the permeable border between internal and external becomes a rigid opposition" (ibid., 102). I take this language of "overbuilding" from Winnicott, who speaks of "the *overgrowth* of the mental function reactive to erratic mothering." D. W. Winnicott, "Mind and Its Relation to the Psyche-Soma," in *Through Paediatrics to Psycho-Analysis: Collected Papers* (New York: Brunner-Routledge, 1992), 246 (my emphasis). Lacan also refers to the ego as an "overly strong structure." Jacques Lacan, *Écrits*, trans. Bruce Fink (New York: Norton, 2002), 265.

32. Loewald, *Papers on Psychoanalysis*, 23. In "The Concept of Cumulative Trauma," Masud Khan argues for the exact opposite of what is being proposed here: that the mother and the associated "holding environment" are equivalent to Freud's *Reizschutz*. M. Masud R. Khan, "The Concept of Cumulative Trauma," *Psychoanalytic Study of the Child* 18 (1963): 290. For Loewald, parents are not themselves "stimulus barriers" in Freud's sense but rather prevent an overbuilding of this barrier (which is itself a kind of protection).

33. To follow this idea to its unfortunate conclusion: a certain amount of dread is necessary to healthy psychic development, as this dread is an indicator of attempts at parental mutuality, attempts that have failed in a particular instance but that may be part of a more general care structure that is "good enough." Excessive dread would then mean a parental inability to allow individuation and an icy lack of dread that the tension-within position has never been properly maintained.

34. Loewald, *Papers on Psychoanalysis*, 29.

35. I am unprepared to say how precisely we ought to understand this claim: although he seems to indicate that it is a *social* crisis that has produced an overly defensive individual, it is difficult to avoid the conclusion that it is also a *familial* crisis (i.e., the result of more parental frustration than gratification). Isaac Balbus has convincingly argued for the relation between these two in *Marxism and Domination: A Neo-Hegelian, Feminist, Psychoanalytic Theory of Sexual, Political, and Technological Liberation* (Princeton: Princeton University Press, 1982) and also "Patriarchal 'Production' in Marx," in *Mourning and Modernity: Essays in the Psychoanalysis of Contemporary Society* (New York: Other Press, 2005). In general, Loewald's brief forays into cultural critique are as vague as his psychoanalytic insights are incisive.

36. Bass, *Difference and Disavowal*, 102, 103. Rahel Jaeggi, *Alienation*, ed. Frederick Neuhouser, trans. Frederick Neuhouser and Alan E. Smith (New York: Columbia University Press, 2014), 6, 202.

37. Loewald, *Papers on Psychoanalysis*, 30.

38. In *Walled States, Waning Sovereignty*, Wendy Brown turns to Sigmund and Anna Freud's respective theories of defense to explain what "psychic reassurances or palliative walls provide amid . . . the loss of horizons, order, and identity attending the decline of state sovereignty." Wendy Brown, *Walled States, Waning Sovereignty* (Brooklyn: Zone, 2010), 107. One might object, with Loewald, that "walling" is not a defensive reaction to the supposed weakness of a sublimated father figure but rather an overbuilding of structure in response to failed mutuality.

39. I am making a connection here and before between identification and imitation as they lead to internalization, one that is, while not explicit in Loewald, implied in his heavy reliance on Werner and Kaplan's *Symbol Formation*, where the capacity for delayed imitation "at some temporal remove from the presentation of content" is said to manifest the existence of "some kind of *internal model or 'schema.'*" Heinz Werner and Bernard Kaplan, *Symbol Formation: An Organismic-Developmental Approach to Language and the Expression of Thought* (New York: Wiley, 1964), 91. In other words, the psyche's architecture is a product of imitative behaviors that have gained the child a certain independence; in Werner and Kaplan's words, "the liberation of gestural depiction from concretely presented content," i.e., the ability to do more than just respond co-actively or reactively to the present (ibid., 91).

40. See the conclusion, n1.

41. Loewald, *Papers on Psychoanalysis*, 11. Or, as Freud writes: "The backward path that leads to complete satisfaction is as a rule obstructed by the resistances

which maintain the repressions. So there is no alternative but to advance in the direction in which growth is still free—though with no prospect of bringing the process to a conclusion or of being able to reach the goal." Sigmund Freud, *The Standard Edition of the Complete Psychological Works of Sigmund Freud*, ed. and trans. James Strachey, 24 vols. (London: Hogarth and the Institute of Psycho-Analysis, 1966), 18:42.

42. Michael Eigen, *The Electrified Tightrope*, ed. Adam Phillips (London: Karnac, 2004), xix.

43. The "rewriting" of the death drive accomplished therein is characterized by what Freud called *Nachträglichkeit*, or "afterwardsness," in Jean Laplanche's translation. Freud had introduced this term in the *Project for a Scientific Psychology* in discussion of the case of Emma, who, at eight years of age, is sexually assaulted by a shopkeeper (about whom she can only remember his laugh; Freud, *Standard Edition*, 1:353). On a shopping trip at eighteen years, someone happens to laugh at her clothes, and this seemingly benign gesture sets off hysterical symptoms. The temporality of this episode is what interests Freud most: it is not that her encounter at age eight *becomes* sexual at eighteen, but rather that it becomes *retroactively* sexual at eight. She is guilty *après-coup*. To put it in the awkward tense of the future perfect, her episode at eight *will have been* traumatic. In a similar way, it is not that the *arche* of the tension-within position becomes the ego-ideal *telos* after a certain developmental accomplishment, but that *the arche will have been the telos*, that the primordial density toward which the child bears an urge to union is "rewritten" as the ideal future toward which the ego strives.

44. "Sublimation . . . involves an internal re-creative return toward [the mother-infant matrix], a reconciliation of the polarized elements produced by individuation and, one may suspect, by sexual differentiation. Sublimation thus brings together what had become separate" (Loewald, *Sublimation*, 21–22).

45. Loewald, *Papers on Psychoanalysis*, 45.

46. Søren Kierkegaard, *The Concept of Dread*, trans. Walter Lowrie (Princeton: Princeton University Press, 1957), 90. Mark C. Taylor draws the parallel between Kierkegaard's stages and the psychoanalytic developmental model in *Kierkegaard's Pseudonymous Authorship: A Study of Time and the Self* (Princeton: Princeton University Press, 1975), 73–74.

47. Loewald explains the interpenetrating and temporal nature of the relation between id, ego, and superego as follows:

> The id, if it can be said to represent the inherited past, the degree and quality of organization with which we are born, has a future insofar as we make it ours by acquiring it, by imprinting on it the stamp of ego organization. Insofar as this is an unfinished task, and to the extent to which we experience it as an unfinished, never-finished task, our superego is developed. The superego then would represent the past as seen from a future, the id as it is *to be organized*, whereas the ego proper represents the id as organized at present.

(Loewald, *Papers on Psychoanalysis*, 49)

48. The overlap here with the views of Jean Laplanche is striking and deserving of longer treatment, but in brief: for Laplanche, drives are formed in response to the "difference between that which is symbolizable and that which is not in the originary enigmatic messages" received from adults. Jean Laplanche, *Nouveaux fondements pour la psychanalyse* (Paris: Press Universitaires de France, 1987), 141. This conception of drive is at the base of his rejuvenation of the seduction theory as a "generalized" one. In his formulation, the death drive and Eros should be understood as elicited by the same "object-source" (the parents), though the death drive responds to that source as Kleinian "part-object" (thus leading to "unbinding" [*déliaison*]) while Eros does the same for the "total-object" (ibid., 144). While Loewald would appreciate Laplanche's "relational" understanding of drive, agreeing with Laplanche that drives emerge in response to the demands of early developmental life, I believe that he would worry that too much emphasis is being placed on the infant's confrontation with "messages that do not make any sense to him" to the neglect of the infant's affective pull toward the caretaker (ibid., 148). Similarly, while he would also agree that the death drive and Eros share more than they are typically thought to, he would object to the idea that the death drive is one of "unbinding," since it is actual *union* that is its aim. He would thus oppose death drive and Eros not along the axis *déliaison/liaison* but rather actual union/symbolic union.

49. Eigen, *The Electrified Tightrope*, 78. Loewald would agree with Jean Gillibert that both Eros and the death drive "*limit* the madness of mastery," but disagree that this mastery should be understood *primarily* as a "possessive power." Jean Gillibert, "De l'objet pulsionnel de la pulsion d'emprise," *Revue Française de Psychanalyse* 46, no. 6 (1982): 1223.

50. As Loewald argues, to have a superego is to recognize that autonomy is a crime against the sacred parental bond, to feel guilt about the conflict between id dependence and ego independence, and to attempt to atone for this "parricide" by transmuting oedipal relations "into internal, intrapsychic structural relations" (Loewald, *Papers on Psychoanalysis*, 389). I mean by "the appropriation of its own method of construction" here what Loewald calls "secondary internalization" (ibid., 266).

51. See Whitebook, *Perversion and Utopia*, 246–57.

52. One might call this process, with Hegel, a "purification of the drives" (*Reinigung der Triebe*), by which he means (negative connotations of the term *purification* aside) not their elimination but rather their being freed from immediacy and contingency as the individual "makes them his own, puts them in himself as his own" or, in language less appealing to a psychoanalyst, as the drives are taken up into "the rational system of the will's volitions." G. W. F. Hegel, *The Philosophy of Right*, trans. T. M. Knox (Oxford: Oxford University Press, 1967), 28, 229, 29.

53. A distinction must be made between binding in the service of mastery and binding into ever greater unities, i.e., binding in the service of Eros, though the two are related: it is the latter that prevents the former from leading to ego rigidity.

54. Loewald, *Papers on Psychoanalysis*, 187.

55. Cf. Walter Benjamin, "On Language as Such and the Language of Man," in *Selected Writings*, ed. Marcus Bullock and Michael Jennings, 4 vols. (Cambridge: Belknap, 2004), 1:68; Martin Jay, *Songs of Experience: Modern American and European Variations on a Universal Theme* (Berkeley: University of California Press, 2005), 320.

56. "Language . . . develops within the growing differentiation between self and object-world" (Loewald, *Papers on Psychoanalysis*, 191).

57. Ibid., 180.

58. Like Robert Pogue Harrison, Loewald thus posits an "underlying nexus between grief and human vocalization." Robert Pogue Harrison, *The Dominion of the Dead* (Chicago: University of Chicago Press, 2003), 62. According to Harrison, "it is through that shared, objective language of grief that the work of separation begins to take place" (ibid., 58).

59. Freud, *Standard Edition*, 19:46.

60. As Freud himself spells out this connection, "the ego is that portion of the id which was modified by the proximity and influence of the external world, which is adapted for the reception of stimuli and as a protective shield against stimuli, comparable to the cortical layer by which a small piece of living substance is surrounded" (ibid., 22: 75).

61. Loewald, *Papers on Psychoanalysis*, 190.

62. Ibid., 188.

63. Ibid., 189.

64. Unlike Lacan and Žižek, who conceive of language as a "mortifying mechanism," the speaking subject being an effect of subjection to "symbolic death," Loewald sees in the waning of the Oedipus complex a revivification, an entrance into a second life. Slavoj Žižek, *Organs Without Bodies: On Deleuze and Consequences* (New York: Routledge, 2004), 120.

65. "The Greek *symbolon* is actually a shard. It was the custom, when a friendship was ritually confirmed, to break a small clay tablet in two parts. Each of the two friends took one piece along on his life's journey, and when the friends, or their descendants, met again, the clay tablet could be reconstructed by fitting the two broken edges together, thus affirming the friendship. The primary layer of meaning of *symbolon* thus includes both the break and the wish for an unbroken union." Christoph Türcke, *Philosophy of Dreams*, trans. Susan Gillespie (New Haven: Yale University Press, 2013), 31.

66. Samuel Weber, *The Legend of Freud* (Minneapolis: University of Minnesota Press, 1982), 45.

67. Loewald, *Papers on Psychoanalysis*, 188.

68. Ibid.

69. Loewald, *Sublimation*, 60.

70. Theodor W. Adorno, "Theses on the Language of the Philosopher," in *Adorno and the Need in Thinking: Critical Essays*, ed. Donald Burke et al. (Toronto: University of Toronto Press, 2007), 38.

71. John Bowlby, "The Nature of the Child's Tie to His Mother," *International Journal of Psychoanalysis* 39 (1958): 350, 351, 369.

72. Ibid., 364.

73. Ibid., 366.

74. Bowlby nonetheless did his best to reconcile his theories with those of Freud, pandering: "In stressing the survival value of the five component instinctual responses we are put in mind of Freud's concepts of libido and Life instinct. Not only is there the same emphasis on survival, but the means of achieving it—a binding together—is the same: 'Eros desires contact because it strives to make the ego and the loved object one, to abolish the barriers of distance between them.' Despite the starting points of the two theories being so different, and their having different implications, the themes appear to be the same" (ibid., 369). It is a gross misinterpretation, of course, to say that Freud's "Life instinct" is a "survival instinct," no less than that the abolition of barriers of distance between ego and object is the means to achieve some kind of evolutionary advantage.

75. Ibid., 362 and 369.

76. Ibid., 371.

77. Taking up the survivalist emphasis of attachment theory in *The Psychic Life of Power*, Butler attributes attachment to a Spinozist "desire to persist in one's own being," one that she wrongly attributes to Freud (Butler, *The Psychic Life of Power*, 28). Attachment, in my view, is precisely the opposite of a desire to persist in one's being: it is a desperate attempt to refuse the overwhelming nature of *one's* being for the comfort of being-with (or perhaps, as Winnicott has argued, simply *being*). D. W. Winnicott, *Human Nature* (New York: Brunner/Mazel, 1988), 127.

78. Bowlby, of course, takes it as axiomatic that "psychological characteristics are subject to the" "interests of species propagation" (Bowlby, "Separation Anxiety," 95).

79. Adrian Johnston, *Time Driven: Metapsychology and the Splitting of the Drive* (Evanston: Northwestern University Press, 2005), 166.

80. According to Laplanche, "from the start, there is something more than an 'attachment' in the simply literal sense of the term." Jean Laplanche, *Freud and the Sexual: Essays 2000–2006*, ed. John Fletcher, trans. John Fletcher et al. (New York: International Psychoanalytic, 2011), 17.

81. Mary Ainsworth further distanced attachment theory from this line of thought by describing "an attachment bond not as dyadic, but rather as characteristic of the individual, 'entailing representation in the internal organization of the individual.'" Jude Cassidy, "The Nature of the Child's Ties," in *Handbook of Attachment, Second Edition: Theory, Research, and Clinical Applications*, ed. Jude Cassidy and Phillip R. Shaver (New York: Guilford, 2008), 12.

82. Bowlby, "The Nature of the Child's Tie to His Mother," 359.

83. Daniel Stern, *The Interpersonal World of the Infant: A View from Psychoanalysis and Developmental Psychology* (London: Karnac, 1998), 10.

84. Ibid., 46. I am especially wary of this latter projection claim: when dealing with the world of the infant, most every description could be accused of the same (and attributing a sense of "self" to the neonate seems particularly ripe for this kind of criticism).

85. Jessica Benjamin, *The Bonds of Love: Psychoanalysis, Feminism, and the Problem of Domination* (New York: Pantheon, 1988), 184. See also Michael Eigen's critique of Marion Milner's use of "undifferentiation" in *The Electrified Tightrope*, 164–71.

86. Jessica Benjamin, *Like Subjects, Love Objects: Essays on Recognition and Sexual Difference* (New Haven: Yale University Press, 1995), 99.

87. Cf. Isaac Balbus, "Between Enemies and Friends: Carl Schmitt, Melanie Klein, and the Passion(s) of the Political," *Theoria and Praxis* 1, no. 1 (2013): 47, n115. For this reason, though I will be avoiding the term *undifferentiation* in what follows, I will retain other terms like *oneness, wholeness,* and *unity,* all of which accurately describe the feeling of what I am calling the tension-within position.

88. Bass, *Difference and Disavowal,* 117; Bracha Ettinger, "Matrixial Trans-subjectivity," *Theory, Culture, and Society* 23, nos. 2–3 (2006): 219; Eigen, *The Electrified Tightrope,* 171; Stern, *The Interpersonal World of the Infant,* 27. Loewald would also be in agreement with Ettinger that object relations theorists tend to reduce the caretaker to a function—Bion's "container" or Winnicott's "holding environment"—when early developmental life ought to be understood as a dynamic coemergence within a caretaker-infant "matrix" (Loewald, *Sublimation,* 33).

89. Eigen, *The Electrified Tightrope,* 157.

90. Just as I find the turn to the closely allied relational theory an overreaction to the theory of intrapsychic drives; see, for instance, Lynne Layton, "Relational Thinking: from Culture to Couch and Couch to Culture," in *Object Relations and Social Relations: The Implications of the Relational Turn in Psychoanalysis,* ed. Simon Clarke et al. (London: Karnac, 2008), 3. In claiming that drives are "connection-seeking" relational phenomena, Loewald did a great deal to preemptively defuse the drive versus relational theory debate. Stephen A. Mitchell and Margaret J. Black, *Freud and Beyond: A History of Modern Psychoanalytic Thought* (New York: Basic Books, 1995), 189–90.

91. As Loewald rightly points out, however, it is unclear that primary narcissism was ever meant in this way. As Freud describes it in "Civilization and Its Discontents," primary narcissism is related to "a feeling of an indissoluble bond, of being one with the external world as a whole" (Freud, *Standard Edition,* 21:65). Indeed, in the many divergent directions in which this idea is developed by later thinkers, it rarely indicates the atomism it is commonly supposed to signify; see D. W. Winnicott, "Metapsychological and Clinical Aspects of Regression Within the Psycho-Analytical Set-Up," *International Journal of Psycho-Analysis* 36 (1955): 19; Margaret S. Mahler, Fred Pine, and Anni Bergman, *The Psychological Birth of the Human Infant: Symbiosis and Individuation* (New York: Basic Books, 1975), 42; Heinz Kohut, "Forms and Transformations of Narcissism," *Journal of the American Psychoanalytic Association* 14 (1966): 245–46; Béla Grunberger, *Narcissism: Psychoanalytic Essays,* trans. Joyce S. Diamanti (New York: International Universities Press, 1979), 107.

92. For an excellent critique of intersubjectivism in both psychoanalysis and critical theory, see Joel Whitebook, "Mutual Recognition and the Work of

the Negative," in *Pluralism and the Pragmatic Turn: Essays in Honor of Thomas McCarthy*, ed. James Bohman and William Rehg (Cambridge: MIT Press, 2001), 257–83.

93. Sigmund Freud and Lou Andreas-Salomé, *Sigmund Freud and Lou Andreas-Salomé: Letters*, ed. Ernst Pfeiffer, trans. William and Elaine Robson-Scott (London: Hogarth, 1966), 154.

94. As Laplanche puts it, "there is surely a death of the psyche by disintegration, death by the death drive, but there is also a kind of psychic death by rigidification and excessive synthesis, psychic death by the ego" (Laplanche, *Nouveaux fondements pour la psychanalyse*, 146).

95. Just as it is the inorganic *Reizschutz* that creates the conditions for the favorable "reception of stimuli" for Freud.

96. For both thinkers, it is wrong then to oppose psychic maturity *qua* bounded and stable ego and *qua* dynamic and many-sided relatedness: in Eli Zaretsky's words, "the ego reaches down into its earliest, most primal, and essentially immortal dependencies precisely when it is strongest and most independent. Eli Zaretsky, *Political Freud: A History* (New York: Columbia University Press, 2015), 147.

97. Freud, *Standard Edition*, 19:53. On one level, the claim that the death drive finds expression in the superego has been upheld, though with new conception of the death drive.

98. While Freud tended to present the superego in an overwhelmingly negative light, as the enforcer of an inwardly directed aggression, he also hinted at another side of the superego, one that could, "in humour, [speak] such kindly words of comfort to the intimidated ego" (ibid., 21: 166). His conclusion was an open one: "we have still a great deal to learn about the nature of the super-ego" (ibid., 21: 166). After Freud, a great many analysts found it helpful to distinguish "good" and "bad" sides of the superego, or to separate the "ego-ideal" from the superego, in recognition that some part of what Freud described under the name superego was a positive influence on the psyche as a whole. See J. C. Flugel, *Studies in Feeling and Desire* (London: Duckworth, 1955), 145; Roy Schafer, "The Loving and Beloved Superego in Freud's Structural Theory," *Psychoanalytic Study of the Child* 15 (1960): 163–88; Joseph Sandler, Alex Holder, and Dale Meers, "The Ego Ideal and the Ideal Self," *Psychoanalytic Study of the Child* 18 (1963): 139–58; Jacob A. Arlow, "Problems of the Superego Concept," *Psychoanalytic Study of the Child* 37 (1982): 229–44. The death drive itself has also found some explicitly positive valuation: for instance, in Le Guen, "Du bon usage de la pulsion de mort," 554; Benno Rosenberg, *Masochisme mortifère et masochisme gardien de la vie* (Paris: Presses Universitaires de France, 1991), 156; and Donna Bentolila López, "The Enigma of the Death Drive: A Revisiting," *Psychoanalysis and Contemporary Thought* 19 (1996): 17.

99. Mitchell similarly understands Loewald as emphasizing "dialectical tensions between discontinuous organizations rather than synthesis." Stephen A. Mitchell, "Juggling Paradoxes: Commentary on the Work of Jessica Benjamin," *Studies in Gender and Sexuality* 1, no. 3 (2000): 260.

100. His understanding of the agencies as temporally oriented attests most strongly to the truth of this claim: if "the superego would represent the past as seen from the future, the id as it is *to be organized,* and the ego proper represents the id as organized at present," then the collapse of any of these agencies into the other would mean the closing of a temporal mode (Loewald, *Papers on Psychoanalysis,* 49). Loewald argues here that seeing these three psychic structures as delimiting and modifying one another allows "a more refined concept of self" (ibid., 50).

101. Lacan, *Écrits,* 82.

3. Aggressivity in Psychoanalysis (Reprised)

1. Konrad Lorenz, *On Aggression,* trans. Marjorie Kerr Wilson (London: Routledge, 2002).

2. Hannah Arendt, *On Violence* (New York: Harcourt Brace Jovanovich, 1970), 69.

3. Erich Fromm, *The Anatomy of Human Destructiveness* (New York: Holt, Rinehart and Winston, 1973), 81.

4. Lorenz, *On Aggression,* 235; Arendt, *On Violence,* 5; Fromm, *The Anatomy of Human Destructiveness,* appendix.

5. As opposed to aggression (*agression*), which "originates in the frustration of a [biological] impulse," aggressivity has its origin in psychic conflict. Richard Boothby, *Death and Desire: Psychoanalytic Theory in Lacan's Return to Freud* (London: Routledge, 1991), 38. Although this term is admittedly rather awkward, I find it better than Bruce Fink's translation, "aggressiveness," which erases some of the distinction Lacan was trying to impose. At times, Fink himself tellingly translates *agressivité* as "aggression"; see, for instance, Jacques Lacan, *Écrits,* trans. Bruce Fink (New York: Norton, 2002), 387.

6. The best treatment of these influences of which I am aware is Dany Nobus, "Life and Death in the Glass: A New Look at the Mirror Stage," in *Key Concepts of Lacanian Psychoanalysis,* ed. Dany Nobus (New York: Other Press, 1999), 101–38.

7. Lacan typically situates the death drive in relation to the symbolic ("the death drive . . . is articulated at a level that can only be defined as a function of the signifying chain"), though a good case could also be made for its more essential relation to the real. Jacques Lacan, *The Seminar of Jacques Lacan, Book VII: The Ethics of Psychoanalysis,* ed. Jacques-Alain Miller, trans. Dennis Porter (New York: Norton, 1997), 211; Lionel Bailly, *Lacan* (Oxford: Oneworld, 2009), 99, 140. Although I would agree that investigating these other connections (between Freudian death drive and Lacanian symbolic/Lacanian real) rather than the present one (between Freudian death drive and Lacanian imaginary) might more adequately elucidate Lacan's own understanding of the death drive, this task, as I explain here, is not the one I take up in this chapter.

8. Jacques Lacan, *The Seminar of Jacques Lacan, Book I: Freud's Papers on Technique, 1953–1954,* ed. Jacques-Alain Miller, trans. John Forrester (New York: Norton, 1991), 148.

9. Jonathan Lear recognizes this fact in "The Thought of Hans W. Loewald," but argues that faulting him for this "grievous lapse" is "not a good way to read him:" "Rather, we should see Loewald as struck by the beauty of an ur-observation: that when human beings are located in a field of psychological complexity, there is a tendency for them to grow in complexity themselves. The differential in complexity thus serves as the occasion for dynamism. Psychological growth is regularly blocked, inhibited and sometimes attacked; but the tendency toward it is there." Jonathan Lear, "The Thought of Hans W. Loewald," *International Journal of Psychoanalysis* 93 (2012): 178. It seems to me, however, that the theorization of a major developmental obstacle to this growth should be part of his conception of growth. Furthermore, it is difficult to avoid those passages where he goes out of his way to avoid any talk of hatred and aggression: for instance, in "The Waning of the Oedipus Complex," when he interprets parricide (a rupturing of the "sacred bond" tying the child to the parents) in terms of guilt over one's autonomy and not in terms of any aggressive urges.

10. What I say of the concept "mother" in *n*5 of the previous chapter goes here as well.

11. Lacan, *Écrits*, 75–76.

12. Lacan, *Seminar I*, 79. Or in Philippe Julien's: "The mirror effects a victory over the fragmentation of the disjointed members and assures motor coordination." Philippe Julien, *Jacques Lacan's Return to Freud: The Real, the Symbolic, and the Imaginary*, trans. Devra Beck Simiu (New York: New York University Press, 1994), 31.

13. Lacan, *Écrits*, 120. Although his exemplary case is a nonvisually impaired child before an *actual* mirror, Lacan would claim both that "all sorts of things in the world behave like mirrors" and also that merely knowing that one "is an object of other people's gazes" is a sufficient condition of imaginary identification (and thus, contrary to the claims of some critics, that the blind do indeed have egos). Jacques Lacan, *The Seminar of Jacques Lacan, Book II: The Ego in Freud's Theory and in the Technique of Psychoanalysis, 1954–1955*, ed. Jacques-Alain Miller, trans. Sylvana Tomaselli (New York: Norton, 1991), 49; Lacan, *Écrits*, 56; Raymond Tallis, *Not Saussure: A Critique of Post-Saussurean Literary Theory* (London: Palgrave Macmillan, 1995), 153; Richard Webster, "The Cult of Lacan: Freud, Lacan, and the Mirror stage," *richardwebster.net*, 2002, http://www.richardwebster.net/the cultoflacan.html.

14. Lacan, *Écrits*, 78. Without investing itself in this image, the child would lack a "bridge to the Symbolic" (Bailly, *Lacan*, 96).

15. Lacan, *Écrits*. 94, 92. Julien argues that around 1964, the function of the mirror stage is detached from the task of "mastery through vision" and situated in the gap created by the gaze of the Other (Julien, *Jacques Lacan's Return to Freud*, 161–62). As I will argue in a moment, Lacan was already focusing on the gap created by the gaze of the Other as early as the 1956–57 seminar, not as an alternative to the mastery paradigm but as a supplement to it.

16. Lacan, *Écrits*, 89.

17. Ibid., 118.

18. Ibid., 91, 78.

19. Boothby, *Death and Desire*, 39. Boothby makes it seem as if the second interpretation of aggressivity is a gross misconstrual of Lacan's intentions, but there are passages to support both positions: though there are times when he speaks of a "need to aggressively strike out at this ideal," there are many others where he finds aggressivity in the pursuit of an ideal, most notably in "good-Samaritan" activities: "[aggressivity] underlies the activities of the philanthropist, the idealist, the pedagogue, and even the reformer" (Lacan, *Écrits*, 138, 79, 81).

20. Ibid., 286; Boothby, *Death and Desire*, 45.

21. Jacques Lacan, *The Seminar of Jacques Lacan, Book X: Anxiety, 1962–1963*, ed. Jacques Alain-Miller, trans. A. R. Price (Cambridge: Polity, 2014), 32. Cf. Lacan, *Écrits*, 55–56.

22. Bailly, *Lacan*, 36.

23. Jacques Lacan, *Le Séminaire de Jacques Lacan, livre IV: La relation d'objet*, ed. Jacques-Alain Miller (Paris: Seuil, 1994), 186.

24. Ibid., 169.

25. Ibid., 193. A child's relationship with its mother is, according to Lacan, "constituted in analysis not by the child's biological dependence, but by its dependence on her love, that is, by its desire for her desire," spurring the child to identify "with the imaginary object of her desire insofar as the mother herself symbolizes it in the phallus" (Lacan, *Écrits*, 462–63).

26. Lacan, *Séminaire IV*, 194.

27. Ibid.

28. Lacan, *Seminar I*, 81–82. Cf. "What the subject finds in this altered image of his body is the paradigm of all the forms of resemblance that will cast a shade of hostility onto the world of objects, by projecting onto them the avatar of his narcissistic image" (Lacan, *Écrits*, 685).

29. Quoted in Boothby, *Death and Desire*, 43.

30. Lacan, *Séminaire IV*, 194.

31. Mikkel Borch-Jacobsen, *Lacan: The Absolute Master*, trans. Douglas Brick (Stanford: Stanford University Press, 1991), 37. Samuel Weber and Jacob Rogozinski express similar concerns: Weber sees the symbolic as but "a lure of the Imaginary, the discursive continuation of the ambivalent strategy of narcissism," and Rogozinski wonders "why we do not stop identifying ourselves with these scintillating figures that are projected on the screen of the phantasm or the scene of the Spectacle, as if they are projected on the wall at the bottom of a cave where we are held prisoner." Samuel Weber, *The Legend of Freud* (Minneapolis: University of Minnesota Press, 1982), 98; Jacob Rogozinski, *The Ego and the Flesh: An Introduction to Egoanalysis*, trans. Robert Vallier (Stanford: Stanford University Press, 2010), 61.

32. Lacan, *Seminar I*, 174. He also asserts—misleadingly I think—"the earliest dissonance between the ego and being . . . to be the fundamental note that resounds in the whole harmonic scale across the phases of psychical history" (Lacan, *Écrits*, 152–53).

33. Lacan, *Séminaire IV*, 193.

34. Lacan, *Écrits*, 697.

35. In its baldest formulation: "a theory of human development in which a child's relationship to a mirror is held to be more significant than its relationship to its parents is inherently implausible" (Webster, "The Cult of Lacan"). Borch-Jacobsen also accuses Lacan of eliminating the affective beneath the specular, which leads, in his view, to the "statue-fication" of the world: if only static, specular imagoes are at the root of ego development, the ego and its world can, in turn, only be static, rigidified entities (Borch-Jacobsen, *Lacan*, 59). Rogozinski similarly asserts that the neglect of the affective makes "the Lacanian body... always immobile, frozen, and petrified as if under a *death sentence*" (Rogozinski, *The Ego and the Flesh*, 57).

36. Lacan, *Séminaire IV*, 185.

37. Ibid., 192.

38. Ibid., 195.

39. Lacan, *Seminar VII*, 67.

40. Lacan, *Écrits*, 247.

41. Lacan, *Seminar VII*, 68.

42. In an early article, "Family Complexes in the Formation of the Individual" (1938), Lacan himself sees both positive and negative sublimations of this bond. Jacques Lacan, "Les complexes familiaux dans la formation de l'individu," in *Autres Écrits* (Paris: Seuil, 2001), 35–36. As Borch-Jacobsen has noted, this article is remarkable, in general, for the way in which it very clearly describes an affective, bodily connection to the mother that both precedes and conditions specular identification (Borch-Jacobsen, *Lacan*, 66–71). Although I disagree with Borch-Jacobsen that Lacan *eliminates* the affective in his later work, I agree that Lacan would never theorize the affective in the same manner.

43. Lacan, *Seminar II*, 107–8.

44. Boothby, *Death and Desire*, 53–54.

45. Lacan, *Seminar II*, 107. About this, at least, he is correct: one *shouldn't* give credit to Freud for imposing an alien theory upon his own.

46. See Paul Denis, "Emprise et théorie des pulsions," *Revue Française de Psychanalyse* 56, no. 5 (1992): 1337.

47. What's worse, he does so with a clean conscience: as he fathomed himself to be rescuing Freudian drive theory from a bad biologism, he felt free to impose. See Elizabeth Roudinesco, *Jacques Lacan & Co.: A History of Psychoanalysis in France, 1925–1985*, trans. Jeffrey Mehlman (Chicago: University of Chicago Press, 1990), 146.

48. Boothby, *Death and Desire*, 51. Weber connects Lacan's mirror stage with the problem of mastery as it is discussed in the *Fort-Da* game of *Beyond the Pleasure Principle*, but follows Lacan in seeing more aggressivity than mastery: "Active control, revenge, rivalry, and the desire to 'make themselves master of the situation' dominates Freud's conjectures as to the impulses behind the playing of children" (Weber, *The Legend of Freud*, 95–96).

49. Lacan, *Séminaire IV*, 185, 169.

50. Lacan, *Écrits*, 574.

51. To review: Loewald follows Karen Horney in postulating a "dread of the vulva," but we need not go there to affirm something like a "dread of union." As the infant grows increasingly independent, and especially as fantasied mastery grows exponentially in comparison to actual mastery, the parent's once helpful interventions come to be seen as impositions, arbitrary and threatening limitations on freedom and desire. This perceived impingement on autonomy is what I have in mind when I speak of "engulfment" here.

52. See Roger Dorey, "The Relationship of Mastery," trans. Philip Slotkin, *International Review of Psychoanalysis* 13 (1986): 326 and 329.

53. In theorizing this "mechanism of defense," wherein the infant "assimilates" or "identifies" itself with the "dreaded external object," Freud explicitly invokes passages from *Beyond the Pleasure Principle* where her father describes the transformation of the passive reception of a threat into an active mastery over it. Anna Freud, *The Ego and the Mechanisms of Defense*, trans. Cecil Baines (London: Karnac, 1993), 110.

54. If this connection holds, then perhaps a better explanation of the overcoming of aggressivity can be tendered: if aggressivity has its energetic source in the urge to union, then the sublimation of the urge to union would entail a decrease in aggressivity. The "dream of absolute self-adequacy" would thus be abandoned for "an original being-at-a-loss" only when narcissistic aggressivity dries up at its instinctual source (Boothby, *Death and Desire*, 149). In other words, a drive for complete independence loses its motivating force without a drive for complete dependence.

55. In this view, it is not that all of the "statue-fied" features of Lacan's world are products of identification with a fixed image, but rather that the infant comes to see the world in petrified form, and perhaps even comes to emphasize static visual representation over dynamic affective interaction in the first place, as a result of an aggressive overbuilding of psychic structure. In short, *alienation follows from aggressivity and not vice versa.*

56. With Greenberg and Mitchell's claim that *"drives, for Klein, are relationships"* in mind, one might legitimately wonder if Klein belongs in this category. Jay R. Greenberg and Stephen A. Mitchell, *Object Relations in Psychoanalytic Theory* (Cambridge: Harvard University Press, 1983), 146. This question deserves more space than I have here, but briefly: although Klein counters Freud in claiming that drives "contain objects as a constitutive part of their nature," she does not explain why aggressivity seems invariably to be one of the two predominant "relational passions" (alongside love), and thus gives the impression that we simply *are* aggressive, even if that aggressivity is always elicited by and directed toward others. That being said, I imagine the Kleinian framework could easily incorporate the basic claim of this chapter: namely, that aggressivity is not an inborn *response* to objects but rather that there is something in the structure of the object-relation that necessarily gives rise to aggressivity.

57. See Jeremy Elkins, "Motility, Aggression, and the Bodily I: An Interpretation of Winnicott," *Psychoanalytic Quarterly* 84, no. 4 (2015): 943–73.

58. As Eli Zaretsky represents his argument, Reich thought "sexual repression turned a neutral drive toward mastery into aggression." Eli Zaretsky, *Secrets of the Soul: A Social and Cultural History of Psychoanalysis* (New York: Vintage, 2004), 224.

59. See W. R. Bion, *Learning from Experience* (London: Tavistock, 1962), chapter 12.

60. "The intersubjective view maintains that the individual grows in and through the relationship to other subjects. Most important, this perspective observes that the other whom the self meets is also a self, a subject in his or her own right. It assumes that we are able and need to recognize that other subject as different and yet alike, as an other who is capable of sharing similar mental experience. Thus the idea of intersubjectivity reorients the conception of the psychic world from a subject's relations to its object toward a subject meeting another subject." Jessica Benjamin, *The Bonds of Love: Psychoanalysis, Feminism, and the Problem of Domination* (New York: Pantheon, 1988), 19–20.

61. Ibid., 22.

62. Ibid., 33.

63. Ibid., 32 (my emphasis).

64. G. W. F. Hegel, *The Phenomenology of Spirit*, trans. A. V. Miller (Oxford: Oxford University Press, 1977), 114. According to Stephen Mitchell, "in Benjamin's particular vision of intersubjectivity, minds tend toward an autonomous omnipotence in which other minds (and bodies) are treated as objects rather than as subjects in their own right." Stephen A. Mitchell, "Juggling Paradoxes: Commentary on the Work of Jessica Benjamin," *Studies in Gender and Sexuality* 1, no. 3 (2000): 261.

65. Jessica Benjamin, *Like Subjects, Love Objects: Essays on Recognition and Sexual Difference* (New Haven: Yale University Press, 1995), 88.

66. Ibid., 89.

67. Ibid.

68. Benjamin discusses this kind of identification but does not attribute to it the same developmental importance: "The child may switch places with the mother, from active to passive. The omnipotence once attributed to the 'good' all-giving mother now resides instead in the child" (ibid., 38).

69. Mitchell, "Juggling Paradoxes," 261; Benjamin, *The Bonds of Love*, 55.

70. Ibid., 67. See also Benjamin, *Like Subjects, Love Objects*, 191. Responding to Stephen Mitchell's criticism of her use of Freudian drive theory, Benjamin has since recognized that she "could have entirely dispensed with Freud in developing [the] thesis that the loss of intersubjective tension is like death"; see Mitchell, "Juggling Paradoxes," 263 and Jessica Benjamin, "Response to Commentaries by Mitchell and by Butler," *Studies in Gender and Sexuality* 1, no. 3 (2000): 295.

71. Sigmund Freud, *The Standard Edition of the Complete Psychological Works of Sigmund Freud*, ed. and trans. James Strachey, 24 vols. (London: Hogarth and the Institute of Psycho-Analysis, 1966), 14:91.

72. René Girard, *Violence and the Sacred*, trans. Patrick Gregory (Baltimore: Johns Hokpins University Press, 1977), 148.

73. Ibid., 18.

74. Ibid., 180.

75. Ibid., 214.

76. Girard presents the "double bind" of the human being as follows: "Man cannot respond to that universal human injunction, 'Imitate me!' without almost immediately encountering an inexplicable counterorder: 'Don't imitate me!' (which really means, 'Do not appropriate my object')" (ibid., 147). According to the theory of aggressivity offered here, by contrast, imitation is the motor not only of the differentiation of I and other but also of the genesis of an external reality in which objects can be desired. If there is a "double bind" of imitation, it is that it is carried out in relation to an other that is both "other" and *other* as a result of projection.

77. Ibid., 176.

78. Ibid.

79. Girard does, of course, think the Oedipus complex lacks sufficient explanatory power: in his view, it is simply "not functional. One does not really know why it should go on generating substitute triangles." René Girard, "Superman in the Underground: Strategies of Madness-Nietzsche, Wagner, and Dostoevsky," *MLN* 91, no. 6 (December 1976): 1168. Whether we believe that our earliest relationships are unconsciously internalized, as relationalists do, or that drives are both formed in and survive those relationships, as I believe drive theorists ought to, a simple response is easily furnished.

80. René Girard, *Things Hidden Since the Foundation of the World*, trans. Stephen Bann and Michael Metteer (Stanford: Stanford University Press, 1987), 155, 157.

81. Ibid., 219 and 215.

82. Ibid., 217.

83. John Milbank, *Theology and Social Theory: Beyond Secular Reason* (Oxford: Basic Blackwell, 1990), 393–94.

84. This essentially theological point is made explicitly so by John Milbank, who, in his own account of the vicissitudes of despair (liberalism, positivism, sociology, postmodernism), offers us a simple choice: the peace of Christianity or the violence of everything else. Against Girard and Milbank, we should see the choice between violence and peace as itself part of the Christian *mythos*. The "either" here is determined by the "or."

85. To be clear, Girard thinks something like the Oedipus complex does indeed play out in childhood, but only because the parents are the content to the model of desire's form; as Mark Anspach explains, "Girard's imitating Oedipus is liable to find himself caught in the same triangle as Freud's desiring Oedipus." Mark R. Anspach, "Editor's Introduction: Imitating Oedipus," in René Girard, *Oedipus Unbound: Selected Writings on Rivalry and Desire*, ed. Mark R. Anspach (Stanford: Stanford University Press, 2004), xxxvi.

86. Bruce Fink, *A Clinical Introduction to Lacanian Psychoanalysis: Theory and Technique* (Cambridge: Harvard University Press, 1997), 89.

87. Bailly, *Lacan*, 87.

88. Bruce Fink, *Lacan to the Letter: Reading* Écrits *Closely* (Minneapolis: University of Minnesota Press, 2004), 137.

89. The symbolic might be said to find more equanimous expression for contradiction in the real through what Adrian Johnston calls the "transubstantiation of *das Ding* into *die Sache*." Adrian Johnston, *Time Driven: Metapsychology and the Splitting of the Drive* (Evanston: Northwestern University Press, 2005), 193.

90. Rogozinski, *The Ego and the Flesh*, 236.

91. In his most fully formed articulation of his understanding of aggression, a dense little piece called "The Use of an Object," Winnicott argues that destruction is necessary to the creation of external reality. It is not, he contends (in much the same manner as Loewald), that the infant enters an already existent reality and becomes aggressive in butting up against it, but that external reality emerges in tandem with a mature "object user." However, whereas Loewald thinks of emergence from the primordial density in terms of a process of coping and mastery, Winnicott, like Lacan, emphasizes the need for destruction: "it is the destructive drive that creates the quality of externality." D. W. Winnicott, "The Use of an Object," *International Journal of Psychoanalysis* 50 (1969): 715.

92. Without, of course, recognizing the *source* of its negative projection.

93. Wilfred Bion, "Attacks on Linking," in *Melanie Klein Today: Developments in Theory and Practice*, ed. Elizabeth Bott Spillius, 2 vols. (London: Routledge, 1988), 1:96–97.

94. Bion, *Learning from Experience*, chapter 12.

95. To my knowledge, the phrase comes from Žižek, though the title of Lacan's nineteenth seminar is " . . . ou pire." Slavoj Žižek, *Enjoy Your Symptom! Jacques Lacan in Hollywood and Out* (London: Routledge, 2013), 88.

96. Friedrich Kluge, *Etymologisches Wörterbuch der deutschen Sprache* (Berlin: de Gruyter, 2002), 106. Both *Bewältigung* and *Gewalt* harken back to the Indo-German root *val* meaning "to be strong."

4. The Psyche in Late Capitalism I

1. Freud himself makes the connection between money and feces in "Character and Anal Erotism." Sigmund Freud, *The Standard Edition of the Complete Psychological Works of Sigmund Freud*, ed. and trans. James Strachey, 24 vols. (London: Hogarth and the Institute of Psycho-Analysis, 1966), 9:173. See also Sándor Ferenczi's "The Ontogenesis of the Interest in Money," in *First Contributions to Psycho-Analysis* (London: Hogarth and the Institute of Psycho-Analysis, 1952) and Otto Fenichel, "The Drive to Amass Wealth," *Psychoanalytic Quarterly* 7 (1938): 69–95.

2. As Adam Phillips argues in "Adam Phillips on money," YouTube video, 44:35, February 7, 2013, posted by "E.W.R. Many," https://youtu.be/K8wGZt-4ASg.

3. Jean-Jacques Rousseau, "Discourse on the Origin and the Foundations of Inequality Among Men," in *The Discourses and Other Early Political Writings*, ed.

and trans. Victor Gourevitch (Cambridge: Cambridge University Press, 1997), 143–44.

4. For a variety of reasons, though the most important being that his interpretation of Freudian metapsychology is nearly opposed to my own. See chapter 5, n7.

5. This chapter might be understood as a response to Jay Bernstein's assertion that "Adorno needs a social psychology—a workable conception of identification, internalization, projection, etc., in relation to an account of socialization and ego formation—which his own writings fail to provide." J. M. Bernstein, *Adorno: Disenchantment and Ethics* (Cambridge: Cambridge University Press, 2001), 130. As opposed to more recent critical theorists like Axel Honneth, who adopt an entirely new psychological frame, I am returning here to the psychology that Adorno and Horkheimer themselves employed. It is for this reason that I consider this chapter an immanent critique.

6. "The strength to stand out as an individual against one's environment and, at the same time, to make contact with it through approved forms of intercourse and thereby to assert oneself in it—in criminals this strength was eroded. They represented a tendency deeply inherent in living things, the overcoming of which is the mark of all development: the tendency to lose oneself in one's surroundings instead of actively engaging with them, the inclination to let oneself go, to lapse back into nature. Freud called this the death impulse [*sic*], Caillois *le mimétisme*." Theodor Adorno and Max Horkheimer, *Dialectic of Enlightenment: Philosophical Fragments*, trans. Edmund Jephcott (Stanford: Stanford University Press, 2002), 188–89.

7. According to Adorno and Horkheimer, "Odysseus resists Circe's magic. And he therefore receives actually what her magic promises only deceptively to those who fail to resist" (ibid., 56). This reading accords Odysseus too much agency, as he is only able to "renounce himself" on account of the "moly" he receives from Hermes, but since my aim here is to follow out the implications of their interpretation of *The Odyssey* and not to challenge it, I will play along.

8. Robert Hullot-Kentor, *Things Beyond Resemblance: On Theodor W. Adorno* (New York: Columbia University Press, 2006), 38–39.

9. Adorno and Horkheimer, *Dialectic of Enlightenment*, 54.

10. Ibid., 11.

11. Ibid., 65.

12. Ibid., 48. In truth, Adorno and Horkheimer are by no means consistent here: Odysseus is presented both as a bourgeois fantasy, embodying risk, the ruthless pursuit of self-interest, etc., as well as a bourgeois reality, representing as he does an "absolute loneliness," a "radical alienation," etc. (ibid., 49).

13. As Adorno writes elsewhere: "In his limitless and implacable demands the petty-bourgeois sticks his chest out, identifying himself with a power that he does not have, outdoing it in his arrogance to the point of absolute spirit and absolute horror." Theodor Adorno, *Minima Moralia: Reflections on a Damaged Life*, trans. E. F. N. Jephcott (London: Verso, 2005), 88.

14. Karl Marx, *Capital Volume One: A Critique of Political Economy*, trans. Ben Fowkes (London: Penguin, 1976), 254.

15. Adorno and Horkheimer, *Dialectic of Enlightenment*, 97. The editors of *Adorno and the Need in Thinking* call attention to this passage for "anticipating the ideology of niche marketing by several decades." Donald Burke, Colin J. Campbell, Kathy Kiloh, Michael K. Palamarek, and Jonathan Short, eds., *Adorno and the Need in Thinking: New Critical Essays* (Toronto: University of Toronto Press, 2007), 10–11.

16. Adorno and Horkheimer, *Dialectic of Enlightenment*, 97.

17. According to Simon Jarvis, "the culture industry thus generates a world of false specificity in which the advertised uniqueness of an individual product—the distinctive individual voice of a new poet, the inimitable style of a star conductor, or the sheer personality of a chat-show host—needs to be foregrounded by the relentless sameness of a whole range of the product's other qualities, from diction to typeface." Simon Jarvis, *Adorno: A Critical Introduction* (New York: Routledge, 1998), 74. The elimination of difference lies not, however, primarily with the "relentless sameness" imprinted on the product itself but rather in the nature of its production.

18. Adorno and Horkheimer, *Dialectic of Enlightenment*, 107.

19. Shane Gunster, *Capitalizing on Culture: Critical Theory for Cultural Studies* (Toronto: University of Toronto Press, 2004), 9.

20. David Harvey, *The Condition of Postmodernity: An Enquiry Into the Origins of Cultural Change* (Cambridge: Blackwell, 1990), 180; Theodor Adorno, "Theory of Pseudo-Culture," trans. Deborah Cook, *Telos* 95 (Spring 1995): 28.

21. I will use the term *late capitalism* to mean the era of capitalism distinguished by "the appropriation of all culture in the service of commodity production." Stanley Aronowitz, *False Promises: The Shaping of American Working-Class Consciousness* (Durham: Duke University Press, 1992), 15. The period demarcated by this definition roughly corresponds to that to which Ernest Mandel assigns the term (the 1940s to the present), one characterized by the "historic defeats of the working-class by fascism and war," "the acceleration of technological innovation," and "the international concentration and centralization of capital." Ernest Mandel, *Late Capitalism*, trans. Joris De Bres (London: NLB, 1975), 9–10.

22. As Robert Hullot-Kentor has argued along different lines: "The Exact Sense in Which the Culture Industry No Longer Exists," *Cultural Critique* 70 (Fall 2008): 137–57. See also Deborah Cook, "Adorno on Mass Societies," *Journal of Social Philosophy* 32, no. 1 (Spring 2001): 35–52. For rejections of the contemporary relevance of the term *culture industry*, see Jim Collins, *Uncommon Cultures: Popular Culture and Post-Modernism* (New York: Routledge, 1989), 8; Peter Uwe Hohendahl, *Prismatic Thought: Theodor W. Adorno* (Lincoln: University of Nebraska Press, 1995), 145.

23. Adorno, *Minima Moralia*, 206.

24. "Without material to negate, there can be no enlightenment" (Bernstein, *Adorno*, 95).

25. Butler claims that "thinking the theory of power with a theory of the psyche [is] a task that has been eschewed by writers in both Foucauldian and psychoanalytic orthodoxies." Judith Butler, *The Psychic Life of Power: Theories in Subjection* (Stanford: Stanford University Press, 1997), 3. True as this may be, the pretense of blazing a new trail here seems a bit disingenuous with no mention of the Frankfurt school.

26. I would include as causes of this psychic shift four broad, interrelated transformations of the twentieth century: 1. the movement of all work activities outside the home, resulting in the further separation of "public" and "private" life; 2. the rise of Fordist and Taylorist manufacturing practices that lead to the routinization of work, the dissatisfactions with which compelled workers to seek the relief of pleasure in their "private" lives; 3. the rise of a variety of industries (media, leisure, fashion, etc.) devoted to providing those pleasures; and 4. the socialization of education. Thanks to these changes, the family has ceded its economic and socializing functions to the workplace and the school, respectively, and "public life has infiltrated and transformed even the most intimate of private refuges." Antoine Prost, "Public and Private Spheres in France," in *A History of Private Life*, ed. Antoine Prost and Gérard Vincent, trans. Arthur Goldhammer, 5 vols. (Cambridge: Belknap, 1991), 5:132.

27. In Adorno's words, "the representatives of the new type are no longer individuals." Theodor Adorno, "Notizen zur neuen Anthropologie," in *Briefe und Briefwechsel*, 8 vols. (Frankfurt: Suhrkamp, 1994), 4.2:453. "The psychology of the individual has lost what Hegel would have called substance." Theodor Adorno, *The Culture Industry: Selected Essays on Mass Culture*, ed. J. M. Bernstein (London: Routledge, 1991), 152.

28. Jessica Benjamin, "The End of Internalization: Adorno's Social Psychology," *Telos* 32 (Summer 1977): 44. One might think of the "end of internalization" narrative as the undoing of the "hothouse family" described by John Demos in "Oedipus and America: Historical Perspectives on the Reception of Psychoanalysis in America," in *Inventing the Psychological: Toward a Cultural History of Emotional Life in America*, ed. Joel Pfister and Nancy Schnog (New Haven: Yale University Press, 1997).

29. Jessica Benjamin, "Authority and the Family Revisited: Or, a World Without Fathers?," *New German Critique* 13 (Winter 1978): 48. This same critique later found a more deserving target in Christopher Lasch. Michèle Barrett and Mary McIntosh, "Narcissism and the Family: A Critique of Lasch," *New Left Review* 1, no. 135 (September-October 1982), 41.

30. Benjamin, "Authority and the Family Revisited," 51.

31. Benjamin develops this critique further in *The Bonds of Love: Psychoanalysis, Feminism, and the Problem of Domination* (New York: Pantheon, 1988), 147–48 and 190–91.

32. Benjamin, "The End of Internalization," 55.

33. Gillian Rose, "How Is Critical Theory Possible? Theodor W. Adorno and Concept Formation in Sociology," *Political Studies* 24, no. 1 (March 1976): 74.

34. Ibid., 74. Rose's argument preemptively defused the force of Michael Theunissen's criticism that Adorno's "absolute negativity," in "surrendering to apocalypticism, cannot be realized in the medium of philosophical knowledge." Michael Theunissen, "Negativität bei Adorno," in *Adorno-Konferenz 1983,* ed. Ludwig von Friedeburg and Jürgen Habermas (Frankfurt: Suhrkamp, 1983), 56; see also Jarvis, *Adorno,* 211–16.

35. The literal reception of Benjamin's thesis has unfortunately been quite influential: Axel Honneth cites Benjamin to support his view that Adorno heralded an "end of mediation." Axel Honneth, *The Struggle for Recognition: The Moral Grammar of Social Conflicts,* trans. Joel Anderson (Cambridge: MIT Press, 1995), chapter 5. Paul Piccone claims Benjamin's article to be nothing less than "a systematic critique of the Frankfurt School's reception of psychoanalysis." Paul Piccone, "General Introduction," in *The Essential Frankfurt School Reader,* ed. Andrew Arato and Eike Gebhardt (New York: Continuum, 2005), xxi.

36. Martin Jay, *Marxism and Totality: The Adventures of a Concept from Lukács to Habermas* (Berkeley: University of California Press, 1984), 274.

37. Max Horkheimer, "Authoritarianism and the Family Today," in *The Family: Its Function and Destiny,* ed. Ruth Nanda Anshen (New York: Harper, 1949), 365–66.

38. According to Horkheimer, "the only dictatorship in recent times, the Third Reich, which tried to dispense systematically with any mediation between the individual and the state and to push Jacobinism to the extreme, has failed" (ibid., 362). I take this to be a point more about the persistence of mediation than about the failure of the Third Reich.

39. Adorno, "Notizen zur neuen Anthropologie," 454.

40. Max Horkheimer, *Critical Theory: Selected Essays,* trans. Matthew J. O'Connell and Others (New York: Continuum, 1999), 57.

41. Horkheimer, "Authoritarianism and the Family Today," 362–63.

42. David Jenemann, *Adorno in America* (Minneapolis: University of Minnesota Press, 1997), xxix. "To think that the individual is being liquidated without trace is over-optimistic" (Adorno, *Minima Moralia,* 135).

43. Adorno and Horkheimer, *Dialectic of Enlightenment,* 167.

44. Jarvis, *Adorno,* 27.

45. Adorno and Horkheimer, *Dialectic of Enlightenment,* 148.

46. Axel Honneth, *Pathologies of Reason: On the Legacy of Critical Theory,* trans. James Ingram and others (New York: Columbia University Press, 2009), 77–78.

47. Gerhard Schweppenhäuser, *Theodor W. Adorno: An Introduction,* trans. James Rolleston (Durham: Duke University Press, 2009), 48; Susan Buck-Morss, *The Origin of Negative Dialectics: Theodor W. Adorno, Walter Benjamin, and the Frankfurt Institute* (New York: Free Press, 1977), 88.

48. A worry expressed in Iain Macdonald's concern that "even if we dispense with the ideality of the past, it remains unclear how the 'restitution' made to the 'damaged' world could be anything but an attempted return to a *prior* engagement with nature." Iain Macdonald, "Cold, Cold, Warm: Autonomy, Intimacy, and Maturity in Adorno," *Philosophy and Social Criticism* 37, no. 6 (2011): 671. Cf.

Fabian Freyenhagen, *Adorno's Practical Philosophy: Living Less Wrongly* (Cambridge: Cambridge University Press, 2013), 68.

49. Habermas characterizes mimesis as an irrational and quasi-mystical "mindfulness" of nature in which there is no place for the exercise of human reason and its supposed conceptual "violence." Jürgen Habermas, *The Theory of Communicative Action*, trans. Thomas McCarthy, 2 vols. (Boston: Beacon, 1984), 1:366–99. Honneth similarly describes mimesis as involving a "prereflective desire to be freed from conditions that fetter our potential for imitative reason" (Honneth, *Pathologies of Reason*, 69). Allen Dunn and Joel Whitebook offer similar criticisms: Dunn faults Adorno for confusing "the stimulating tremor that strengthens the ego even as it breaks its boundaries" (what I call "postoedipal mimesis" here) and "the suffering that remembers a unity of subject and object" ("preoedipal mimesis"), and Whitebook laments the identification of *la promesse de bonheur* with "the complete *jouissance* that would result from loss of ego, dedifferentiation and merger." Allen Dunn, "The Man Who Needs Hardness: Irony and Solidarity in the Aesthetics of Theodor Adorno," in *Germany and German Thought in American Literature and Cultural Criticism*, ed. Peter Freese (Essen: Die Blaue Eule, 1990), 483; Joel Whitebook, "From Schoenberg to Odysseus: Aesthetic, Psychic, and Social Synthesis in Adorno and Wellmer," *New German Critique* 58 (Winter 1993): 49.

50. The "priority of the object" should not be confused with a "naïve realism": in Adorno's work, there is a reciprocity between subject and object, meaning that the object is determined in part by its conceptual determinations. Brian O'Connor, *Adorno's Negative Dialectic: Philosophy and the Possibility of Critical Rationality* (Cambridge: MIT Press, 2004): 48–50. Thus, the "priority of the object" does not mean hypostasizing the object; this priority is rather "the corrective of the subjective reduction, not the denial of a subjective share." Theodor Adorno, *Critical Models: Interventions and Catchwords*, trans. Henry W. Pickford (New York: Columbia University Press, 1998), 250. It should thus be kept in mind throughout that a critical realism is being defended here.

51. Ibid., 247.

52. Ibid., 254. Just before this, Adorno relates this "knowledge" (*Erkenntnis*) to the subject's "experience" (*Erfahrung*). Cf. "He who wishes to know [*erfahren*] the truth about life in its immediacy must scrutinize its estranged form" (Adorno, *Minima Moralia*, 15).

53. Theodor Adorno, *Negative Dialectics,* trans. E. B. Ashton (London: Routledge, 1973), 365; Adorno, *Critical Models*, 247.

54. Bernstein, *Adorno*, 456. I take Adorno's assertion that childhood mistakes serve as "the model of experience" to mean that preoedipal mimesis serves as the model of postoedipal mimesis; this is how I understand Adorno's claim that "nonidentity is the secret *telos* of identification" and Bernstein's own claim that "reflective judgment is the heir of mimetic understanding" (Adorno, *Negative Dialectics*, 373; ibid., 149; Bernstein, *Adorno*, 312). It is important to emphasize, however, that those mistakes are not themselves real *Erfahrungen*, which are possible only "in the medium of conceptual reflection" (Adorno, *Negative Dialectics*, 13).

According to Anke Thyen, the experience (*Erfahrung*) that is the fruit of negative dialectics is "a discursive, i.e. reflection-led and reflection-determined, experience obtained from a manner of appropriating possible objects of reflection in such a way that the indissolubility of the object is preserved as its freedom." Anke Thyen, *Negative Dialektik und Erfahrung: Zur Rationalität des Nichtidentischen bei Adorno* (Frankfurt: Suhrkamp, 1989), 213.

55. See Max Horkheimer, *The Eclipse of Reason* (New York: Oxford University Press, 1947), chapter 1.

56. Adorno and Horkheimer, *Dialectic of Enlightenment*, 44–45; Jarvis, *Adorno*, 31.

57. Theodor Adorno, "Sociology and Psychology, Part 1," *New Left Review* 1, no. 46 (November-December 1967): 80; Adorno, *The Culture Industry*, 121; Hans Loewald, *Papers on Psychoanalysis* (New Haven: Yale University Press, 1980), 47.

58. Bernstein, *Adorno*, 396. Adorno wrote often of a hardened coldness in the face of suffering, an idea one also finds in Wilhelm Reich. Theodor Adorno, "The Problem of the New Type of Human Being," in *Current of Music*, ed. Robert Hullot-Kentor (Cambridge: Polity, 2009), 466; Wilhelm Reich, "The Characterological Mastery of the Oedipus Complex," *International Journal of Psycho-Analysis* 12 (1931): 454. This coldness is a function of having been "broken in on" by reality, a traumatic breach that leads to excessive protective structure building, or, in this new formulation, ego rigidity. Robert Hullot-Kentor, "Right Listening and a New Type of Human Being," in *The Cambridge Companion to Adorno*, ed. Tom Huhn (Cambridge: Cambridge University Press, 2004), 193; Adorno, "The Problem of the New Type of Human Being," 463.

59. Adorno, *The Culture Industry*, 118; Adorno, *Minima Moralia*, 184. It is for this reason that I find the "tension" model of therapeutic success to suit Adorno's project much better than the "integration" model, one that he relied upon at times and of which he was relentlessly critical at others. Theodor W. Adorno, Else Frenkel-Brunswik, Daniel J. Levinson, and R. Nevitt Sanford, *The Authoritarian Personality* (New York: Harper and Row, 1950), 234; Theodor Adorno, "Sociology and Psychology, Part II," *New Left Review* 1, no. 47 (January-February 1968): 83. One might see the tension model already at work in his opposition of a weak ego not to a strong ego but to a "firm ego," one constituted by a strong "inner tension." Theodor Adorno and Hellmut Becker, "Education for Autonomy," *Telos* 56 (Summer 1983): 108.

60. Adorno, *The Culture Industry*, 95.

61. Loewald, *Papers on Psychoanalysis*, 68.

62. Bernard Stiegler, "The Time of Cinema: On the 'New World' and 'Cultural Exception,'" *Tekhnema: Journal of Philosophy and Technology* 4 (Spring 1998): 62.

63. Cf. Fredric Jameson, *Late Marxism: Adorno, or the Persistence of the Dialectic* (London: Verso, 1990), 140. Here I am following Andreas Huyssen's lead in "pursuing the question, in relation to mass culture, to what extent and for what purposes the products of the culture industry might precisely speak to and activate . . . pre-ego impulses." Andreas Huyssen, "Adorno in Reverse: From

Hollywood to Richard Wagner," in *Adorno: A Critical Reader*, ed. Nigel Gibson and Andrew Rubin (Oxford: Blackwell, 2002), 35.

64. Adorno, *The Culture Industry*, 139, 142.

65. Adorno gets part of the way here when he writes that "people compensate for social powerlessness, which goes to the root of individual drives and conscious motives as well as guilt feelings because they are not what they should be and do not do what they should do according to their self-image. They compensate by turning themselves either in fact or imagination into members of something higher and more encompassing to which they attribute qualities which they themselves lack and from which they profit by vicarious participation" (Adorno, "Theory of Pseudo-Culture," 32–33).

66. Adorno, *The Culture Industry*, 183. Sherry Turkle similarly speaks of the "flow state" allowed by computer-mediated interaction, wherein "you are able to act without self-consciousness." Sherry Turkle, *Alone Together: Why We Expect More from Technology and Less from Each Other* (New York: Basic Books, 2011), 226.

67. Stiegler, "The Time of Cinema," 62, 64.

68. Ibid., 64. Cf. Michael Eigen, *The Electrified Tightrope*, ed. Adam Phillips (London: Karnac, 2004), 241.

69. Skeptics of the problematic of "escapism"—that we go to the movies to "escape" real life—often prefer to see the products of the culture industry (especially as it has evolved, with its first-person role-playing games and social networking sites) as providing forums for self-expression and not self-forgetting; see, for instance, Tom Boellstorff, *Coming of Age in Second Life: An Anthropologist Explores the Virtually Human* (Princeton: Princeton University Press, 2008), 27. According to the drive theory articulated in the previous chapters, the alternative is a false one: fantasied identifications no doubt make possible unexplored forms of self-relating as well as contribute to who we become inasmuch as they fail but leave behind a residue as internalizations, but they are also, as I argued in chapter 2, the primary means of escape from oneself. For Loewald, the desperate child turns to the fantasy of directly being the other half in the primordial bond—the Ur-fantasy, upon which all subsequent fantasies are modeled—as a confused way of reversing the process of individuation. While the specific content of fantasy obviously has a great deal to do with self-formation and expression, the very act of fantasying is secondary to the instinctual need that engenders it, and it is this need that I am associating here with "losing oneself." Thus while film, in particular, bears the astonishing ability to transport audiences to strange realities, one that lends the culture industry the awesome power of managing public fantasies, the need for the fantasies it engenders stems from an overwhelming urge to overcome separation and thereby no longer be oneself. Fruitful as a "second life" might be as a form of self-expression, it is also "a way out for those who confront the severe limitations of corporate ideology, determining social structures, and the physical body itself," which, again, is in itself neither a negative nor a positive phenomenon. Anne Balsamo, *Technologies of the Gendered Body: Reading Cyborg Women* (Durham: Duke University Press, 1996), 122.

70. Gunster, *Capitalizing on Culture*, 31. "The moviegoer . . . perceives the street outside as a continuation of the film he has just left" (Adorno and Horkheimer, *Dialectic of Enlightenment*, 99). According to Jack Zipes, "the inevitable outcome of most mass-mediated fairy tales is a happy reconfirmation of the system which produces them." Jack Zipes, "The Instrumentalization of Fantasy: Fairy Tales and the Mass Media," in *The Myths of Information: Technology and Postindustrial Culture*, ed. Kathleen Woodward (London: Routledge and Kegan Paul, 1980), 101.

71. Adorno, *Minima Moralia*, 202.

72. Theodor Adorno, "On Popular Music," in Hullot-Kentor, *Current of Music*, 309. In Gunster's words, there is an exchange of "unfulfilled longing for the pleasures of immediate satisfaction" (Gunster, *Capitalizing on Culture*, 33). The choice of psychopharmaceuticals over psychotherapy for the treatment of say, anxiety, is illustrative here: one is *actually* relieved of a particular psychic pain, but only at the cost of working through the source of that pain and thus the possibility of lasting (nonmedicated) relief from it.

73. Theodor Adorno, *The Culture Industry*, 38.

74. Gunster, *Capitalizing on Culture*, 59; Adorno, *The Culture Industry*, 39.

75. Gunster, *Capitalizing on Culture*, 60–61.

76. As Douglas Kellner argues, the Frankfurt school meant by "false needs" those whose "satisfaction provide[s] momentary pleasure [and which] perpetuate a system whose continuation impedes the fulfillment of individual and social needs and potentials." Douglas Kellner, *Herbert Marcuse and the Crisis of Marxism* (Berkeley: University of California Press, 1984), 244.

77. Theodor Adorno, *Critical Models*, 55. Adorno succinctly states the kind of happiness attained here "is to actual happiness what unemployment is to the abolition of work" (Adorno, "Notizen zur neuen Anthropologie," 459).

78. Adorno himself was highly sensitive to the fact that the "escape" provided by the culture industry was far from simple "ersatz satisfaction": in his own words, "people are not only, as the saying goes, falling for the swindle; if it guarantees them even the most fleeting gratification they desire a deception which is nonetheless transparent to them. . . . Without admitting it they sense their lives would be completely intolerable as soon as they no longer clung to satisfactions which are none at all" (Adorno, *The Culture Industry*, 103).

79. Adorno and Horkheimer, *Dialectic of Enlightenment*, 136.

80. "The very fact that people suffer from universal manipulation is used for manipulation. People's sincerest feelings are being perverted and gratified by swindle." Theodor W. Adorno, "Democratic Leadership and Mass Manipulation," in *Gesammelte Schriften*, 20 vols. (Frankfurt: Suhrkamp, 1997), 20.1:284.

81. Adorno and Horkheimer, *Dialectic of Enlightenment*, xix; Adorno, "Theory of Pseudo-Culture," 27.

82. Adorno, *Critical Models*, 55.

83. In response to the concern about the negative connotations of this phrase, I can only say that I hope to have done enough in the first three chapters to convince the reader that the drive toward the breaking down of self/other boundaries characteristic of the death drive has, in itself, no negative valence and is in fact

a positive phenomenon inasmuch as it is part and parcel of an adequate "holding environment." In this view, "losing oneself" is not an evasion of some authentic oneness with oneself; it is, on the contrary, the manifestation of a primary psychic need.

84. Adorno and Horkheimer, *Dialectic of Enlightenment*, 112, 107, 49. A good argument could be made that psychoanalysis itself proved to be another branch of the culture industry (psychoanalysis to "lose oneself" in the "archaic depths" of the psyche . . .), though I would not go so far as to dub psychoanalysis the spirit of late capitalism; see Eli Zaretsky, "Psychoanalysis and the Spirit of Capitalism," *Constellations* 15, no. 3 (2008): 366–81.

85. Otto Fenichel, "Ego Strength and Ego Weakness," in *The Collected Papers of Otto Fenichel* (New York: Norton, 1954).

86. It would be incorrect, for instance, to say that an overly militarized nation was "weak"; though one could certainly trace back that militarization to concerns about security that stemmed from an internal "weakness," the nation itself is still strong, and, indeed, too strong.

87. Gunster, *Capitalizing on Culture*, 53.

88. "Technology is making gestures precise and brutal, and with them men. It expels from movements all hesitation, deliberation, civility" (Adorno, *Minima Moralia*, 40).

89. They "see the world as it is, but pay the price of no longer seeing how it could be" (Adorno, "The Problem of a New Type of Human Being," 466).

90. Raymond Geuss, *Outside Ethics* (Princeton: Princeton University Press, 2005), 113. It is this conception of society as necessarily producing lies that Adorno claims "has a suspicious tendency to become itself ideology" (Adorno, *Minima Moralia*, 43).

91. The relation between this new anthropological type and what Lacan calls the "subject of science," the subject that succeeds the "alienated" subject in the era of preventive normalization following a "decline of paternal imagoes," is in need of further investigation. Elizabeth Roudinesco, *Jacques Lacan & Co.: A History of Psychoanalysis in France, 1925–1985*, trans. Jeffrey Mehlman (Chicago: University of Chicago Press, 1990), 485.

92. Adorno, "Notizen zur neuen Anthropologie," 468. Thanks to Lisa Cerami for walking me through the intricacies of this phrase.

93. Ibid., 471.

94. Adorno approvingly cites Simmel's idea that ego immaturity stems from superego weakness in Adorno, *Critical Models*, 386; see also Ernst Simmel, "Anti-Semitism and Mass Psychopathology," in *Anti-Semitism: A Social Disease*, ed. Ernst Simmel (New York: International Universities Press, 1946), 49.

95. No doubt Adorno would have been initially hostile to the move I am making here: following Freud, he saw in the superego nothing but "blindly, unconsciously internalized social coercion" and lamented the attempt to distinguish good and bad forms of the superego (Adorno, *Negative Dialectics*, 272; see also Adorno, "Sociology and Psychology, Part II," 82). What Adorno laments in this distinction is the attempt to separate good forms of social coercion from bad ones.

What I am doing in this chapter and the next, by contrast, is separating that part of the superego that serves social coercion from that part that resists it. More generally, however, I find that the "integration" model of therapeutic success (wherein the ego purges itself of the superego) that Adorno relies upon to launch this critique of revisionist psychoanalysts fits his general project quite poorly (see n59). If we admit, as he does, that the ego's "reality testing" is no socially neutral function, the call to "raze" the agency that criticizes the ego should look quite frightening.

96. Adorno, *Minima Moralia*, 207.

97. Corresponding roughly to what Adorno called "reflex-like" thinking and real reflexivity. Seyla Benhabib, *Critique, Norm, Utopia: A Study of the Foundations of Critical Theory* (New York: Columbia University Press, 1986), 209.

98. Jonathan Lear, *A Case for Irony* (Cambridge: Harvard University Press, 2011), 45.

99. Jonathan Lear, "A Lost Conception of Irony," *berfrois*, January 12, 2012, http://www.berfrois.com/2012/01/jonathan-lear-lost-conception-irony/.

100. Ibid. Lear emphasizes that this critical distance is not "disenchantment with given social pretenses" but rather a "committed questioning" (Lear, *A Case for Irony*, 38).

101. Lear himself is skeptical of the idea that the superego could be an agent of ironic reflection: "while the ego may be considered a faculty of pretense—governing how we put ourselves forward in the world—the idea that the superego in any of its guises might be a faculty for pretense-transcending aspiring would be met by Freud with skepticism bordering on derision. Far from being a faculty of pretense-transcendence, the superego is dedicated to keeping us in line" (ibid., 45). I have addressed this concern in the conclusion of chapter 2.

102. Ibid., 14.

103. Lear, "A Lost Conception of Irony" and *A Case for Irony*, 32.

104. In one of their pithier quotables, Adorno and Horkheimer claim that "the culture industry does not sublimate; it suppresses" (Adorno and Horkheimer, *Dialectic of Enlightenment*, 111). While this is not exactly inaccurate, it might be more precise to say: "the culture industry does not sublimate; it manages gratification as a means of curbing sublimation."

105. Marx, *Capital Volume One*, 792–93.

106. One of the primary objections to the "end of internalization" thesis is that it cannot explain breaks from increasing homogeneity: in other words, it does quite well with the drab conformism of the forties and fifties, but cannot explain the emergence of sixties counterculture. According to Douglas Kellner, Adorno's "theoretical optic cannot adequately account for the genesis and popularity of many forms of popular music such as the blues, jazz, rock and roll, punk, and other forms of music connected with oppositional subcultures." Douglas Kellner, "Theodor W. Adorno and the Dialectics of Mass Culture," in Gibson and Rubin, *Adorno: A Critical Reader*, 101. I believe that this new problematic of "losing oneself" and "living straight ahead" helps here: the failure of the culture industry that the critical theorists knew and despised (the industry of the forties)

was that it did not provide *enough* incentive for "living straight ahead," that its "immediate satisfactions" were insufficient to compensate for the conformity demanded. The sixties might then be seen coming to its aid: in forging more powerful modes of "losing oneself," whether through political "joining" or LSD, "counterculture" proved itself only a temporary trial run; its "explosiveness" would soon be appropriated to serve commodity production. I would hope that the history of the "oppositional subcultures" mentioned by Kellner serves as evidence of this point and, more generally, to tame the uncritical assumption that we ought *always* to attend to a "work's contradictions, critical or oppositional moments, or potential to provide insight into social conditions or to elicit a critical response" (ibid., 101).

107. Adorno and Horkheimer, *Dialectic of Enlightenment*, 116 (my emphasis). They continue: "Once, film spectators saw their own wedding in that of others. Now the happy couple on the screen are specimens of the same species as everyone in the audience" (ibid., 116).

108. Harvey, *The Condition of Postmodernity*, part 3.

109. Loewald, *Papers on Psychoanalysis*, 49; Helga Nowotny, "From the Future to the Extended Present," in *The Formulation of Time Preferences in a Multidisciplinary Perspective*, ed. Guy Kirsch, Peter Nijkamp, and Klaus Zimmermann (Aldershot: Avebury, 1988), 27.

110. It is thus unnecessary for the culture industry to propagate "an anti-utopian, intrinsically conservative image of human nature" in order to convince us that strong social forces are needed to curb "submerged destructive forces lying just beneath consciousness" (Aronowitz, *False Promises*, 113). The culture industry works just as well with a utopian image (see, for instance, *The Matrix* series). Its force lies not in its content, overt or covert, but in the kind of identification it makes possible, which can take place within a wide variety of narratives.

111. Theodor W. Adorno, "The Actuality of Philosophy," trans. Benjamin Snow, *Telos* 31 (March 1977): 129.

112. Jay, *Marxism and Totality*, 209.

113. Horkheimer, *The Eclipse of Reason*, 112–13. Compare with the twenty-year-old Horkheimer's longing for a different existence: "By my craving for truth will I live, and search into what I desire to know; the afflicted will I aid, satisfy my hatred against injustice, and vanquish the Pharisees, but above all search for love, love and understanding" (quoted in Buck-Morss, *The Origin of Negative Dialectics*, 9).

114. See Martin Shuster, *Autonomy After Auschwitz: Adorno, German Idealism, and Modernity* (Chicago: University of Chicago Press, 2014), 134.

115. I do not believe there is any reason to believe, as Fabian Freyenhagen does, that "while Adorno seemed to think of the critical individuals on roughly the model of his own life, there is clearly room for extending the ambit beyond white males from a privileged background and educated in modernist high culture" (Freyenhagen, *Adorno's Practical Philosophy*, 179). Rather than open luck to other demographics, I am attempting here to do away with the luck altogether.

116. Adorno, *Negative Dialectics*, 41.

117. Jürgen Habermas, *Philosophical-Political Profiles,* trans. Frederick G. Lawrence (Cambridge: MIT Press, 1983), 106. I thus take the following to be one way of addressing the problem of the "normative foundations" of critical theory.

118. Adorno, *Negative Dialectics,* 4. "Conceited . . . is the illusion that anyone— and by this one means oneself—might be exempt from the tendency to socialized pseudo-culture" (Adorno, "Theory of Pseudo-Culture," 37).

119. Adorno and Horkheimer, *Dialectic of Enlightenment,* 99.

120. Despite the fact that it was his intention to work collaboratively on an "open-ended" version of the dialectic with Adorno (which the latter eventually wrote on his own), it is clear that Horkheimer never fully understood or accepted Adorno's emphasis on negation (See Buck-Morss, *The Origin of Negative Dialectics,* 68). Concepts like reason, truth, and the whole were generally less problematic for Horkheimer, ethical anchors in a fragmented world: "Harmony and significant existence, which metaphysics wrongly designates as true reality against the con-tradictions of the phenomenal world, are not meaningless" (Horkheimer, *Critical Theory,* 178). It is thus very difficult to see Horkheimer, who much preferred the straightforward march of ideology critique, following Adorno down the rabbit hole. Simon Jarvis recounts an occasion when Horkheimer, in conversation with Adorno about the possibility of a materialist dialectic, was "driven to an exasper-ated outburst: 'So all we can do is just say 'no' to everything!'" (Jarvis, *Adorno,* 211). One might take the following passage from *Minima Moralia,* obviously written with Hegel in mind, to apply equally to Horkheimer:

> Even when sophistication is understood in the theoretically acceptable sense of that which widens horizons, passes beyond the isolated phenom-enon, considers the whole, there is still a cloud in the sky. It is just this passing-on and being able to linger, this tacit assent to the primacy of the general over the particular, which constitutes not only the deception of idealism in hypostasizing concepts, but also its inhumanity, that has no sooner grasped the particular than it reduces it to a through-station, and finally comes all too quickly to terms with suffering and death for the sake of a reconciliation occurring merely in reflection—in the last analysis, the bourgeois coldness that is only too willing to underwrite the inevitable.
>
> (Adorno, *Minima Moralia,* 74)

Adorno's worry, in essence, is that anyone in rabid pursuit of wholeness, as Horkheimer imagined himself to be, will find himself irritated with the particu-lars along the way. Adorno thus does not, like Horkheimer, want to pit the par-ticular (the resistant individual) against a false universal for the sake of a true universal but rather aims to turn the particular against itself for the sake of rec-onciliation with other particulars.

121. Adorno, *Negative Dialectics,* 140.

122. Jarvis, *Adorno,* 202. What's more, anyone who promises to get us "to the things themselves" in this way can only, in the present world, be hawking ideol-ogy. In essence, we have here Adorno's critique of Heidegger (in his mind, the quintessential sick subject): while his impulse to break out of Kantian subjectivity

is also Adorno's, by denying mediation and desperately grasping for the things themselves, Heidegger ends up enthroning "the being-thus-and-not-otherwise of whatever may, as culture, claim to make sense" (Adorno, *Negative Dialectics*, 86). In aiming for a regression past subjectivity, Heidegger, with his desire to answer the "ontological need," with his affirmation of the "purity" of being, with his immediate, visual categories, with his doctrine of "the *ens realissimum* under the name of Being," and with his glance cast longingly back at Greece, provides little more than a new form of domesticated risk, and thus his philosophy is already primed for success on the market (ibid., 79).

123. I thus disagree, in both spirit and substance, with Robert Pippin's assessment of negative dialectics: that it "seems little more than applying concepts in such a way that an asterisk is always somehow present or implied, as if to add to the invoking of a term such as 'factory' or 'welfare' or 'husband' or 'statue': *Caution: Concepts just used not adequate to the sensuous particulars that might fall under them.*" Robert Pippin, *The Persistence of Subjectivity: On the Kantian Aftermath* (Cambridge: Cambridge University Press 2005), 105. I imagine something similar could be said of psychoanalysis: that its aim is little more than to bring about the realization "My understanding of my relationship to my mother is not adequate to the sensuous particulars that fall under it." In both psychoanalysis and negative dialectics (which I am admittedly attempting to interpret as a historically specific mode of psychoanalysis), the aim is to bring about a real change in the way the subject relates to the world, though I suppose that neither will ever be immune from the charge that they are fanciful ways of leaving everything as it is (but with asterisks!).

124. Hullot-Kentor, "Right Listening and a New Type of Human Being," 194.

125. Robert Hullot-Kentor, "A New Type of Human Being and Who We Really Are," *Brooklyn Rail*, November 10, 2008, http://www.brooklynrail.org/2008/11 /art/a-new-type-of-human-being-and-who-we-really-are.

126. Adorno, *The Culture Industry*, 197.

127. Adorno, "The Problem of a New Type of Human Being," 468.

128. Theodor W. Adorno, *Problems of Moral Philosophy*, ed. Thomas Schröder, trans. Rodney Livingston (Stanford: Stanford University Press, 2001), 169. This reading would make sense of Adorno's "wish that, as its ultimate act, the dialectic would cancel itself out altogether": if "unswerving negation" could not recreate the kind of psychic tension that allows a non-projective, mimetic relationship to the world, then there would be no "ultimate act" of negative dialectics (Jameson, *Late Marxism*, 120; Adorno, *Negative Dialectics*, 159).

129. Adorno, "The Actuality of Philosophy," 130. It is only the achievement of this postoedipal mimesis that would allow noncoercive communication. If Adorno was "hostile" to the "dialogic, communicative function of language," it was because he understood, in good psychoanalytic fashion, that destruction precedes communication (and, indeed, the kind of destruction that may require the renunciation of communication as an aim) (Jay, *Marxism and Totality*, 272; Whitebook, "From Schoenberg to Odysseus," 59; Bernstein, *Adorno*, 283). The problem with the communicative intersubjectivity that second-generation critical

theorists suggest ought to replace Adorno's utopian thinking, in short, is that it eliminates from the sphere of "social action" the act of self-effacement. We see in Habermas's subsumption of the emancipatory interest he associates with psychoanalytic illumination in *Knowledge and Human Interests* to practical interest in his "mature" work the characteristic gesture of the communicative turn. Jürgen Habermas, *Knowledge and Human Interests*, trans. Jeremy J. Shapiro (Boston: Beacon, 1971), chapter 9. It is also noteworthy that power becomes "derivative from the more anthropologically basic communicative interaction" in this same move. Amy Allen, *The Politics of Our Selves: Power, Autonomy, and Gender in Contemporary Critical Theory* (New York: Columbia University Press, 2008), 176.

130. Gillian Rose, *Hegel Contra Sociology* (London: Athlone, 1981), 33.

131. Adorno, *Minima Moralia*, 39 (the original phrase deals literally with the relation to one's home, but it works metaphorically as well). Andrew Douglas makes this same point—that Adorno's dialectical approach is "germane to a particular historical moment, an approach that recommends itself in light of the contradictions that we now experience"—but is quite vague about the present conditions that demand this approach. Andrew J. Douglas, *In the Spirit of Critique: Thinking Politically in the Dialectical Tradition* (Albany: SUNY Press, 2013), 81. The "redemptive energy" of dialectical thinking "in the face of despair" is not enough, to my mind, to justify its historical specificity (ibid., 65). In this section I am arguing that negative dialectics is not simply germane to but rather *made possible by* the conditions of late capitalism.

132. In addition to defending Adorno and Horkheimer against the charge that they, like Lasch, mounted a "reactionary defence of the bourgeois, patriarchal, Christian form of the family," my reworking of their crisis of internalization narrative has addressed Benjamin's criticisms of it in reconceiving of the superego as that which allows successful navigation of the conflict between tendencies traditionally associated with mother (union) and father (differentiation) and demonstrating that the weakening of the superego presents a unique opportunity for the achievement of autonomy (Barrett and McIntosh, "Narcissism and the Family," 43).

133. I thus disagree with Stéphane Haber that Adorno "yielded to the temptation to exonerate *retrospectively and strategically* the bourgeois superego" (and also, relatedly, his literal interpretation of the end of internalization thesis). Stéphane Haber, *Freud et la théorie sociale* (Paris: La Dispute, 2012), 186, 231.

134. Adorno, *Problems of Moral Philosophy*, 170.

135. Adorno, *Minima Moralia*, 66. Stiegler proposes a similar idea when he argues for the need "*to produce a superego through the critique of the superego* inherited from previous modes of life." Bernard Stiegler, *Réenchanter le monde: La valeur esprit contre le populisme industriel* (Paris: Flammarion, 2006), 70.

136. Adorno admittedly spurns the idea that he is proposing something like "psychoanalysis on a mass scale," which he deems "not feasible," but at the same time claims that the attempt "to foster self-reflection in those whom we want to emancipate from the grip of all-powerful conditioning" necessarily involves "a substantial piercing of . . . powerful defense mechanisms" (Adorno, "Democratic

Leadership and Mass Manipulation," 277, 272). While it is true that "abstract insight into one's own irrationalities, without going into their motivation, would not necessarily function in a cathartic way," since, as Adorno and Horkheimer themselves point out, the irrationality of mass culture intimately shapes our personal lives from an early age, I believe Adorno is wrong to downplay the psychological change involved in his approach (ibid., 279). In late capitalist society the critique of mass culture is a necessary part of "Wo Es war, soll Ich werden."

137. Aronowitz, *False Promises*, 119.

138. "There is no telling yet whether it will be a disaster or a liberation" (Adorno, *Negative Dialectics*, 346).

139. As I said in the first section, I am acutely aware that this narrative needs to be updated, and my aim here was to have laid a foundation for those additions. While I am hesitant even to hint at what they might look like, I can offer a brief note about how they ought to be formulated. The strength of the critical theorists' appropriation of psychoanalysis was to have revealed a dynamic *internal* to psychoanalytic theory rather than to have simply "revised" Freud and criticized him either for what he supposedly got wrong or for being outdated. It is easy to gather a list of adjectives that the *New York Times* uses to describe "youth" (distracted, aimless, plugged in), compare this list to the psychological theories of Freud or the Frankfurt school, and conclude that the latter leave something to be desired. The more difficult task, and the one upon which the legacy of the first-generation critical theorists hangs, is to work *within* their theories toward the present.

140. I take the possibility of this transformation to be what Adorno has in mind when he invokes "the mass potential of autonomy and spontaneity which is very much alive" (Adorno, "Democratic Leadership and Mass Manipulation," 272). At this point, I hope it is clear that Shane Gunster is wrong to claim that Adorno's "criticism of commodification leaves one convinced of its dangers but largely fails to explore any immanent dynamic within this social process that might play a part in its dialectical suspension" (Gunster, *Capitalizing on Culture*, 71). If the reification Adorno describes is understood as incomplete, as I believe it must (following Rose), then we can see dialectical possibility where Gunster sees none.

141. Theodor Adorno, *The Culture Industry*, 203. This is also how I understand the claim that "the man who enjoys [happiness] is acceding to the terms of the empirical world—terms that he wants to transcend, though they alone give him the chance of transcending" (Adorno, *Negative Dialectics*, 374).

142. By which Adorno meant not self-sufficiency but proper object relation (what I am calling a capacity for postoedipal mimesis): "Detached from the object, autonomy is fictitious" (ibid., 223).

143. See Russell Berman, "Adorno's Politics," in Gibson and Rubin, *Adorno: A Critical Reader.*

144. According to Volker Heins, Adorno rejected both "decisionistic and moralistic conceptions of politics" in favor of a "democratic pedagogy" that "focuses less on the restoration of democratic institutions than on the transformation of the ideas and habits of citizens." Volker Heins, "Saying Things That Hurt: Adorno as Educator," *Thesis Eleven* 110, no. 1 (2012): 70, 72.

145. While I appreciate the desire to counter the picture of Adorno as pessimistic elitist, I believe recent efforts to recover a "democratic" Adorno—such as those of Andrew Douglas, Volker Heins, and Shannon Mariotti—overstate the case. Douglas, for instance, claims that "ordinary citizens must work on a mode of critical reflection that can expose and blast open the continuum of democratic apathy," a statement that Adorno would find extremely suspect (Douglas, *In the Spirit of Critique*, 89). See also Heins, "Saying Things That Hurt" and Shannon Mariotti, "Critique from the Margins: Adorno and the Politics of Withdrawal," *Political Theory* 36, no. 3 (June 2008): 456–65.

146. Freud, *Standard Edition*, 21:49.

147. Macdonald, "Cold, Cold, Warm," 684. Adorno offers a very concrete proposal in Adorno and Becker, "Education for Autonomy," 109.

148. Macdonald, "Cold, Cold, Warm," 684. It is for this reason that I find it premature, though not wrong exactly, to portray reason's "turning upon itself" as a "self-critique through which actuality can be reendowed with ethical substantiality" (Bernstein, *Adorno*, 233).

149. See chapter 3, *n*96.

5. The Psyche in Late Capitalism II

1. "Mechanization . . . impinged upon the very center of the human psyche." Siegfried Giedion, *Mechanization Takes Command: A Contribution to Anonymous History* (New York: Norton, 1969), 42. "Technology [is] deeply modified at every stage of its development by dreams, wishes, impulses, religious motives that spring directly . . . from the recesses of man's unconscious." Lewis Mumford, *The Culture of Cities* (New York: Harcourt Brace, 1970), 415. "Ecologists . . . tend to polarize their efforts on limited objectives without taking into account all the consequences of technology on the human psyche. Jacques Ellul and Patrick Troude-Chastenet, *Jacques Ellul on Politics, Technology, and Christianity: Conversations with Patrick Troude-Chastenet* (Eugene: Wipf and Stock, 2005), 119.

2. As I suspect is also true of many of the readers of this chapter, I have been part of too many conversations where a seemingly thoughtful interlocutor transforms, in front of my eyes, into a human billboard: "Have you seen the new x? Have you heard that scientists did y?"

3. Karl Marx, *Capital Volume One: A Critique of Political Economy*, trans. Ben Fowkes (London: Penguin, 1976), 492.

4. Cf. Sigmund Freud, *The Standard Edition of the Complete Psychological Works of Sigmund Freud*, ed. and trans. James Strachey, 24 vols. (London: Hogarth and the Institute of Psycho-Analysis, 1966), 21:87–88.

5. See, for instance, his underdeveloped claims that "the mother is the goal of Eros and of the death instinct" and that "there are two kinds of mastery: a repressive and a liberating one." Herbert Marcuse, *Five Lectures: Psychoanalysis, Politics, and Utopia*, trans. Jeremy J. Shapiro and Shierry M. Weber (Boston:

Beacon, 1970), 25; Herbert Marcuse, *One-Dimensional Man: Studies in the Ideology of Advanced Industrial Society* (London: Routledge, 2002), 240.

6. Joel Whitebook, "The Marriage of Marx and Freud: Critical Theory and Psychoanalysis," in *The Cambridge Companion to Critical Theory*, ed. Fred Rush (Cambridge: Cambridge University Press, 2004), 89.

7. In this chapter I will thus not be directly confronting Marcuse's own reinterpretation of Freudian drive theory, but I can briefly indicate the major differences between his presentation and my own. Whereas Marcuse interprets the death drive as a "result of the trauma of primary frustration," I see it as that which is primarily frustrated, and thus as preceding the trauma that Marcuse contends is its source. Herbert Marcuse, *Eros and Civilization: A Philosophical Inquiry Into Freud* (Boston: Beacon, 1966), 139. Furthermore, whereas Marcuse, in articulating the historically specific possibility of freeing Eros from surplus repression, believes that a "strengthened Eros" could "absorb the objective of the death instinct," I argue that Eros, being a sublimation of the death drive, always already *has absorbed* its force but with a changed objective (ibid., 235). Finally, whereas Marcuse expresses hope in the free thrust of the "libidinal energy generated by the id," my own limited hopes lie in the liberating possibilities that *attend* instinctual frustration; which is to say, not in "exploding the reality ego" but in derigidifying it (ibid., 48).

8. Herbert Marcuse, *An Essay on Liberation* (Boston: Beacon, 1969), 13.

9. Herbert Marcuse, *Negations: Essays in Critical Theory*, trans. Jeremy J. Shapiro (London: Penguin, 1968), 198.

10. Ibid., 194.

11. Freud, *Standard Edition*, 21:121. Erich Fromm rejects this line of thought:

[According to Freud,] the aim of the instinct is not weakened, but it is directed toward other socially valuable aims, in this case the "domination over nature." This sounds, indeed, like a perfect solution. Man is freed from the tragic choice between destroying either others or himself, because the energy of the destructive instinct is used for the control over nature. But, we must ask, can this really be so? Can it be true that destructiveness becomes transformed into constructiveness? What can "control over nature" mean? Taming and breeding animals, gathering and cultivating plants, weaving cloth, building huts, manufacturing pottery, and many more activities including the construction of machines, railroads, airplanes, skyscrapers. All these are acts of constructing, building, unifying, synthesizing, and indeed, if one wanted to attribute them to one of the two basic instincts, they might be considered as being motivated by Eros rather than by the death instinct.

Erich Fromm, *The Anatomy of Human Destructiveness* (New York: Holt, Rinehart and Winston, 1973), 465–66.

12. Ernest Jones, *Sigmund Freud: Life and Work*, 3 vols. (London: Hogarth, 1957), 3:493–94.

13. Freud, *Standard Edition*, 14:94.

14. Ibid., 21:97.

15. And I do not mean simply that coitus leads to reproduction: in late capitalism, sexuality is deployed in myriad ways to promote commodity consumption.

16. F. J. Hacker, "Sublimation Revisited," *International Journal of Psycho-Analysis* 53 (1972): 219.

17. Ernest Jones, *Papers on Psycho-Analysis* (London: Baillière, Tindall and Cox, 1913), 426.

18. Hacker, "Sublimation Revisited," 220.

19. Morton Schoolman chalks this fact up to Marcuse's generally confused understanding of sublimation. Morton Schoolman, *The Imaginary Witness: The Critical Theory of Herbert Marcuse* (New York: Free Press, 1980), 107.

20. Marcuse, *Eros and Civilization*, 85–86.

21. Marcuse, *Negations*, 198.

22. "Assuming that the Destruction Instinct (in the last analysis: the Death Instinct) is a large component of the energy which feeds the technical conquest of man and nature, it seems that society's growing capacity to manipulate technical progress also increases its *capacity to manipulate and control this instinct*, i.e. to satisfy it 'productively'" (Marcuse, *One-Dimensional Man*, 82).

23. Freud, *Standard Edition*, 21:91–92.

24. Marcuse himself denies the existence of a force like aggressivity: "One can dispense with the notion of an innate 'power-drive' in human nature. This is a highly dubious psychological concept and grossly inadequate for the analysis of social developments" (Marcuse, *One-Dimensional Man*, 48).

25. According to Cornelius Castoriadis, "the idea of *total* mastery remains the hidden motor of modern technological development." Cornelius Castoriadis, *Philosophy, Politics, Autonomy*, ed. David Ames Curtis (Oxford: Oxford University Press, 1991), 192–93 (my emphasis).

26. Advertisements readily exploit this feeling: "convenience at your fingertips," "fit for a king," and, perhaps the most telling phrase, "with the touch of a button."

27. Marcuse, *One-Dimensional Man*, 159.

28. Marcuse, *Negations*, 153; Douglas Kellner, *Herbert Marcuse and the Crisis of Marxism* (Berkeley: University of California Press, 1984), 332.

29. Marcuse, *Five Lectures*, 238; see n57.

30. As Marcuse explains,

For the vast majority of the population, [the competitive struggle for existence] means life-long labor in the process of material production, and on this necessity rests not only the material reproduction of this society but also its moral and political structure: the institutions of domination and their mental counterpart, the repressive work-ethics of scarcity and of earning a living. And it is precisely this necessity which technical progress threatens to render unnecessary, irrational by the double power to mechanize human labor and to conquer scarcity. The result would be the tendentious abolition of business and industrial labor, and the pacification of existence. This end is by no means inherent in technical progress. Technology can be used, and is largely used for sustaining and even increasing the quantity of socially required labor and for denying gratification and pacification.

Herbert Marcuse, *Collected Papers of Herbert Marcuse*, ed. Douglas Kellner, 6 vols. (London: Routledge, 2014), 2:46. Cf. Marcuse, *An Essay on Liberation*, 19.

31. Ibid., 1:41.

32. Kellner, *Herbert Marcuse and the Crisis of Marxism*, 330.

33. Marcuse, *Five Lectures*, 56.

34. Ibid., 68. Following Gilbert Simondon, Marcuse thus thinks of liberation as a kind of *completion* of technics: "in constituting themselves *methodically* as political enterprise, science and technology would *pass beyond* the stage at which they were, because of their neutrality, *subjected* to politics and against their intent functioning as political instrumentalities" (Marcuse, *One-Dimensional Man*, 238).

35. "Now there is, in advanced technological societies of the West, *indeed a large desublimation* (compared with the preceding stages) in sexual mores and behavior. . . . But does this mode of desublimation signify the ascendancy of the life-preserving and life-enhancing Eros over its fatal adversary" (Marcuse, *Five Lectures*, 57)? In short, no: Eros is supposed to represent the individual's autonomy from society, but "in the technological desublimation today, the all but opposite tendency seems to prevail. The conflict between pleasure and the reality principle is managed by a controlled liberalization which increases satisfaction with the offerings of society. . . . With the integration of [pleasure] into the realm of business and entertainment, the repression is itself repressed: society has enlarged, not individual freedom, but its control over the individual" (ibid., 57). Thus, in Marcuse's view, both freedom and bondage today can be conceived in terms of desublimation; whereas one returns the subject's drives, the other seeks further control over them.

36. Marcuse, *One-Dimensional Man*, 162.

37. "The very judgment that the automobile is the most effective means of traveling from point A to point B structures in advance the visible and the invisible, what can be seen and what cannot. The most effective means of achieving a desired end, in this case reaching a destination, itself is a moment of world disclosure." Samir Gandesha, "Marcuse, Habermas, and the Critique of Technology," in *Herbert Marcuse: A Critical Reader*, ed. John Abromeit and W. Mark Cobb (London: Routledge, 2004), 203.

38. In order to distinguish these two elements, Feenberg introduces a distinction "between the aspect of technology stemming from the functional relation to reality, which [he calls] the 'primary instrumentalization,' and the aspect stemming from its social involvements and implementation, which [he calls] the 'secondary instrumentalization.'" Andrew Feenberg, *Between Reason and Experience: Essays in Technology and Modernity* (Cambridge: MIT Press, 2010), 72. This distinction allows him to hold off both the constructivist reduction of the technical to the social as well as the naïve elimination of the social from the technical.

39. Andrew Feenberg, "The Bias of Technology," in *Marcuse: Critical Theory and the Promise of Utopia*, ed. Robert Pippin et al. (London: Macmillan, 1988), 230, 238.

Habermas understands Marcuse's assertion that technology *is* ideology as meaning that "technocratic consciousness makes this practical interest [in "the maintenance of intersubjectivity of mutual understanding as well as . . . the creation of communication without domination"] disappear behind the interest in the expansion of our power of technical control." Jürgen Habermas, "Technology and Science as Ideology," in *Toward a Rational Society*, trans. Jeremy J. Shapiro (Cambridge: Polity, 1987), 113. Habermas thus reduces the whole problem of "technological rationality" to a confusion of "technical and practical problems," thereby conceding that "experts can resolve all technical questions properly and appropriately so long as they do not overstep the bounds of their authority and 'colonize the lifeworld'" (ibid., 120; Feenberg, *Between Reason and Experience*, 167). To ask more of technology—for instance, that it be "aestheticized"—would, for Habermas, be to seek the "resurrection of fallen nature" (Habermas, "Technology and Science as Ideology," 86). As Feenberg and Kellner both argue, this move leaves "no room at all for the social dimension of science and technology" and is ultimately conservative in casting the idea of repurposing technological progress to the end of meeting human needs as "utopian speculation" (Feenberg, *Between Reason and Experience*, 138; Kellner, *Herbert Marcuse and the Crisis of Marxism*, 331). Kellner abruptly concludes that "Habermas and others who defame the notion of a 'new technology' are in effect capitulating to current forms of technology and labour as inevitable and inalterable" (ibid., 332). For a longer critique of Habermas on this point, see Ben Agger, "Marcuse and Habermas on New Science," *Polity* 9, no. 2 (Winter 1976): 158–81.

40. Feenberg, *Between Reason and Experience*, 29, 151, 153.

41. Bernard Stiegler, *Réenchanter le monde: La valeur esprit contre le populisme industriel* (Paris: Flammarion, 2006), 128.

42. In Feenberg's terms, this means that primary instrumentalization cannot be separated from secondary instrumentalization *even analytically*.

43. Feenberg claims that "only in our fantasies do we transcend the strange loops of reason and experience. In the real world, there is no escape from the logic of finitude" (Feenberg, *Between Reason and Experience*, xxiii). My claim here is that this fantasy is not therefore without consequence and that excluding this fantasy from our understanding of technology reinforces the very "neutrality" of technology that Feenberg rejects (ibid., 6).

44. For other articulations of this basic idea, see Castoriadis, *Philosophy, Politics, Autonomy*, 192–95; Anthony Elliott, *Subject to Ourselves: Social Theory, Psychoanalysis, and Postmodernity* (Cambridge: Polity, 1996), 79.

45. Marcuse, *Five Lectures*, 39.

46. Herbert Marcuse, *Counterrevolution and Revolt* (Boston: Beacon, 1972), 68–69. Thanks to Isaac Balbus for pointing me to this passage.

47. For Marx,

living labour [in the sense of labor that produces use-values] must seize on these things, awaken them from the dead, change them from merely possible into real and effective use-values. Bathed in the fire of labour, appropriated as part of its organism, and infused with vital energy for the performance of the functions appropriate to their concept and to their vocation in the process, they are indeed consumed, but to some purpose, as elements in the formation of new use-values, new products, which are capable of entering into individual consumption as means of subsistence or into a new labour process as means of production.

(Marx, *Capital Volume One*, 289–90)

48. Marcuse, *Counterrevolution and Revolt*, 60.

49. A separation repeated by Feenberg: "No doubt human nature remains the same as always, but the means at our disposal are now much more powerful than in the past." Andrew Feenberg, "Heidegger and Marcuse: The Catastrophe and Redemption of Technology," in Abromeit and Cobb, *Herbert Marcuse: A Critical Reader*, 67.

50. Marcuse, *Collected Papers*, 1:47.

51. Marx, *Capital Volume One*, 165.

52. Marcuse, *Eros and Civilization*, 95.

53. Ibid., 32.

54. See Sherry Turkle, *Alone Together: Why We Expect More from Technology and Less from Each Other* (New York: Basic Books, 2011), 266–67.

55. Indeed, he goes out of his way to interpret the structural model in dualistic terms: "Throughout the various stages of Freud's theory, the mental apparatus appears as a dynamic union of opposites of the unconscious and the conscious structures; of primary and secondary processes; of inherited, 'constitutionally fixed' and acquired forces; of soma-psyche and the external reality. This dualistic construction continues to prevail even in the later tripartite topology of id, ego, and superego; the intermediary and 'overlapping' elements tend toward the two poles" (Marcuse, *Eros and Civilization*, 21–22). An adherence to rather than an ultimate rejection of the structural model would have led Marcuse to interpret advanced capitalist society not as one-dimensional but two-dimensional, fixed between the poles of a rigid instrumentalism at work (ego) and fleeting pleasure in one's leisure (id) without the critical dimension needed to transcend this bipolar existence (superego) (see Marcuse, *Collected Papers*, 5:111).

56. Bernard Stiegler, "Spirit, Capitalism and Superego," *ars industrialis*, May 2006, http://arsindustrialis.org/node/2928.

57. Exaggerating this claim even further, Jeremy Shapiro argues that the individual today is "no more than a unit or locus in a field of total design whose laws determine his or its meaning and our reaction." Jeremy J. Shapiro, "One-Dimensionality: The Universal Semiotic of Technological Experience," in *Critical Interruptions: New Left Perspectives on Herbert Marcuse*, ed. Paul Breines (New York: Herder and Herder, 1970), 166. As I argued in the previous chapter, I do not believe it productive to ape the Frankfurt school's rhetoric about a total elimination of individuality when their own theories demand the assumption of the continued existence of (damaged) individuality.

58. Or, more precisely, that the problem of technological rationality is one of linguistic deficit.

59. Erik Erikson helpfully describes the difference between the different wholes sought by Eros and Thanatos in distinguishing between "wholeness" and "totality":

Wholeness seems to connote an assembly of parts, even quite diversified parts, that enter into a fruitful association and organization. This concept is most strikingly expressed in such terms as wholeheartedness, wholemindedness, wholesomeness, and the like. As a *Gestalt*, then, wholeness emphasizes a sound, organic, progressive mutuality between diversified functions and parts within an entirety, the boundaries of which are open and fluent. Totality, on the contrary, evokes a *Gestalt* in which an absolute boundary is emphasized; given a certain degree of arbitrary delineation, nothing that belongs inside must be left outside, nothing that must be outside can be tolerated inside.

Erik Erikson, "Wholeness and Totality: A Psychiatric Contribution," in *Totalitarianism*, ed. Carl J., Friedrich (New York: Grosset and Dunlap, 1954), 161–62.

60. To use Sherry Turkle's words, the language of Thanatos "promise[s] relationships where we will be in control, even if that means not being in relationships at all" (Turkle, *Alone Together*, 17).

61. Marcuse, *One-Dimensional Man*, 172.

62. Ibid., 98. Jeremy Shapiro calls this the "universal semiotic of technological experience" (Shapiro, "One-Dimensionality," 152).

63. Marcuse, *One-Dimensional Man*, 97. In the era of text message abbreviation, this trend has reached somewhat absurd heights.

64. Christoph Türcke, *Philosophy of Dreams*, trans. Susan Gillespie (New Haven: Yale University Press, 2013), 239. Karl Korn analyzes this phenomenon in the phrase *auf Draht*, or "on the ball," "up to speed": today, "being well-informed, having one's ears and connections everywhere, is crucial." Karl Korn, *Sprache in der verwalteten Welt* (Olten: Walter, 1959), 86. One cannot be successful without being up to date, the concern for which is fueled by an anxiety over being left behind: "the phrase 'on the ball' will be around as long as there is a general prosperity that creates the illusion that an individual could escape the fate of the masses through information" (ibid., 87).

65. Cf. David Harvey, *The Condition of Postmodernity: An Enquiry Into the Origins of Cultural Change* (Cambridge: Blackwell, 1989), part 3.

66. Marcuse, *One-Dimensional Man*, 92.

67. Ibid., 95.

68. A phenomenon that Jaeggi calls "rigidification." Rahel Jaeggi, *Alienation*, trans. Frederick Neuhouser and Alan E. Smith, ed. Frederick Neuhouser (New York: Columbia University Press, 2014), 59.

69. Marcuse, *One-Dimensional Man*, 96. Cf. Theodor Adorno, *Minima Moralia: Reflections on a Damaged Life*, trans. E. F. N. Jephcott (London: Verso, 2005), 137–38.

70. Analytic philosophy, as exemplified in Austin and Wittgenstein, is a primary target of Marcuse's, which, he believes, colludes with this closure: in Wittgenstein's assurance that philosophy "leaves everything as it is," one finds the essentially conservative nature of a "self-styled poverty of philosophy" that masochistically reduces speech to the "humble and common" (Marcuse, *One-Dimensional Man*, 182). This conservativism is exacerbated by the "therapeutic

character" with which these philosophers conceive their project: "to cure from illusions, deceptions, obscurities, unsolvable riddles, unanswerable questions, from ghosts and spectres" (ibid., 187–88). Against this contemporary effort to reduce the scope of philosophy (and to thereby "cure" it), Marcuse upholds the difference between everyday and philosophical thinking (ibid., 183). The latter is preoccupied with the "question of universals," with abstract nouns like "justice," "beauty," and "freedom," all of which are not just components of everyday language games but rather "ideas which transcend their particular realizations as something that is to be surpassed, overcome" (ibid., 218). The persistence of these "untranslatable universals" in the face of linguistic instrumentalization attests to the continuing "unhappy consciousness of a divided world in which 'that which is' falls short of, and even denies, 'that which can be'" (ibid., 214).

71. Theodor Adorno, "Theory of Pseudo-Culture," *Telos* 95 (Spring 1995): 33.

72. Jürgen Habermas, *The Theory of Communicative Action*, trans. Thomas McCarthy (Boston: Beacon, 1984), 1:287.

73. Albrecht Wellmer, "Truth, Semblance and Reconciliation: Adorno's Aesthetic Redemption of Modernity," in *The Persistence of Modernity: Essays on Aesthetics, Ethics, and Postmodernism* (Cambridge: MIT Press, 1993), 20.

74. Joel Whitebook, "From Schoenberg to Odysseus: Aesthetic, Psychic, and Social Synthesis in Adorno and Wellmer," *New German Critique* 58 (Winter 1993): 56.

75. See chapter 4, *n*129 and chapter 5, *n*70.

76. See Freud, *Standard Edition*, 21:145.

77. Nicole M. Aschoff, "The Smartphone Society," *Jacobin* 17 (Spring 2015): 35.

78. Jerrold Seigel, *The Idea of the Self: Thought and Experience in Western Europe Since the Seventeenth Century* (Cambridge: Cambridge University Press, 2005), 10. According to Balbus, "computer-mediated communication dramatically accelerates the compression of time and space endemic to modernity . . . and promotes the proliferation and intensification of fantasies of infantile omnipotence off which modernity feeds and to which it contributes." Isaac Balbus, *Mourning and Modernity: Essays in the Psychoanalysis of Contemporary Society* (New York: Other, 2005), 117. Although I agree with Balbus's basic argument, I believe it is important to distinguish, as he does not, between omnipotence and self-loss, and to see these features as equally prevalent in what he calls the "infancy of modernity."

79. Martin Heidegger, "The Question Concerning Technology," in *Basic Writings*, ed. David Farrell Krell (New York: Harper Collins, 2008), 307–42.

Conclusion

1. The adoption of the term *triangulation* in recent psychoanalytic discourse reflects a desire to rescue the fundamentals of what Freud theorized under the concept "Oedipus complex" while discarding the reification of heterosexual complementarity; see Jay Greenberg, *Oedipus and Beyond: A Clinical Theory* (Cambridge: Harvard University Press, 1991), 180; Lewis Aron, "The Internalized Primal Scene," *Psychoanalytic Dialogues* 5 (1995): 195–237; Jessica Benjamin,

"Response to Commentaries by Mitchell and by Butler," *Studies in Gender and Sexuality* 1, no. 3 (2000): 306. My own way of doing so has been to translate mother and father into "other" and *other*, respectively, and thus to see the conflict that Freud assigns to two separate people as generated by the schizoid relation to one and the same other.

2. *Le Gai Savoir*, directed by Jean-Luc Godard (1969; Neuilly-sur-Seine: Gaumont, 2012).

3. The figure above should thus be imagined as generally atrophied in the upper half, but more swollen in the upper-right quadrant.

4. Sigmund Freud, *The Standard Edition of the Complete Psychological Works of Sigmund Freud*, ed. and trans. James Strachey, 24 vols. (London: Hogarth and the Institute of Psycho-Analysis, 1966), 21:166.

5. For sexuality as bodily pleasure, see the third section of the second essay of the *Three Essays*, "Infantile Sexuality" (Freud, *Standard Edition*, 7:183–85); for the importance of limitations, see the first section of the same essay, where Freud speaks of the "mental forces which are later to impede the course of the sexual instinct and, like dams, restrict its flow—disgust, feelings of shame and the claims of aesthetic and moral ideals" (ibid., 7:177).

6. See introduction, *n*43.

7. Leo Bersani, "Why Sex?" presentation, First Annual Conference of the Society for Psychoanalytic Inquiry, University of Chicago, May 17–19, 2013.

8. Herbert Marcuse, *One-Dimensional Man: Studies in the Ideology of Advanced Industrial Society* (London: Routledge, 2002), 255 (my emphasis).

9. Claus Offe, "Technology and One-Dimensionality," in *Marcuse: Critical Theory and the Promise of Utopia*, ed. Robert Pippin et al. (London: Macmillan, 1988), 218.

10. Herbert Marcuse, *Collected Papers of Herbert Marcuse*, ed. Douglas Kellner (London: Routledge, 2014), 5:223.

11. Marcuse, *One-Dimensional Man*, 250.

12. Theodor Adorno, *Minima Moralia: Reflections on a Damaged Life*, trans. E. F. N. Jephcott (London: Verso, 2005), 135–36.

13. I would hope, nonetheless, that the possibility I have outlined in chapter 4 indicates that we have more to do than simply "drag" ourselves along "under the burden of what is." Theodor Adorno, *Negative Dialectics*, trans. E. B. Ashton (London: Routledge, 1973), 345.

14. I find this passage from Douglas Kellner to be remarkable in this regard:

> While there is no question but that Adorno has overly one-sided and excessively negative and critical views of both the texts and the audiences of media culture, occasionally I have a nightmare that in some sense Adorno is right, that media culture by and large keeps individuals gratified and subservient to the logic and practices of market capitalism, that the culture industry has become thoroughly commodified and absorbs and deflects all oppositional culture to subservient ends. At times, web-surfing, channel-shifting on cable systems, or scanning commercial radio can provide the

impression that Adorno is correct, that most media culture is reified rub-
bish and blatant ideology, that culture has been fundamentally commercial-
ized, homogenized, and banalized by contemporary capitalism.

Douglas Kellner, "Theodor W. Adorno and the Dialectics of Mass Culture," in
Adorno: A Critical Reader, ed. Nigel Gibson and Andrew Rubin (Oxford: Blackwell,
2002), 105–6. Bernstein lists the standard complaints against Adorno in J. M.
Bernstein, *Adorno: Disenchantment and Ethics* (Cambridge: Cambridge University
Press, 2001), 57.

15. It is for this reason that I am skeptical of Axel Honneth's assertion that
critical theory "cannot be maintained today in the theoretical form in which
the members of the Frankfurt School originally developed it." Axel Honneth,
Pathologies of Reason: On the Legacy of Critical Theory, trans. James Ingram (New
York: Columbia University Press, 2009), 42. Although I agree that their project
needs to be updated, it strikes me as obfuscating to emphasize their essential
outdatedness.

16. Shane Gunster, *Capitalizing on Culture: Critical Theory for Cultural Studies*
(Toronto: University of Toronto Press, 2004), 12. Like Robyn Marasco, I am thus
interested in what "critical theory can do when freed from the demand that it fur-
nish a way out of despair." Robyn Marasco, *The Highway of Despair: Critical Theory
After Hegel* (New York: Columbia University Press, 2015), 21.

17. Freud, *Standard Edition*, 21:145.

Bibliography

Abraham, Nicolas, and Maria Torok. *The Wolf Man's Magic Word: A Cryptonomy*. Trans. Nicholas Rand. Minneapolis: University of Minnesota Press, 1986.

Adorno, Theodor W. "The Actuality of Philosophy." Trans. Benjamin Snow. *Telos* 31 (March 1977): 120–33.

——. *Critical Models: Interventions and Catchwords*. Trans. Henry W. Pickford. New York: Columbia University Press, 1998.

——. *The Culture Industry: Selected Essays on Mass Culture*. Ed. J. M. Bernstein. London: Routledge, 1991.

——. *Current of Music*. Ed. Robert Hullot-Kentor. Cambridge: Polity, 2009.

——. "Democratic Leadership and Mass Manipulation." In *Gesammelte Schriften*, 20.1:267–86. Frankfurt: Suhrkamp, 1997.

——. *Minima Moralia: Reflections on a Damaged Life*. Trans. E. F. N. Jephcott. London: Verso, 2005.

——. *Negative Dialectics*. Trans. E. B. Ashton. London: Routledge, 1973.

——. "Notizen zur neuen Anthropologie." In *Briefe und Briefwechsel*, 4:453–71. Frankfurt: Suhrkamp, 1994.

——. *Problems of Moral Philosophy*. Ed. Thomas Schröder. Trans. Rodney Livingston. Stanford: Stanford University Press, 2001.

——. "Sociology and Psychology, Part 1." *New Left Review* 1, no. 46 (November-December 1967): 67–80.

——. "Sociology and Psychology, Part 2." *New Left Review* 1, no. 47 (January-February 1968): 79–97.

——. "Theory of Pseudo-Culture." Trans. Deborah Cook. *Telos* 95 (Spring 1995): 15–38.

——. "Theses on the Language of the Philosopher." In *Adorno and the Need in Thinking: Critical Essays,* 35–40. Ed. Donald Burke, Colin J. Campbell, Kathy Kiloh, Michael K. Palamarek, and Jonathan Short. Toronto: University of Toronto Press, 2007.

Adorno, Theodor W., and Hellmut Becker. "Education for Autonomy." *Telos* 56 (Summer 1983): 103–10.

Adorno, Theodor W., and Else Frenkel-Brunswik, Daniel J. Levinson, and R. Nevitt Sanford. *The Authoritarian Personality.* New York: Harper and Row, 1950.

Adorno, Theodor W., and Max Horkheimer. *Dialectic of Enlightenment: Philosophical Fragments.* Trans. Edmund Jephcott. Stanford: Stanford University Press, 2002.

Agger, Ben. "Marcuse and Habermas on New Science." *Polity* 9, no. 2 (Winter 1976): 158–81.

Alexander, Franz. *Fundamentals of Psychoanalysis.* New York: Norton, 1963.

——. "The Need for Punishment and the Death-Instinct." *International Journal of Psycho-Analysis* 10 (1929): 256–69.

Alford, C. Fred. *Narcissism: Socrates, the Frankfurt School, and Psychoanalytic Theory.* New Haven: Yale University Press, 1988.

Allen, Amy. *The Politics of Our Selves: Power, Autonomy, and Gender in Contemporary Critical Theory.* New York: Columbia University Press, 2008.

Anspach, Mark R. "Editor's Introduction: Imitating Oedipus." In René Girard, *Oedipus Unbound: Selected Writings on Rivalry and Desire,* vii–liv. Ed. Mark R. Anspach. Stanford: Stanford University Press, 2004.

Arendt, Hannah. *On Violence.* New York: Harcourt Brace Jovanovich, 1970.

Arlow, Jacob A. "Problems of the Superego Concept." *Psychoanalytic Study of the Child* 37 (1982): 229–44.

Aron, Lewis. "The Internalized Primal Scene." *Psychoanalytic Dialogues* 5 (1995): 195–237.

Aronowitz, Stanley. *False Promises: The Shaping of American Working Class Consciousness.* Durham: Duke University Press, 1992.

Aschoff, Nicole M. "The Smartphone Society." *Jacobin* 17 (Spring 2015): 35–41.

Assoun, Paul-Laurent. *Freud and Nietzsche.* Trans. Richard L. Collier. London: Continuum, 2002.

——. *Freud et les sciences sociales: Psychanalyse et théorie de la Culture.* Paris: Armand Colin, 1993.

Aulagnier, Piera. *The Violence of Interpretation: From Pictogram to Statement.* Trans. Alan Sheridan. Hove: Brunner-Routledge, 2001.

Bailly, Lionel. *Lacan.* Oxford: Oneworld, 2009.

Balbus, Isaac. "Between Enemies and Friends: Carl Schmitt, Melanie Klein, and the Passion(s) of the Political." *Theoria and Praxis* 1, no. 1 (2013): 18–47.

——. *Marxism and Domination: A Neo-Hegelian, Feminist, Psychoanalytic Theory of Sexual, Political, and Technological Liberation.* Princeton: Princeton University Press, 1982.

——. *Mourning and Modernity: Essays in the Psychoanalysis of Contemporary Society.* New York: Other, 2005.

Balsamo, Anne. *Technologies of the Gendered Body: Reading Cyborg Women.* Durham: Duke University Press, 1996.

Barrett, Michèle, and Mary McIntosh. "Narcissism and the Family: A Critique of Lasch." *New Left Review* 1, no. 135 (September-October 1982): 35–48.

Bass, Alan. *Difference and Disavowal: The Trauma of Eros.* Stanford: Stanford University Press, 2000.

Bataille, Georges. *Theory of Religion.* Trans. Robert Hurley. New York: Zone, 1989.

Beirnaert, Louis. "La pulsion de mort chez Freud." *Études* 342 (March 1975): 397–406.

Benhabib, Seyla. *Critique, Norm, Utopia: A Study of the Foundations of Critical Theory.* New York: Columbia University Press, 1986.

Benjamin, Jessica. "Authority and the Family Revisited: Or, a World Without Fathers?" *New German Critique* 13 (Winter 1978): 35–57.

——. *The Bonds of Love: Psychoanalysis, Feminism, and the Problem of Domination.* New York: Pantheon, 1988.

——. "The End of Internalization: Adorno's Social Psychology." *Telos* 32 (Summer 1977): 42–64.

——. *Like Subjects, Love Objects: Essays on Recognition and Sexual Difference.* New Haven: Yale University Press, 1995.

——. "Response to Commentaries by Mitchell and by Butler." In *Studies in Gender and Sexuality* 1, no. 3 (2000): 291–308.

Benjamin, Walter. "On Language as Such and the Language of Man." *Selected Writings,* 1:62–74. Ed. Marcus Bullock and Michael Jennings. Cambridge: Belknap Press of Harvard University, 2004.

Berman, Russell. "Adorno's Politics." In *Adorno: A Critical Reader,* 110–31. Ed. Nigel Gibson and Andrew Rubin. Oxford: Blackwell, 2002.

Bernfeld, Siegfried. *Psychologie des Säuglings.* Vienna: Julius Springer, 1925.

Bernstein, J. M. *Adorno: Disenchantment and Ethics.* Cambridge: Cambridge University Press, 2001.

Bersani, Leo. *The Freudian Body: Psychoanalysis and Art.* New York: Columbia University Press, 1986.

——. "Why Sex?" First Annual Conference of the Society for Psychoanalytic Inquiry. University of Chicago. May 17–19, 2013.

Bilgrami, Akeel. *Secularism, Identity, and Enchantment.* Cambridge: Harvard University Press, 2014.

Bion, Wilfred. "Attacks on Linking." *Melanie Klein Today: Developments in Theory and Practice,* 1:87–101. Ed. Elizabeth Bott Spillius. London: Routledge, 1988.

——. *Learning from Experience.* London: Tavistock, 1962.

Bloch, Ernst. *The Principle of Hope.,* Trans. Neville Plaice, Stephen Plaice, and Paul Knight. 3 vols. Cambridge: MIT Press, 1996.

Blum, Harold P. "The Borderline Childhood of the Wolf Man." In *Freud and His Patients,* 341–58. Ed. Mark Kanzer, and Jules Glenn. New York: Jason Aronson, 1980.

Boellstorff, Tom. *Coming of Age in Second Life: An Anthropologist Explores the Virtually Human*. Princeton: Princeton University Press, 2008.

Boothby, Richard. *Death and Desire: Psychoanalytic Theory in Lacan's Return to Freud*. London: Routledge, 1991.

Borch-Jacobsen, Mikkel. *Lacan: The Absolute Master*. Trans. Douglas Brick. Stanford: Stanford University Press, 1991.

Borch-Jacobsen, Mikkel, and Sonu Shamdasani. *The Freud Files: An Inquiry Into the History of Psychoanalysis*. Cambridge: Cambridge University Press, 2012.

Bowlby, John. "The Nature of the Child's Tie to His Mother." *International Journal of Psychoanalysis* 39 (1958): 350–73.

——. "Separation Anxiety." *International Journal of Psycho-Analysis* 41 (1960): 89–113.

Brooks, Peter. "Fictions of the Wolfman: Freud and Narrative Understanding." *Diacritics* 9, no. 1 (1979): 71–81.

Brown, Wendy. *Walled States, Waning Sovereignty*. Brooklyn: Zone, 2010.

Buck-Morss, Susan. *The Origin of Negative Dialectics: Theodor W. Adorno, Walter Benjamin, and the Frankfurt Institute*. New York: Free Press, 1977.

Butler, Judith. "The Pleasures of Repetition." In *Pleasure Beyond the Pleasure Principle*, 259–75. Ed. Robert A. Glick and Stanley Bone. New Haven: Yale University Press, 1990.

——. *The Psychic Life of Power: Theories in Subjection*. Stanford: Stanford University Press, 1997.

Caropreso, Fátima, and Richard Theisen Simanke. "Life and Death in Freudian metapsychology." In *On Freud's "Beyond the Pleasure Principle,"* 86–107. Ed. Salman Akhtar and Mary Kay O'Neil. London: Karnac, 2011.

Cassidy, Jude. "The Nature of the Child's Ties." In *Handbook of Attachment: Theory, Research, and Clinical Applications*, 3–22. 2d ed. Ed. Jude Cassidy and Phillip R. Shaver. New York: Guilford, 2008.

Castoriadis, Cornelius. *Philosophy, Politics, Autonomy*. Ed. David Ames Curtis. Oxford: Oxford University Press, 1991.

Chodorow, Nancy. "The Psychoanalytic Vision of Hans Loewald." *International Journal of Psychoanalysis* 84 (2003): 897–913.

Collins, Jim. *Uncommon Cultures: Popular Culture and Post-Modernism*. New York: Routledge, 1989.

Cook, Deborah. "Adorno on Mass Societies." *Journal of Social Philosophy* 32, no. 1 (Spring 2001): 35–52.

Crews, Frederick, ed. *Unauthorized Freud: Doubters Confront a Legend*. London: Penguin, 1999.

Culler, Jonathan. *The Pursuit of Signs: Semiotics, Literature, Deconstruction*. London: Routledge, 1981.

Deleuze, Gilles, and Félix Guattari. *Anti-Oedipus: Capitalism and Schizophrenia*. Trans. Robert Hurley, Mark Seem, and Helen R. Lane. Minneapolis: University of Minnesota Press, 1983.

Demos, John. "Oedipus and America: Historical Perspectives on the Reception of Psychoanalysis in America." In *Inventing the Psychological: Toward a Cultural*

History of Emotional Life in America, 63–78. Ed. Joel Pfister and Nancy Schnog. New Haven: Yale University Press, 1997.

Denis, Paul. "Emprise et théorie des pulsions." *Revue Française de Psychanalyse* 56, no. 5 (1992): 1295–422.

Derrida, Jacques. *Archive Fever: A Freudian Impression*. Trans. Eric Prenowitz. Chicago: University of Chicago Press, 1996.

——. "Autoimmunity: Real and Symbolic Suicides—a Dialogue with Jacques Derrida." Trans. Pascale-Anne Brault and Michael Naas. In *Philosophy in a Time of Terror*, 85–136. Ed. Giovanna Borradori. Chicago: University of Chicago Press, 2003.

——. "Différance." In *Speech and Phenomena and Other Essays on Husserl's Theory of Signs*, 129–60. Trans. David B. Allison. Evanston: Northwestern University Press, 1973.

——. *The Post Card: From Socrates to Freud and Beyond*. Trans. Alan Bass. Chicago: University of Chicago Press, 1987.

——. *Rogues: Two Essays on Reason*. Trans. Pascale-Anne Brault and Michael Naas. Stanford: Stanford University Press, 2005.

Dinnerstein, Dorothy. *The Mermaid and the Minotaur*. New York: Other, 1999.

Dolto, Françoise. *La Vague et l'océan: Séminaire sur les pulsions de mort*. Paris: Gallimard, 2003.

Dorey, Roger. "Le désir d'emprise." *Revue Française de Psychanalyse* 56, no. 5 (1992): 1423–32.

——. "The Relationship of Mastery." Trans. Philip Slotkin. *International Review of Psychoanalysis* 13 (1986): 323–32.

Douglas, Andrew J. *In the Spirit of Critique: Thinking Politically in the Dialectical Tradition*. Albany: SUNY Press, 2013.

Dufresne, Todd. *Tales from the Freudian Crypt: The Death Drive in Text and Context*. Stanford: Stanford University Press, 2000.

Dunn, Allen. "The Man Who Needs Hardness: Irony and Solidarity in the Aesthetics of Theodor Adorno." In *Germany and German Thought in American Literature and Cultural Criticism*, 470–84. Ed. Peter Freese. Essen: Die Blaue Eule, 1990.

Eagleton, Terry. *The Ideology of the Aesthetic*. Malden, MA: Blackwell, 1990.

Eigen, Michael. *The Electrified Tightrope*. Ed. Adam Phillips. London: Karnac, 2004.

——. *Psychic Deadness*. London: Karnac, 2004.

Eissler, K. R. "Comments on Erroneous Interpretations of Freud's Seduction Theory." *Journal of the American Psychoanalytic Association* 41, no. 2 (1993): 571–83.

Elkins, Jeremy. "Motility, Aggression, and the Bodily I: An Interpretation of Winnicott." *Psychoanalytic Quarterly* 84, no. 4 (2015): 943–73.

Ellenberger, Henri. *The Discovery of the Unconscious: The History and Evolution of Dynamic Psychiatry*. New York: Basic Books, 1970.

Elliott, Anthony. *Subject to Ourselves: Social Theory, Psychoanalysis, and Postmodernity*. Cambridge: Polity, 1996.

Ellul, Jacques, and Patrick Troude-Chastenet. *Jacques Ellul on Politics, Technology, and Christianity: Conversations with Patrick Troude-Chastenet.* Eugene: Wipf and Stock, 2005.

Erikson, Erik. "Wholeness and Totality: A Psychiatric Contribution." In *Totalitarianism*, 156–71. Ed. Carl J. Friedrich. New York: Grosset and Dunlap, 1954.

Esposito, Roberto. *Immunitas: The Protection and Negation of Life.* Trans. Zakiya Hanafi. Cambridge: Polity, 2011.

Ettinger, Bracha. "Matrixial Trans-subjectivity." *Theory, Culture, and Society* 23, nos. 2–3 (2006): 218–22.

Feenberg, Andrew. *Between Reason and Experience: Essays in Technology and Modernity.* Cambridge: MIT Press, 2010.

——. "The Bias of Technology." In *Marcuse: Critical Theory and the Promise of Utopia*, 225–56. Ed. Robert Pippin, Andrew Feenberg, and Charles P. Webel. London: Macmillan, 1988.

——. "Heidegger and Marcuse: The Catastrophe and Redemption of Technology." In *Herbert Marcuse: A Critical Reader*, 67–80. Ed. John Abromeit and W. Mark Cobb. London: Routledge, 2004.

Fenichel, Otto. "The Drive to Amass Wealth." *Psychoanalytic Quarterly* 7 (1938): 69–95.

——. "Ego Strength and Ego Weakness." In *The Collected Papers of Otto Fenichel*, 70–80. New York: Norton, 1954.

——. *The Psychoanalytic Theory of Neurosis.* London: Routledge and Kegan Paul, 1946.

Ferenczi, Sándor. "The Ontogenesis of the Interest in Money." In *First Contributions to Psycho-Analysis*, 319–31. London: Hogarth and the Institute of Psycho-Analysis, 1952.

——. *Thalassa: A Theory of Genitality.* London: Karnac, 1989.

Fink, Bruce. *A Clinical Introduction to Lacanian Psychoanalysis: Theory and Technique.* Cambridge: Harvard University Press, 1997.

——. *Lacan to the Letter: Reading Écrits Closely.* Minneapolis: University of Minnesota Press, 2004.

Fletcher, John. *Freud and the Scene of Trauma.* New York: Fordham University Press, 2013.

Flugel, J. C. *Studies in Feeling and Desire.* London: Duckworth, 1955.

Forrester, John. *Dispatches from the Freud Wars: Psychoanalysis and its Passions.* Cambridge: Harvard University Press, 1997.

Freud, Anna. *The Ego and the Mechanisms of Defense.* Trans. Cecil Baines. London: Karnac, 1993.

Freud, Sigmund. *Gesammelte Werke: Chronologisch Geordnet.* 18 vols. London: Imago, 1991.

——. *A Phylogenetic Fantasy: Overview of the Transference Neuroses.* Ed. Ilse Grubrich-Simitis. Trans. Axel and Peter Hoffer. Cambridge: Belknap, 1987.

——. *The Standard Edition of the Complete Psychological Works of Sigmund Freud.* Ed. and Trans. James Strachey. 24 vols. London: Hogarth and the Institute of Psycho-Analysis, 1966.

Freud, Sigmund, and Karl Abraham. *A Psycho-Analytic Dialogue: The Letters of Sigmund Freud and Karl Abraham, 1907–1926.* Ed. Hilda C. Abraham and Ernst L. Freud. Trans. Bernard Marsh and Hilda C. Abraham. New York: Basic Books, 1965.

Freud, Sigmund, and Lou Andreas-Salomé. *Sigmund Freud and Lou Andreas-Salomé: Letters.* Ed. Ernst Pfeiffer. Trans. William and Elaine Robson-Scott. London: Hogarth, 1966.

Freud, Sigmund, and Sándor Ferenczi. *The Correspondence of Sigmund Freud and Sándor Ferenczi.* Ed. Ernst Falzeder and Eva Brabant. Trans. Peter T. Hoffer. 3 vols. Cambridge: Belknap, 1996.

Freyenhagen, Fabian. *Adorno's Practical Philosophy: Living Less Wrongly.* Cambridge: Cambridge University Press, 2013.

Fromm, Erich. *The Anatomy of Human Destructiveness.* New York: Holt, Rinehart and Winston, 1973.

——. *Escape from Freedom.* New York: Henry Holt, 1969.

——. "The Method and Function of an Analytic Social Psychology: Notes on Psychoanalysis and Historical Materialism." In *The Essential Frankfurt School Reader,* 477–96. Ed. Andrew Arato and Eike Gebhardt. New York: Continuum, 2005.

Gaddini, Eugenio. "On Imitation." *International Journal of Psychoanalysis* 50 (1969): 475–84.

Le Gai Savoir. Directed by Jean-Luc Godard. 1969. Neuilly-sur-Seine: Gaumont, 2012.

Gandesha, Samir. "Marcuse, Habermas, and the Critique of Technology." In *Herbert Marcuse: A Critical Reader,* 188–208. Ed. John Abromeit and W. Mark Cobb. London: Routledge, 2004.

Gardiner, Muriel, ed. *The Wolf-Man: With the Case of the Wolf-Man by Sigmund Freud.* New York: Basic Books, 1971.

Gay, Peter. *Freud: A Life for Our Time.* New York: Norton, 1988.

——. *Freud for Historians.* Oxford: Oxford University Press, 1985.

Geuss, Raymond. *Outside Ethics.* Princeton: Princeton University Press, 2005.

Giedion, Siegfried. *Mechanization Takes Command: A Contribution to Anonymous History.* New York: Norton, 1969.

Gillibert, Jean. "De l'objet pulsionnel de la pulsion d'emprise." *Revue Française de Psychanalyse* 46, no. 6 (1982): 1211–43.

Girard, René. "Superman in the Underground: Strategies of Madness-Nietzsche, Wagner, and Dostoevsky." *MLN* 91, no. 6 (December 1976): 1161–85.

——. *Things Hidden Since the Foundation of the World.* Trans. Stephen Bann and Michael Metteer. Stanford: Stanford University Press, 1987.

——. *Violence and the Sacred.* Trans. Patrick Gregory. Baltimore: Johns Hokpins University Press, 1977.

Goldstein, Jan. *The Post-Revolutionary Self: Politics and Psyche in France, 1750–1850.* Cambridge: Harvard University Press, 2005.

Goux, Jean-Joseph. *Symbolic Economies: After Marx and Freud.* Trans. Jennifer Curtiss Gage. Ithaca: Cornell University Press, 1990.

Green, André. *Life Narcissism, Death Narcissism*. Trans. Andrew Weller. London: Free Association Books, 2001.

Greenberg, Jay. *Oedipus and Beyond: A Clinical Theory*. Cambridge: Harvard University Press, 1991.

Greenberg, Jay R., and Stephen A. Mitchell. *Object Relations in Psychoanalytic Theory*. Cambridge: Harvard University Press, 1983.

Grubrich-Simitis, Ilse. "Trauma or Drive—Drive and Trauma: A Reading of Sigmund Freud's Phylogenetic Fantasy of 1915." *Psychoanalytic Study of the Child* 43 (1988): 3–32.

Grunberger, Béla. *Narcissism: Psychoanalytic Essays*. Trans. Joyce S. Diamanti. New York: International Universities Press, 1979.

Gunster, Shane. *Capitalizing on Culture: Critical Theory for Cultural Studies*. Toronto: University of Toronto Press, 2004.

Haber, Stéphane. *Freud et la Théorie Sociale*. Paris: La Dispute, 2012.

Habermas, Jürgen. *Knowledge and Human Interests*. Trans. Jeremy J. Shapiro. Boston: Beacon, 1971.

——. *Philosophical-Political Profiles*. Trans. Frederick G. Lawrence. Cambridge: MIT Press, 1983.

——. "Technology and Science as Ideology." In *Toward a Rational Society*, 81–122. Trans. Jeremy J. Shapiro. Cambridge: Polity, 1987.

——. *The Theory of Communicative Action*. Trans. Thomas McCarthy. 2 vols. Boston: Beacon, 1984.

Hacker, F. J. "Sublimation Revisited." *International Journal of Psycho-Analysis* 53 (1972): 219–23.

Hacking, Ian. *The Social Construction of What?* Cambridge: Harvard University Press, 1999.

Hansen, Miriam Bratu. "Benjamin and Cinema: Not a One-Way Street." *Critical Inquiry* 25 (Winter 1999): 306–43.

Harrison, Robert Pogue. *The Dominion of the Dead*. Chicago: University of Chicago Press, 2003.

Hartmann, Heinz. "Comments on the Psychoanalytic Theory of Instinctual Drives." *Psychoanalytic Quarterly* 17 (1948): 368–88.

Harvey, David. *The Condition of Postmodernity: An Enquiry Into the Origins of Cultural Change*. Cambridge: Blackwell, 1990.

Hegel, G. W. F. *The Phenomenology of Spirit*. Trans. A. V. Miller. Oxford: Oxford University Press, 1977.

——. *The Philosophy of Right*. Trans. T. M. Knox. Oxford: Oxford University Press, 1967.

Heidegger, Martin. "The Question Concerning Technology." In *Basic Writings*, 307–42. Ed. David Farrell Krell. New York: Harper Collins, 2008.

Heins, Volker. "Saying Things That Hurt: Adorno as Educator." *Thesis Eleven* 110, no. 1 (2012): 68–82.

Hendrick, Ives. "The Discussion of the 'Instinct to Master.'" *Psychoanalytic Quarterly* 12 (1943): 561–65.

——. "Work and the Pleasure Principle." *Psychoanalytic Quarterly* 12 (1943): 311–29.

Hoffman, Thomas. "Revival of the Death Instinct: A View from Contemporary Biology." *Neuropsychoanalysis* 6 (2004): 63–75.

Hohendahl, Peter Uwe. *Prismatic Thought: Theodor W. Adorno.* Lincoln: University of Nebraska Press, 1995.

Honneth, Axel. *Pathologies of Reason: On the Legacy of Critical Theory.* Trans. James Ingram and Others. New York: Columbia University Press, 2009.

——. *The Struggle for Recognition: The Moral Grammar of Social Conflicts.* Trans. Joel Anderson. Cambridge: MIT Press, 1995.

——. "The Work of Negativity." In *Recognition, Work, Politics: New Directions in French Critical Theory,* 127–36. Ed. Jean-Philippe Deranty, Danielle Petherbridge, John Rundell, and Robert Sinnerbrink. Leiden: Brill, 2007.

Horkheimer, Max. "Authoritarianism and the Family Today." In *The Family: Its Function and Destiny,* 359–74. Ed. Ruth Nanda Anshen. New York: Harper, 1949.

——. *Critical Theory: Selected Essays.* Trans. Matthew J. O'Connell and Others. New York: Continuum, 1999.

——. *The Eclipse of Reason.* New York: Oxford University Press, 1947.

Horney, Karen. "Der Kampf in Der Kultur [Culture and Aggression]: Einige Gedanken und Bedenken zu Freud's Todestrieb und Destruktionstrieb." Trans. Bella S. Van Bark. *American Journal of Psychoanalysis* 20 (1960): 130–38.

——. "Observations on a Specific Difference in the Dread Felt by Men and by Women Respectively for the Opposite Sex." *International Journal of Psycho-Analysis* 13 (1932): 348–60.

Hullot-Kentor, Robert. "The Exact Sense in Which the Culture Industry No Longer Exists." *Cultural Critique* 70 (Fall 2008): 137–57.

——. "A New Type of Human Being and Who We Really Are." *Brooklyn Rail,* November 10, 2008. http://www.brooklynrail.org/2008/11/art/a-new-type-of-human-being-and-who-we-really-are.

——. "Right Listening and a New Type of Human Being." In *The Cambridge Companion to Adorno,* 181–97. Ed. Tom Huhn. Cambridge: Cambridge University Press, 2004.

——. *Things Beyond Resemblance: On Theodor W. Adorno.* New York: Columbia University Press, 2006.

Huyssen, Andreas. "Adorno in Reverse: From Hollywood to Richard Wagner." In *Adorno: A Critical Reader,* 29–56. Ed. Nigel Gibson and Andrew Rubin. Oxford: Blackwell, 2002.

Ikonen, Pentti, and Eero Rechardt. *Thanatos, Shame, and Other Essays: On the Psychology of Destructiveness.* London: Karnac, 2010.

Jaeggi, Rahel. *Alienation.* Ed. Frederick Neuhouser. Trans. Frederick Neuhouser and Alan E. Smith. New York: Columbia University Press, 2014.

James, William. *Varieties of Religious Experience: A Study in Human Nature.* London: Routledge, 2002.

Jameson, Fredric. *Late Marxism: Adorno, or the Persistence of the Dialectic.* London: Verso, 1990.

Jarvis, Simon. *Adorno: A Critical Introduction.* New York: Routledge, 1998.

Jay, Martin. *The Dialectical Imagination: A History of the Frankfurt School and the Institute of Social Research, 1923–1950*. Berkeley: University of California Press, 1996.

——. *Marxism and Totality: The Adventures of a Concept from Lukács to Habermas*. Berkeley: University of California Press, 1984.

——. *Songs of Experience: Modern American and European Variations on a Universal Theme*. Berkeley: University of California Press, 2005.

Jenemann, David. *Adorno in America*. Minneapolis: University of Minnesota Press, 1997.

Johnston, Adrian. *Time Driven: Metapsychology and the Splitting of the Drive*. Evanston: Northwestern University Press, 2005.

Jones, Ernest. *Papers on Psycho-Analysis*. London: Baillière, Tindall and Cox, 1913.

——. *Sigmund Freud: Life and Work*. 3 vols. London: Hogarth, 1957.

Jones, James W. "Hans Loewald: The Psychoanalyst as Mystic." *Psychoanalytic Review* 88 (2001): 793–809.

Julien, Philippe. *Jacques Lacan's Return to Freud: The Real, the Symbolic, and the Imaginary*. Trans. Devra Beck Simiu. New York: New York University Press, 1994.

Jung, C. G. *Psychology of the Unconscious: A Study of the Transformations and Symbolisms of the Libido*. Trans. Beatrice M. Hinkle. New York: Moffat, Yard, 1917.

Kanzer, Mark. "Further Comments on the Wolf Man: The Search for a Primal Scene." In *Freud and His Patients*, 359–66. Ed. Mark Kanzer and Jules Glenn. New York: Jason Aronson, 1980.

Kellner, Douglas. *Herbert Marcuse and the Crisis of Marxism*. Berkeley: University of California Press, 1984.

——. "Theodor W. Adorno and the Dialectics of Mass Culture." In *Adorno: A Critical Reader*, 86–109. Ed. Nigel Gibson and Andrew Rubin. Oxford: Blackwell, 2002.

Kerr, John. "Beyond the Pleasure Principle and Back Again: Freud, Jung, and Sabina Spielrein." In *Freud: Appraisals and Reappraisals*, 3:3–79. Ed. Paul E. Stepansky. Hillsdale: Analytic, 1988.

Khan, M. Masud R. "The Concept of Cumulative Trauma." *Psychoanalytic Study of the Child* 18 (1963): 286–306.

Kierkegaard, Søren. *The Concept of Dread*. Trans. Walter Lowrie. Princeton: Princeton University Press, 1957.

King, Pearl, and Riccardo Steiner, eds. *The Freud-Klein Controversies, 1941–45*. London: Routledge, 1992.

Kisiel, Theodore. *The Genesis of Heidegger's* Being & Time. Berkeley: University of California Press, 1993.

Klein, Melanie. *Envy and Gratitude and Other Works, 1946–1963*. New York: Free Press, 1975.

Kluge, Friedrich. *Etymologisches Wörterbuch der deutschen Sprache*. Berlin: de Gruyter, 2002.

Kofman, Sarah. *Freud and Fiction*. Trans. Sarah Wykes. Cambridge: Polity, 1991.

Kohut, Heinz. "Forms and Transformations of Narcissism." *Journal of the American Psychoanalytic Association* 14 (1966): 243–72.

——. "Introspection, Empathy, and Psychoanalysis—an Examination of the Relationship Between Mode of Observation and Theory." *Journal of the American Psychoanalytic Association* 7 (1959): 459–83.

Kolakowski, Leszek. *Main Currents of Marxism: Its Rise, Growth, and Dissolution.* Trans. P. S. Falla. 3 vols. Oxford: Oxford University Press, 1978.

Korn, Karl. *Sprache in der verwalteten Welt.* Olten: Walter, 1959.

Kristeva, Julia. *Revolution in Poetic Language.* Trans. Margaret Waller. New York: Columbia University Press, 1984.

Lacan, Jacques. "Les complexes familiaux dans la formation de l'individu." In *Autres Écrits*, 23–84. Paris: Seuil, 2001.

——. *Écrits.* Trans. Bruce Fink. New York: Norton, 2002.

——. *The Seminar of Jacques Lacan, Book I: Freud's Papers on Technique, 1953–1954.* Ed. Jacques-Alain Miller. Trans. John Forrester. New York: Norton, 1991.

——. *The Seminar of Jacques Lacan, Book II: The Ego in Freud's Theory and in the Technique of Psychoanalysis, 1954–1955.* Ed. Jacques-Alain Miller. Trans. Sylvana Tomaselli. New York: Norton, 1991.

——. *Le Séminaire de Jacques Lacan, livre IV: La relation d'objet.* Ed. Jacques-Alain Miller. Paris: Seuil, 1994.

——. *The Seminar of Jacques Lacan, Book VII: The Ethics of Psychoanalysis.* Ed. Jacques-Alain Miller. Trans. Dennis Porter. New York: Norton, 1997.

——. *The Seminar of Jacques Lacan, Book X: Anxiety, 1962–1963.* Ed. Jacques Alain-Miller. Trans. A. R. Price. Cambridge: Polity, 2014.

——. *Seminar XI: The Four Fundamental Concepts of Psychoanalysis.* Trans. Alan Sheridan. New York: Norton, 1981.

Laplanche, Jean. *Freud and the Sexual: Essays, 2000–2006.* Ed. John Fletcher. Trans. John Fletcher, Jonathan House, and Nicholas Ray. New York: International Psychoanalytic, 2011.

——. *Life and Death in Psychoanalysis.* Trans. Jeffrey Mehlman. Baltimore: Johns Hopkins University Press, 1976.

——. *Nouveaux Fondements pour la psychanalyse.* Paris: Presse Universitaires de France, 1987.

——. "La pulsion de mort dans la théorie de la pulsion sexuelle." In *La Pulsion de Mort*, 11–26. Paris: Presses Universitaires de France, 1986.

——. "The So-Called 'Death Drive.'" In *The Death Drive: New Life for a Dead Subject?*, 40–59. Ed. Rob Weatherill. London: Rebus, 1999.

Laplanche, Jean, and Jean-Bertrand Pontalis. *The Language of Psychoanalysis.* Trans. Donald Nicholson-Smith. London: Hogarth and the Institute of Psycho-Analysis, 1973.

Lasch, Christopher. *Haven in a Heartless World: The Family Besieged.* New York: Norton, 1995.

Layton, Lynne. "Relational Thinking: from Culture to Couch and Couch to Culture." In *Object Relations and Social Relations: The Implications of the Relational Turn in Psychoanalysis*, 1–24. Ed. Simon Clarke, Herbert Hahn, and Paul Hoggett. London: Karnac, 2008.

Lear, Jonathan. *A Case for Irony.* Cambridge: Harvard University Press, 2011.

——. "The Introduction of Eros: Reflections on the Work of Hans Loewald." *Journal of the American Psychoanalytic Association* 44 (1996): 673–98.

——. "A Lost Conception of Irony." *berfrois,* January 12, 2012. http://www.berfrois.com/2012/01/jonathan-lear-lost-conception-irony/.

——. *Love and its Place in Nature.* New York: Farrar, Straus and Giroux, 1990.

——. "The Slippery Middle." In Axel Honneth, *Reification: A New Look at an Old Idea,* 131–46. Oxford: Oxford University Press, 2008.

——. "The Thought of Hans W. Loewald." *International Journal of Psychoanalysis* 93 (2012): 167–79.

Leclaire, Serge. *A Child Is Being Killed: On Primary Narcissism and the Death Drive.* Trans. Marie-Claude Hays. Stanford: Stanford University Press, 1998.

Le Guen, Claude. "Du bon usage de la pulsion de mort." *Revue Française de Psychanalyse* 53, no. 2 (1989): 535–56.

Leledakis, Kanakis. *Society and Psyche: Social Theory and the Unconscious Dimension of the Social.* Oxford: Berg, 1995.

Loewald, Hans. Hans W. Loewald Papers (MS 1721). Manuscripts and Archives, Yale University Library.

——. *Papers on Psychoanalysis.* New Haven: Yale University Press, 1980.

——. *Psychoanalysis and the History of the Individual.* New Haven: Yale University Press, 1978.

——. *Sublimation: Inquiries Into Theoretical Psychoanalysis.* New Haven: Yale University Press, 1988.

López, Donna Bentolila. "The Enigma of the Death Drive: A Revisiting." *Psychoanalysis and Contemporary Thought* 19 (1996): 3–27.

Lorenz, Konrad. *On Aggression.* Trans. Marjorie Kerr Wilson. London: Routledge, 2002.

Macdonald, Iain. "Cold, Cold, Warm: Autonomy, Intimacy, and Maturity in Adorno." *Philosophy and Social Criticism* 37, no. 6 (2011): 669–89.

Mahler, Margaret S., and Fred Pine, and Anni Bergman. *The Psychological Birth of the Human Infant: Symbiosis and Individuation.* New York: Basic Books, 1975.

Mahony, Patrick J. *Cries of the Wolf Man.* New York: International Universities Press, 1984.

Makari, George. *Revolution in Mind: The Creation of Psychoanalysis.* New York: HarperCollins, 2008.

Malabou, Catherine. *The New Wounded: From Neurosis to Brain Damage.* Trans. Steven Miller. New York: Fordham University Press, 2002.

Mandel, Ernst. *Late Capitalism.* Trans. Joris De Bres. London: NLB, 1975.

Marasco, Robyn. *The Highway of Despair: Critical Theory After Hegel.* New York: Columbia University Press, 2015.

Marcuse, Herbert. *Collected Papers of Herbert Marcuse.* Ed. Douglas Kellner. 6 vols. London: Routledge, 2014.

——. *Counterrevolution and Revolt.* Boston: Beacon, 1972.

——. *Eros and Civilization: A Philosophical Inquiry Into Freud.* Boston: Beacon, 1966.

——. *An Essay on Liberation.* Boston: Beacon, 1969.

——. *Five Lectures: Psychoanalysis, Politics, and Utopia*. Trans. Jeremy J. Shapiro and Shierry M. Weber. Boston: Beacon, 1970.

——. *Negations: Essays in Critical Theory*. Trans. Jeremy J. Shapiro. London: Penguin, 1968.

——. *One-Dimensional Man: Studies in the Ideology of Advanced Industrial Society*. London: Routledge, 2002.

Mariotti, Shannon. "Critique from the Margins: Adorno and the Politics of Withdrawal." *Political Theory* 36, no. 3 (June 2008): 456–65.

Marty, Pierre. *Les mouvements individuels de vie et de mort: Essay d'économie psychosomatique*. Paris: Payot, 1976.

Marx, Karl. *Capital Volume One: A Critique of Political Economy*. Trans. Ben Fowkes. London: Penguin, 1976.

——. *The Marx-Engels Reader*. Ed. Robert Tucker. New York: Norton, 1978.

Masson, Jeffrey Moussaieff. *The Assault on Truth: Freud's Suppression of the Seduction Theory*. New York: Ballantine, 2003.

Menninger, Karl A. *Man Against Himself*. New York: Harcourt Brace, 1938.

Meyer, Catherine, ed. *Le Livre noir de la psychanalyse*. Paris: Les Arènes, 2005.

Milbank, John. *Theology and Social Theory: Beyond Secular Reason*. Oxford: Basic Blackwell, 1990.

Mitchell, Stephen. "From Ghosts to Ancestors: The Psychoanalytic Vision of Hans Loewald." *Psychoanalytic Dialogues* 8 (1998): 825–55.

——. "Juggling Paradoxes: Commentary on the Work of Jessica Benjamin." *Studies in Gender and Sexuality* 1, no. 3 (2000): 251–69.

Mitchell, Stephen, and Margaret J. Black. *Freud and Beyond: A History of Modern Psychoanalytic Thought*. New York: Basic Books, 1995.

Mumford, Lewis. *The Culture of Cities*. New York: Harcourt Brace, 1970.

Neuhouser, Frederick. *Rousseau's Theodicy of Self-Love: Evil, Recognition, and the Drive for Recognition*. Oxford: Oxford University Press, 2008.

Nieztsche, Friedrich. *On the Genealogy of Morals*. Trans. Walter Kaufmann and R. J. Hollingdale. New York: Vintage, 1989.

Nobus, Dany. "Life and Death in the Glass: A New Look at the Mirror Stage." In *Key Concepts of Lacanian Psychoanalysis*, 101–38. Ed. Dany Nobus. New York: Other, 1999.

Nowotny, Helga. "From the Future to the Extended Present." In *The Formulation of Time Preferences in a Multidisciplinary Perspective*, 17–31. Ed. Guy Kirsch, Peter Nijkamp, and Klaus Zimmermann. Aldershot: Avebury, 1988.

Obholzer, Karin. *The Wolf-Man: Conversations with Freud's Patient—Sixty Years Later*. Trans. Michael Shaw. New York: Continuum, 1982.

O'Connor, Brian. *Adorno's Negative Dialectic: Philosophy and the Possibility of Critical Rationality*. Cambridge: MIT Press, 2004.

Offe, Claus. "Technology and One-Dimensionality." In *Marcuse: Critical Theory and the Promise of Utopia*, 215–24. Ed. Robert Pippin, Andrew Feenberg, and Charles P. Webel. London: Macmillan, 1988.

Offenkrantz, William. "Problems of the Therapeutic Alliance: Freud and the Wolf Man." *International Journal of Psychoanalysis* 54 (1973): 75–78.

Ogden, Thomas. *Subjects of Analysis*. Lanham: Rowman and Littlefield, 1977.

Oliver, Kelly, and Steve Edwin, eds. *Between the Psyche and the Social: Psychoanalytic Social Theory*. Lanham: Rowman and Littlefield, 2002.

Phillips, Adam. "Adam Phillips on Money." YouTube video. 44:35. February 7, 2013. Posted by "E.W.R. Many." https://youtu.be/K8wGZt-4ASg.

——. "Keeping it Moving." In Judith Butler, *The Psychic Life of Power*, 151–59. Stanford: Stanford University Press, 1997.

——. *Kissing, Tickling, and Being Bored: Psychoanalytic Essays on the Unexamined Life*. Cambridge: Harvard University Press, 1993.

——. *Terrors and Experts*. Cambridge: Harvard University Press, 1995.

Piccone, Paul. "General Introduction." In *The Essential Frankfurt School Reader*, ix–xxi. Ed. Andrew Arato and Eike Gebhardt. New York: Continuum, 2005.

Pippin, Robert. *The Persistence of Subjectivity: On the Kantian Aftermath*. Cambridge: Cambridge University Press 2005.

Pontalis, J. B. "On Death-Work in Freud, in the Self, in Culture." In *Psychoanalysis, Creativity, and Literature: A French-American Inquiry*, 85–95. Ed. Alan Roland. New York: Columbia University Press, 1978.

Poster, Mark. *Critical Theory of the Family*. New York: Seabury Press, 1978.

Postone, Moishe. "Critique and Historical Transformation." *Historical Materialism* 12, no. 3 (2004): 53–72.

Prost, Antoine. "Public and Private Spheres in France." In *A History of Private Life*, 5:1–143. Ed. Antoine Prost and Gérard Vincent. Trans. Arthur Goldhammer. Cambridge: Belknap, 1991.

Psychology Wiki. "Death Drive." http://psychology.wikia.com/wiki/Death_drive.

Rabain, Jean-François. "Compte rendu du colloque sur la pulsion de mort." *Revue Française de Psychanalyse* 53, no. 2 (1989): 761–67.

Reich, Wilhelm. "The Characterological Mastery of the Oedipus Complex." *International Journal of Psycho-Analysis* 12 (1931): 452–67.

——. *Reich Speaks of Freud*. Ed. Mary Higgins and Chester Raphael. New York: Farrar, Straus and Giroux, 1967.

——. *The Sexual Revolution: Toward a Self-Governing Character Structure*. New York: Farrar, Straus and Giroux, 1963.

Rice, James L. *Freud's Russia: National Identity in the Evolution of Psychoanalysis*. New Brunswick, NJ: Transaction, 1993.

Ricoeur, Paul. *Freud and Philosophy: An Essay on Interpretation*. Trans. Denis Savage. New Haven: Yale University Press, 1970.

Rogozinski, Jacob. *The Ego and the Flesh: An Introduction to Egoanalysis*. Trans. Robert Vallier. Stanford: Stanford University Press, 2010.

Rose, Gillian. *Hegel Contra Sociology*. London: Athlone, 1981.

——. "How is Critical Theory Possible? Theodor W. Adorno and Concept Formation in Sociology." *Political Studies* 24, no. 1 (March 1976): 69–85.

——. *The Melancholy Science: An Introduction to the Thought of Theodor W. Adorno*. New York: Columbia University Press, 1978.

Rose, Jacqueline. *Why War?—Psychoanalysis, Politics, and the Return to Melanie Klein*. Oxford: Blackwell, 1993.

Rose, Nikolas. *Inventing Our Selves: Psychology, Power, and Personhood*. Cambridge: Cambridge University Press, 1996.

Rosenberg, Benno. *Masochisme mortifère et masochisme gardien de la vie*. Paris: Presses Universitaires de France, 1991.

Roudinesco, Elizabeth. *Jacques Lacan & Co.: A History of Psychoanalysis in France, 1925–1985*. Trans. Jeffrey Mehlman. Chicago: University of Chicago Press, 1990.

Rousseau, Jean-Jacques. "Discourse on the Origin and the Foundations of Inequality Among Men." In *The Discourses and Other Early Political Writings*, 113–88. Ed. and trans. Victor Gourevitch. Cambridge: Cambridge University Press, 1997.

Roustang, François. *Dire Mastery: Discipleship from Freud to Lacan*. Arlington: American Psychiatric, 1986.

Sandler, Joseph, and Alex Holder, and Dale Meers. "The Ego Ideal and the Ideal Self." *Psychoanalytic Study of the Child* 18 (1963): 139–58.

Scarfone, Dominique. *Jean Laplanche*. Paris: Press Universitaires de France, 1997.

Schafer, Roy. "The Loving and Beloved Superego in Freud's Structural Theory." *Psychoanalytic Study of the Child* 15 (1960): 163–88.

Schoolman, Morton. *The Imaginary Witness: The Critical Theory of Herbert Marcuse*. New York: Free Press, 1980.

Schweppenhäuser, Gerhard. *Theodor W. Adorno: An Introduction*. Trans. James Rolleston. Durham: Duke University Press, 2009.

Segal, Hanna. *Melanie Klein*. New York: Penguin, 1979.

Seigel, Jerrold. *The Idea of the Self: Thought and Experience in Western Europe Since the Seventeenth Century*. Cambridge: Cambridge University Press, 2005.

Serres, Michel. *Conversations on Science, Culture, and Time: Michel Serres with Bruno Latour*. Trans. Roxanne Lapidus. Ann Arbor: University of Michigan Press, 1995.

Shapiro, Jeremy J. "One-Dimensionality: The Universal Semiotic of Technological Experience." In *Critical Interruptions: New Left Perspectives on Herbert Marcuse*, 136–86. Ed. Paul Breines. New York: Herder and Herder, 1970.

Sherrat, Yvonne. *Adorno's Positive Dialectic*. Cambridge: Cambridge University Press, 2002.

Shuster, Martin. *Autonomy After Auschwitz: Adorno, German Idealism, and Modernity*. Chicago: University of Chicago Press, 2014.

Simmel, Ernst. "Anti-Semitism and Mass Psychopathology." In *Anti-Semitism: A Social Disease*, 33–78. Ed. Ernst Simmel. New York: International Universities Press, 1946.

Sloterdijk, Peter. *Bubbles*, vol. 1 of *Spheres*. Trans. Wieland Hoban. 3 vols. Los Angeles: Semiotext(e), 2011.

Smelser, Neil J. *The Social Edges of Psychoanalysis*. Berkeley: University of California Press, 1998.

Stern, Daniel. *The Interpersonal World of the Infant: A View from Psychoanalysis and Developmental Psychology*. London: Karnac, 1998.

Stiegler, Bernard. *Réenchanter le monde: La valeur esprit contre le populisme industriel*. Paris: Flammarion, 2006.

——. "Spirit, Capitalism and Superego." *ars industrialis*, May 2006. http://arsindustrialis.org/node/2928.

——. "The Time of Cinema: On the 'New World' and 'Cultural Exception.'" *Tekhnema: Journal of Philosophy and Technology* 4 (Spring 1998): 62–114.

Sulloway, Frank. "Exemplary Botches." In *Unauthorized Freud: Doubters Confront a Legend*, 174–85. Ed. Frederick Crews. London: Penguin, 1999.

——. *Freud, Biologist of the Mind: Beyond the Psychoanalytic Legend*. New York: Basic Books, 1979.

Tallis, Raymond. *Not Saussure: A Critique of Post-Saussurean Literary Theory*. London: Palgrave Macmillan, 1995.

Taylor, Mark C. *Kierkegaard's Pseudonymous Authorship: A Study of Time and the Self*. Princeton: Princeton University Press, 1975.

Theunissen, Michael. "Negativität bei Adorno." In *Adorno-Konferenz 1983*, 41–65. Ed. Ludwig von Friedeburg and Jürgen Habermas. Frankfurt: Suhrkamp, 1983.

Thyen, Anke. *Negative Dialektik und Erfahrung: Zur Rationalität des Nichtidentischen bei Adorno*. Frankfurt: Suhrkamp, 1989.

Tiefer, Leonore. *Sex Is not a Natural Act and Other Essays*. Boulder: Westview, 2004.

Tillich, Paul. *The Protestant Era*. Trans. James Luther Adams. Chicago: University of Chicago Press, 1948.

Tolstoy, Leo. *Confession*. Trans. David Patterson. New York: Norton, 1983.

Türcke, Christoph. *Philosophy of Dreams*. Trans. Susan Gillespie. New Haven: Yale University Press, 2013.

Turkle, Sherry. *Alone Together: Why We Expect More from Technology and Less from Each Other*. New York: Basic Books, 2011.

Weatherill, Rob. *The Sovereignty of Death*. London: Rebus, 1998.

Weber, Samuel. *The Legend of Freud*. Minneapolis: University of Minnesota Press, 1995.

Webster, Richard. "The Cult of Lacan: Freud, Lacan, and the Mirror Stage." *richardwebster.net*, 2002. http://www.richardwebster.net/thecultoflacan.html.

——. *Why Freud Was Wrong: Sin, Science, and Psychoanalysis*. New York: Basic Books, 1996.

Weinstein, Fred. *Freud, Psychoanalysis, Social Theory: The Unfulfilled Promise*. Albany: SUNY Press, 2001.

Wellmer, Albrecht. "Truth, Semblance and Reconciliation: Adorno's Aesthetic Redemption of Modernity." In *The Persistence of Modernity: Essays on Aesthetics, Ethics, and Postmodernism*, 1–35. Cambridge: MIT Press, 1993.

Werner, Heinz, and Bernard Kaplan. *Symbol Formation: An Organismic-Developmental Approach to Language and the Expression of Thought*. New York: Wiley, 1964.

Wheeler, William Morton. "On Instincts." *Journal of Abnormal Psychology* 15 (1917): 295–318.

White, Kristin. "Notes on 'Bemächtigungstrieb' and Strachey's Translation as 'Instinct for Mastery.'" *International Journal of Psychoanalysis* 91, no. 4 (May 2010): 811–20.

Whitebook, Joel. "From Schoenberg to Odysseus: Aesthetic, Psychic, and Social Synthesis in Adorno and Wellmer." *New German Critique* 58 (Winter 1993): 45–64.

———. "The Marriage of Marx and Freud: Critical Theory and Psychoanalysis." In *The Cambridge Companion to Critical Theory*, 74–102. Ed. Fred Rush. Cambridge: Cambridge University Press, 2004.

———. "Mutual Recognition and the Work of the Negative." In *Pluralism and the Pragmatic Turn: Essays in Honor of Thomas McCarthy*, 257–83. Ed. James Bohman and William Rehg. Cambridge: MIT Press, 2001.

———. *Perversion and Utopia: A Study in Psychoanalysis and Critical Theory*. Cambridge: MIT Press, 1996.

Winnicott, D. W. *Human Nature*. New York: Brunner/Mazel, 1988.

———. "Metapsychological and Clinical Aspects of Regression Within the Psycho-Analytical Set-Up." *International Journal of Psycho-Analysis* 36 (1955): 16–26.

———. "Mind and Its Relation to the Psyche-Soma." In *Through Paediatrics to Psycho-Analysis: Collected Papers*, 243–54. New York: Brunner-Routledge, 1992.

———. "The Theory of the Parent-Infant Relationship." *International Journal of Psychoanalysis* 41 (1960): 585–95.

———. "The Use of an Object." *International Journal of Psychoanalysis* 50 (1969): 711–16.

Wittels, Fritz. *Sigmund Freud: His Personality, His Teaching, and His School*. London: Allen and Unwin, 1924.

Zaretsky, Eli. *Political Freud: A History*. New York: Columbia University Press, 2015.

———. "Psychoanalysis and the Spirit of Capitalism." *Constellations* 15, no. 3 (2008): 366–81.

———. *Secrets of the Soul: A Social and Cultural History of Psychoanalysis*. New York: Vintage, 2004.

Zipes, Jack. "The Instrumentalization of Fantasy: Fairy Tales and the Mass Media." In *The Myths of Information: Technology and Postindustrial Culture*, 88–110. Ed. Kathleen Woodward. London: Routledge and Kegan Paul, 1980.

Žižek, Slavoj. *Enjoy Your Symptom! Jacques Lacan in Hollywood and Out*. London: Routledge, 2013.

———. *The Indivisible Remainder*. London: Verso, 1996.

———. *Organs Without Bodies: On Deleuze and Consequences*. New York: Routledge, 2004.

———. *The Parallax View*. Cambridge: MIT Press, 2006.

Index

drive and, 126, 155–56n2, 156n3;
fantasy and, 158n17; Freud, S., and,
41–43, 46–47, 51; Jung and, 159n27;
Lacan and, 60, 66, 76; language
of Eros and, 49–53; Laplanche and,
162n48; Lear and, 168n9; mastery
and, 44, 52, 56–58, 158n24; mother
and, 156–57n5; narcissism and,
157n9, 165n91; undifferentiation
and, 54–56
Lorenz, Konrad, 59
Losing oneself, 94–98, 181n66;
death drive and, 97, 182–83n83;
escapism and, 181n69; examples
of, 97; living straight ahead and,
105–6, 124
Love and Its Place in Nature (Lear),
142n52

Macdonald, Iain, 178n48
Machines, 118–20
Malabou, Catherine, 153n80, 155n91
Mandel, Ernest, 176n21
Marcuse, Herbert, 3–4, 20, 82, 109–25,
132, 147n7, 148–49n25, 152n65,
191n7, 193n34; aggressivity and,
192n24; analytic philsophy and,
196–97n70; crisis of internalization
and, 86; Habermas and, 193–
94n39; language of Thanatos
and, 121–23; structural theory and,
195n55
"Marriage of Marx and Freud, The:
Critical Theory and Psychoanalysis"
(Whitebook), 137n10
Marx, Karl, 2–3, 81, 84, 102, 109, 129;
Freud, S., and, 3–4, 81–83, 129–30;
Marcuse and, 117–19; mastery and,
136n4
Masson, Jeffrey Moussaieff, 138n16
Mastery, 1–3; aggressivity and, 33–34,
66–67, 69, 78, 158n24; anality and,
82; as *Bemächtigung*, 1, 3, 24–26;
as *Bewältigung*, 1, 3, 24–26, 78,
148, 158n24; binding and, 162n53;

defining, 56–58; drive to, 18–19,
23–24, 33–35, 37–38, 66–67, 69,
126–29; history of, 24–28, 149–
50n25; Klein and, 152n64, 153n69;
Lacan and, 61, 63, 66–69, 78;
language and, 128; Loewald and,
44, 52, 56–58, 158n24; Marx and,
136n4; mimesis and, 92; pleasure
principle and, 36–37; postoedipal,
57, 92; preemptive, 84; preoedipal,
57; technical, 109–18, 123–24,
192n25
Maturity, 104, 107
Metapsychology, 3, 4–14, 41, 131, 138n23,
145–46n1
Mimesis, 83, 104, 179–80n54, 179n49;
Girard and, 72–75; postoedipal,
91–94, 100, 106, 187–88n129;
preoedipal, 91–98, 100
Mirror stage (Lacan), 61–67, 168n13,
169n31; mastery and, 168n15,
170n48
Modernity: failed mutuality and, 46;
infancy of, 124
Money, 82, 174n1
Mother: death drive and, 157n11;
Loewald and, 156–57n5;
omnipotent, 61–65; as Other, 62,
65, 68; as Thing, 65–66. *See also*
Caretaker
Mourning, 51, 127, 158n21
Mumford, Lewis, 109

Nachträglichkeit. See Afterwardsness
Narcissism, 59–78, 103; castration and,
64–65; primary, 157n9, 165n91
Narcissistic libido, 34
Negative Dialectics (Adorno), 91
Negativity, 91, 100, 104–5, 178n34,
186n120, 187n123
Neuhouser, Frederick, 143n68
New Anthropological Type, 19, 81–108,
183n91
Nietzsche, Friedrich, 141n45
Nirvana principle, 36

Ricoeur, Paul, 146n2
Rigidity. *See* Ego
Rogozinski, Jacob, 76, 169n31, 170n35
Rose, Gillian, 89, 104–5, 144n74
Rose, Nikolas, 15–18
Rosenberg, Benno, 31–32
Rousseau, Jean-Jacques, 82

Sadism, 34, 112
Sartre, Jean-Paul, 59
Scapegoating, 72–73
Schweppenhäuser, Gerhard, 91
Seduction thesis, 13, 142n55
Self-overcoming, 107, 132
Seminar II (Lacan), 66–67
Seminar IV (Lacan), 63–65
Seminar VII (Lacan), 65–66
Sexuality, 130–32, 198n5
Shapiro, Jeremy, 195n57
Sickness Unto Death (Kierkegaard), 74
Smart phone, 124
Social Construction of What, The? (Hacking), 143n65
Social constructivism, 14–18, 143n65
Solms, Mark, 140n43
Stern, Daniel, 54–56
Stiegler, Bernard, 94–95, 116–17, 120, 135n135
Strachey, Alix, 140n43
Strachey, James, 8, 139n26, 140n43, 151n60
Struggle for recognition, 70–72
Subjectivism, 14–15
Sublimation, 47–53, 100, 111–12, 121–23, 128–29, 161n44, 184n104; resistant individuals and, 102–3. *See also* Aggressive sublimation
Submissive individuals, 102
Superego, 47–49, 57, 130, 166n98, 188n135; Adorno and, 183–84n95; automatization of, 118–20; crisis of internalization and, 86–90; death drive sublimation and, 100; id and, 98–101, 161n47; ironic reflection

and, 184n101; living straight ahead and, 98–101; substitute, 101–5
Symbolic, 52, 62, 65, 75–76, 163n65, 174n89

Technological rationality, 114–16
Technology, 20, 109–25, 132–33, 193n34–35; aggressivity and, 109–18, 121–25; as ideology, 193–94n39; technics and, 114–18
Television, 95
Temporality, 48–49, 100–101, 122, 142n53, 161n43, 161n47, 167n100
Tension-between position, 32–33, 38, 45, 55, 67, 152n64, 159n29. *See also other*
Tension model, 58, 180n59
Tension-within position, 17, 32–33, 38, 45, 55–56, 67, 71, 73, 76, 126, 152n64, 159n29; language of Eros and, 50. *See also* "other"
Terrors and Experts (Phillips), 139n42
Thanatos, 121–23, 129–30, 133
Theodicy, 15, 143n68
Theology, 143n67, 173n84
"Theory of the Parent-Infant Relationship" (Winnicott), 149
Theunissen, Michael, 178n34
Thing (*Das Ding*), 49–53, 65–67, 121–23
Things Hidden Since the Foundation of the World (Girard), 74
Three Essays on the Theory of Sexuality (Freud, S.), 25, 140n43
Tiefer, Leonore, 144n78
Todestrieb. See Death drive
Torok, Maria, 138n16
Totality, 195–96n59
Totem and Taboo (Freud, S.), 35
Trieb. See Drive
Türcke, Christoph, 122

Undifferentiation, 54–56, 92, 165n85
Unification, 122–23

GPSR Authorized Representative: Easy Access System Europe, Mustamäe tee
50, 10621 Tallinn, Estonia, gpsr.requests@easproject.com